Sharing Pedagogies

Sharing Pedagogies

Students & Teachers
Write about Dialogic Practices

Edited and with an Introduction by
Gail Tayko and John Paul Tassoni

Foreword by Ira Shor

Boynton/Cook Publishers
HEINEMANN
Portsmouth, NH

Boynton/Cook Publishers
A subsidiary of Reed Elsevier Inc.
361 Hanover Street
Portsmouth, NH 03801-3912
Offices and agents throughout the world

Editor: Peter Stillman
Cover design: Darci Mehall
Cover illustration: T. Watson Bogaard
Manufacturing: Louise Richardson

The authors and publisher wish to thank those who generously gave permission to reprint borrowed material:

Excerpt from "Emotions". From *Singing Yet* by Stan Rice. Copyright © 1992 by Stan Rice. Reprinted by permission of Alfred A. Knopf, Inc.

Excerpt from "Map" by Claire Bateman. From *The Bicycle Slow Race.* Copyright © 1991 by Claire Bateman, Wesleyan University Press. Reprinted by permission of University Press of New England.

Excerpt from "O Taste and See" by Denise Levertov. From *Poems 1960–1967.* Copyright © 1966 by Denise Levertov. Reprinted by permission of New Directions Publishing Corp.

Library of Congress Cataloging-in-Publication Data
Sharing pedagogies: students and teachers write about dialogic practices/edited by Gail Tayko and John Paul Tassoni: foreword by Ira Shor.
     p. cm.
     Includes bibliographical reference
     ISBN 0-86709-412-5
     1. English language—Composition and exercises—Study and teaching (Secondary)—Unites States. 2. English language—Rhetoric—Study and teaching—United States. 3. Education—Study and teaching (Higher)—United States. 4. Teacher-student relationships—United States. 5. Critical pedagogy—United States. 6. Teaching—United States. 7. Dialogue. I. Tayko, Gail. II. Tassoni, John Paul.
PE1405.U6S53 1997   96-30442
371.1'023—dc20   CIP

Printed in the United States of America on acid-free paper
00 99 98 97 DA 1 2 3 4 5

For Our Parents,
Mary and Suzanne and Manuel and Rosario

Contents

Foreword

Where Does Subject Matter Come from and What Do We Do with It?

This is a passionate, risky, and promising book. It's about the passion, the risk, and the promise of sharing power in the classroom. The classes described in these chapters question the unequal power relations dominating schools. Questioning power, the authors in this volume search for something students and teachers need and may yet win—a culture of democratic authority—certainly a prize worth the risk, and a risk that explains the passion.

Chapter by chapter, this book offers stories of conflict, collaboration, success, and failure. The actors in these pedagogical dramas struggle with their doubts and convictions. What a refreshing contrast to the passionless classrooms too familiar in education (which Jerome Bruner complained about in the 1950s, which John Goodlad saw again in the 1980s, and which we can still witness today). How many students enter our classrooms expecting the "same old, same old"? In these pages and classrooms, the voices of students and teachers find new life.

The papers collected here show students and teachers reconstructing power relations by asking, Who has the right to speak about what in the classroom? Whose voices, what contents, and which processes should be deployed? How can we overcome entrenched teacher-talk (the dominant one-way monologue dubbed "narration sickness" by Paulo Freire and denounced by him as "the banking model" of pedagogy)? This book is facing what I think of as the central question of democratic teaching: Where does subject matter come from and what do we do with it to become empowered, critical, and more humane?

Questioning canons and methods is risky because the standard curriculum comes from and supports the status quo, which Freire referred to as "the power that is now in power." The traditional structures of education have the weight of 150 years on their side, the time it took to establish teacher-centered classrooms, subject-centered curricula, invasive testing and textbook industries, biased institutional tracking, unequal funding of working-class versus elite education, business-oriented subject matter, and top-down hierarchies for administration and policy-making. Such authoritarian devices are not accidents of history. They reflect and support the unequal concentration of power in society at large. Because democratic relations and egalitarian policies disturb the friendly fit of schooling with the status quo, shared pedagogy is oppositional, involving transformed power. As a curriculum of resistance, shared pedagogy practices an alternative model of social relations—collaboration and negotiation rather than one-way transmissions of knowledge and commands.

The democratic alternative of shared power has an honorable history dating back at least to John Dewey. From his early to his late texts, Dewey emphasized the synergy of democracy and education—with one requiring the other to work. In *Experience and Education* (1938), he wrote that

> There is, I think, no point in the philosophy of progressive education which is sounder than its emphasis upon the importance of the participation of the learner in the formation of the purposes which direct his activities in the learning process, just as there is no defect in traditional education greater than its failure to secure the active co-operation of the pupil in construction of the purposes involved in his studying. (67)

Dewey was clear about the need to begin with a cooperative, experimental, and experiential process centered in the students, not in the teacher, the academic subject, or the official textbook. He advised teachers to discover subject matter close to student experience, which he called their "vital interests":

> Think of the absurdity of having to teach language as a thing by itself. If there is anything the child will do before he goes to school, it is to talk of the things that interest him. But when there are no vital interests appealed to in the school, when language is used simply for the repetition of lessons, it is not surprising that one of the chief difficulties of school work has come to be instruction in the mother-tongue. Since the language taught is unnatural, not growing out of the real desire to communicate vital impressions and convictions, the freedom of children in its use gradually disappears, until finally the high school teacher has to invent all kinds of devices to assist in getting any spontaneous and full use of speech. (*The School and Society*, 1900, 55–56)

Dewey's discussion of lifeless high-school classrooms in his time foreshadows the ocean of reports appearing in the 1980s and 1990s that examined the malaise of secondary education especially and higher education to a lesser degree. By the time students reach college, they have spent 12,000 hours inside a one-way curriculum, disorienting them from participatory learning. In the area of freshman English, the absence of "vital interests" came to the attention of Richard Ohmann (*English in America* 1976), who observed an urgent search for compelling subject matter in the most widely used writing texts of that decade.

The problem of vital subject matter lay beneath Freire's own turn to "generative themes" in the 1950s when he first designed literacy programs for Brazilian peasants and workers. In Freire's dialogic method, subject matter is discovered from and with the students, taken from the lives, language, and conditions of students themselves. This points to the second great concern of the reports in this book following the first concern for negotiation—how to situate subject matter inside student experience. In the Freirean model, personal experience or "subjectivity" is the material through which to launch a critical inquiry. Critical pedagogies evolving from Freirean (as well as from feminist and multicultural) roots situate the personal in the social and the social in the personal for an historical reading of experience.

Negotiated and situated pedagogies involve change, which is possible but certainly not easy. As I mentioned above, the stories of shared pedagogy in this book refreshingly admit doubt and failure as well as success. I admire Rosemarie Lewandowski's admission in Chapter 1 that negotiating with students left her insecure in class, not firmly confident in her professional position. The difficulty of establishing shared authority also bedeviled Chris Zawodniak in Chapter 2, who reports that his teacher Jeff took too low a profile in class, assuming a *laissez-faire* posture in letting students run the course, but apparently allowing himself the right to intervene whenever he wanted. Students felt watched and poorly guided at the same time, it seems. "We students must have active teacher involvement at the core of any student-centered classroom," Zawodniak observes. The absent teacher can be just as big a problem for a class as the dominating one, an issue that returns with a vengeance in Chapter 10 by Katharine Wilson, whose theme is that "no authority" is not the answer.

Wilson's report reminded me of the socializing influence of education, which Foucault liked to call "normalization" to indicate the process through which people are habituated to the norms of the status quo. Years of nonnegotiable authority in school help prepare us for the nonnegotiable nature of authority in society as a whole, especially at work. In a corporate society where power is monopolized at the top, where schools and colleges lack mechanisms for students to negotiate their education, it is easy to imagine that the opposite of domination is freedom from any control or authority, a *laissez-faire* permissiveness or individualism, as if a free curriculum was like a shopping expedition to the mall where you are free to buy whatever you like or can afford, following only your personal impulses or tastes. But the opposite of antidemocratic structure is not no structure but rather democratic, negotiated structure. I take this as the meaning of Wilson's remarkable report about her experience as a graduate student in the seminar from which Jane Tompkins wrote her famous essay "Pedagogy of the Distressed." This is a story of one antiauthoritarian professor feeding her students more than enough freedom for them to choke on. After Tompkins started the seminar and then abdicated authority to students, Katharine Wilson writes, "No authoritarian teacher ever bullied me, emotionally or intellectually, as badly as my fellow graduate students did in that class." Her painful experience in Tompkins' seminar left her

determined not to let permissiveness rule her own classes, to prevent aggressive students from mauling the others. Her description of how she maintains
her own teacherly authority while inviting shared dialogue with students still
raises questions, it seems to me, revealing a problematic struggle over power
relations, not a simple answer.

Despite Tompkins' homage to Freire as the source of her pedagogy,
Freire has spoken decisively against *laissez-faire* postures by the teacher (see
A Pedagogy for Liberation 1987), insisting that critical educators cannot re-
sign responsibility for the development of themselves and the students in a
mutually transformative process. He called the teacher's responsibility for
leadership "democratic directiveness." A democratic authority is different
from an authoritarian authority (nonnegotiated teacherly governance) or an
absent authority (nonnegotiated domination by aggressive students). As Wilson and others report, students have a hard time constructing democratic relations when authority is simply dumped in their laps by a *laissez-faire*
teacher. In Freirean dialogics, the goal is teacher-student reconciliation/recon-
struction, where the teacher and the students share roles so as to change each
other, both being leaders and followers. Freirean pedagogy requires an engaged critical teacher in the dialogue.

Authority conflicts are also at the center of "Between Student and Teacher Roles" (Chapter 7), which chronicles the failure of a teacher-training program to provide dialogic sites where future educators can develop as
student-centered professionals. The student-interns reporting in this chapter
encountered public school authorities too traditional for isolated novices to
test the shared pedagogy recommended to them by their campus-based authorities. A similar problem of curricular mismatch emerges in Chapter 4
("Creating Dialogue: What the English Curriculum Doesn't Teach"), where
we are told that "Undergraduate English majors have a conflicted relationship
with the demands of their own discipline. They learn to fear writing, distrust
their talents, doubt their successes, and see themselves as impostors." Copy-
ing academic conventions is questioned in this chapter: "The whole notion of
assimilation should be opened to critical examination. . . . Students should be
encouraged to question the value of their assimilation into academia." This
chapter and "Between Student and Teacher Roles" raise the issue of how to
develop students as institutional change agents, a theme that could benefit
from still more exposure in these reports.

At the level of democratic classroom change, Sandy Feinstein's report in
Chapter 5 is concretely helpful. Feinstein constructs a syllabus in two- to
four-week intervals so that she can include students in the planning. "Over the
years," she says, "I have grown accustomed to changing directions in midcourse." She changes with the students and the process, engaged, not sitting
on the sidelines. Another fine example of an engaged teacher is Lucy
Schultz's codevelopment with student Michael Gilland of the "Writing Cin-

cinnati" course (Chapter 6). She reports how the momentum of the planning process shifted toward Michael as he proved to be the expert on the city.

Lastly, I must thank Ann Ott, Beth Boquet, and Mark Hurlbert for reminding me in Chapter 11 of the power of shared food. When I first brought hamburgers to class in the 1970s and experimented with what is now considered a cultural studies approach to composition and critical pedagogy, I didn't invite the students to eat the burgers but only to analyze them. What a missed opportunity! Ann, Beth, and Mark know better—they build community through class dinners. How I wish I had done more critical eating with my classes twenty years ago. But even though Mark brings a full dinner pail to class in one hand, he carries a half-empty syllabus in the other, inviting the students to share in constructing the remainder of the course (reiterating Sandy Feinstein's approach from an earlier chapter).

All in all, these are provocative materials for a discussion of power sharing. I do think that experiments such as these would be of even more help if they pushed the envelope farther, especially in regard to how a teacher reaches out to students to negotiate while also pulling the process toward critical thought about the status quo. Democracy through shared pedagogy must merge with critical thinking about power in society. Classrooms need to be democratic and critical to develop teachers and students as thinkers and citizens. This is why I named the pedagogy I described in *Empowering Education* (1992) "critical-democratic," combining power-sharing with questioning the unequal conditions of society in general.

Power-sharing is a promising means to distribute authority to students; it can also be a means to develop teachers and students as critical thinkers and change agents. Democracy in education is still a marginal practice a century after Dewey first wrote. The absence of democratic classrooms is more than enough to make Dewey turn over in his grave several times. Even if education by itself cannot transform society, an approach like shared pedagogy is one inviting means through which we can improve the conditions for democratic and humane change—and does this age need that kind of pedagogy and change!

Ira Shor

Acknowledgments

Many thanks to those who shared their time and expertise to make this book possible. In particular, we are grateful to all those who allowed us to consider their papers; Peter Stillman for his support; Francis Marion University for providing us with the released time to get this project started; Bridget Burden and Beverly White at FMU for helping us with our mailing list; Miami University–Middletown for the use of its facilities; Tracie Jones and Michelle Day-Curtis for their assistance; David B. Downing for his advice; and Cynthia Lewiecki-Wilson, Jeff D. Sommers, John Heyda, and William H. Thelin for reading and commenting on our introduction.

We especially thank Ira Shor and C. Mark Hurlbert, who provided us with insights, support, and guidance throughout this project.

Introduction

Why Share
Students in Pedagogy Scholarship
John Paul Tassoni and Gail Tayko

Treason, formation, elation, confession, dysfunction.
Entity, clarity, mystery, scarcity, nearness.
Sanity, pity, pleasure, conjunction.
                    —Stan Rice, "Emotions"

1

Sharing Pedagogies is an experiment in creating and sustaining dialogue within English classrooms and pedagogy scholarship. Representing critical responses to dialogic practices in composition, literature, and English education courses, the articles collected here focus on the experiences of graduate and undergraduate students who have participated in decentered classrooms, collaborative projects, and courses that stress issues of student empowerment and cultural diversity. The selections include, for example, Chris Zawodniak's critique of his instructor's student-centered yet student-stifling approach to Freshman Composition; they include stories from Shannon Siebert, Richelle Dowding, Staci Quigley, Melanie Bills, and Mary Anne Browder Brock, developing teachers who weigh the practicality of their training in dialogic pedagogy against the demands of high-school curricula, underprepared students, and their professional goals; and they include dialogues among students and teachers like Lucille M. Schultz, Carman Costello, C. Ann Ott, and Bob Mayberry, who connect university and community interests, discover multiculturalism within their apparently homogeneous classrooms, and personalize writing instruction and doctoral candidacy.

We say this book is an experiment because we have found through working with these authors that writing about dialogic pedagogies involves risk-taking in terms of how teachers teach, how students interact with their teachers, and how pedagogy scholarship represents classroom life. We feel that this book represents a site where dialogue troubles or shifts the subject locations of its authors along the academic hierarchy as students become teachers and teachers become students. In their depictions of academic experiences and in their efforts to represent these experiences, the writers of this volume demonstrate what we carefully, even hesitantly, identify as successes of dialogic thinking and writing, namely, the values of cooperation, negotiation, friendship, a willingness to take risks. To the degree it demonstrates such successes, *Sharing Pedagogies* shows the mutual exchange of knowledge, the "reciprocal influence"—to borrow Françoise Lionnet's phrase—that "unconsciously" creates a "new culture" (1989, 15–16).

We proceed with caution, however, for we observe that vulnerability, conflict, and changing values also measure into the ways our contributors write about teaching. Probably more often than not, students and teachers who participate in and write about dialogic pedagogies experience discomfort or duress, because negotiating each other's interests and concerns implies altering ingrained behaviors and attitudes instilled by the academic hierarchy. For teachers and students alike, a dialogic pedagogy means challenging forces that prevent them from interacting as complex beings who feel pain and affection, make mistakes, change their minds, get confused, teach each other, create (rather than merely absorb or transmit) knowledge. This book also shows, then, the effort, the kind of *postdisciplinary commitment*, involved in practicing a dialogic pedagogy "where every distance must be drawn to scale/and an inch off means someone absent" (Bateman 1994, 24).

2

Having worked with the students who contributed to this volume, we understand that the risks for students who share pedagogies are multiple, for their reciprocal engagement with teachers requests that they assume roles as their instructors' intellectual equals; that they be forthcoming, critical, articulate; that they overload already overloaded schedules; that they risk their relationships with peers mistrustful of their relationships with authority figures; that they risk friendships with teachers they admire. Frequently, students who write about their instructors are as yet under the power of those authoritative figures. This issue of safety and vulnerability speaks to the institutional hierarchy: namely, the felt limitations that remind students that they reside at the lower rungs of the academy and should not trespass their own local boundaries. To one of our undergraduate contributors who offers a stringent critique of a former teacher's methods, we said, "You're still a student, and perhaps that teacher and his colleagues will read your article—are you *sure* you want this article to be published?" (And, in this sense, we had to ask *ourselves*, "Should *we* publish it?") The institution's hierarchical conceptions of student/teacher relations restrict the opportunities for student-researchers and teacher-researchers to come together to write. In doing so, those conceptions restrict the opportunities for them to scrutinize together and, perhaps, change what really goes on in their classrooms.

Dialogic teachers not only need to encourage but also to match their students' risk-taking and vulnerability. It is not necessarily a pleasant or, for some, even a desirable experience for teachers to be honest with students about their grading criteria, their uncertainty about subject matter, or their struggles to bring their personal and professional concerns into a better balance. But with a dialogic pedagogy, teachers often find themselves more honest than they usually are with their students, more vulnerable than they need to be in classrooms where lecture notes and multiple-choice exams prescribe a class's discourse. For teachers, dialogics means asking. Now, exactly how much power do I want to share with this student? Is it safe to speak? Is that what I really wanted to say? Is that what I really wanted to hear? What are the implications of writing collaboratively with my student? How do I write with a student? Is there a student with whom I can write about my teaching? Is there a student who will write with me?

Hierarchical conceptions of student/teacher relations stand alongside other institutional, social, and personal hindrances to student/teacher collaboration in scholarship and to student-researchers who write alone. Although dialogic pedagogy involves exercising the skills and values that students and teachers need to look and act upon the world critically and responsibly, the exercise of these skills and values is rarely incentive enough to propel students, particularly undergraduates whose majors lie outside the discipline (those most English teachers most often teach), into the world of academic scholarship. Unlike faculty and graduate students, whose investment in scholarship translates into discernible rewards, such as job security, career advancement, and funding opportunities, undergraduates who devote time beyond their heavy courseloads and other job and family obligations do so with the most altruistic of motives. And in those cases where funding is available for students to conduct research, collaborators still must contend with the relative instability of students' circumstances: Students leave town, transfer, drop out, overload their course schedules, take second jobs, change majors, develop new interests, and, as C. Mark Hurlbert points out, "even go to war"—factors that make difficult sustaining a collaborative project through the successive revisions necessary to bring it to publication (Hurlbert and Bodnar 1994, 230 n3).

And given the obstacles that do anything but *invite* engagement in dialogue and the honing of student-researchers who can contribute to an understanding of how one learns and teaches—people in our discipline must also ask this: Where are the dialogic models? What models exist for those student- and teacher-researchers who want to represent their dialogic practices dialogically?

3

Pedagogy scholarship has challenged the gap between research and instruction that often divides the experiences of critical theorists and classroom teachers. Teacher-researchers recognize the classroom as a place where students' diverse backgrounds and experiences can add significantly to ways that classroom instructors and critical theorists perceive, teach, and practice reading and writing. Nevertheless, while teacher-researchers like David B. Downing, Patricia Harkin, and James J. Sosnoski recognize that "the transaction between the teacher and the student [is] a dynamic instance, not of preserving, but rather of actually forming cultures discursively" (Downing et al. 1994, 9), research in English pedagogy, overall, limits or excludes students' voices. There do exist publications in which students' perspectives are indeed privileged, and conference panels also provide forums where students periodically share their sides of the story with professional audiences, but in general, students have found little space in our discipline's scholarship to articulate their involvement in the theories and practices that shape their educational experiences and those of their teachers.

We believe student participation in pedagogy scholarship to be not only a logical outcome of, but also an impetus behind, dialogic approaches to composition, literature, and English education courses. In dialogic classrooms, students and teachers interact as collaborators. In dialogic classrooms, as Mary Louise Pratt would say, students "meet, clash, and grapple" with texts, with each other, and with their instructors as they examine and generate discourses vital to their education and, associatively, to their lives outside the classroom (1991, 34). With the relative absence of students' participation in scholarship on dialogic pedagogies, however, the profession risks perpetuating the objectification of students common in the depositor/receptacle (banking) model that Paulo Freire describes in *Pedagogy of the Oppressed* ([1970] 1990, 58).

As Marguerite H. Helmers makes clear in her extensive critique of articles that describe classroom practices, *Writing Students: Composition Testimonials and Representations of Students*, scholarship on English pedagogies rarely features students as critical agents. Most often, work of this nature presents narratives dominated by instructors' points of view. Reproduced in the form of journal entries, summaries of classroom discussions and interviews, or excerpted passages of papers, students' voices are contextualized by teacher-researchers, whose interpretations of events normally hold sway. Of course, these interpretations are important. Teachers have knowledge and educational experiences (experiences as students and as instructors) that qualify them to make such assessments. But classroom narratives, or "testimonials" as Helmers calls them, tend to reduce the dynamic instances of the pedagogical situations they describe. That is, students in particular must undergo "some flattening of life to fit the requirements of the genre." The rhetoric of such testimonials, given to creating and sustaining generic images of studenthood, presents students as *"transhistorical,"* essentialized characters (1994, 26). "It is through teachers' knowledge of the commonly held beliefs of the profession," explains Helmers, "that they [teachers] are able to supply the details that enable a testimonial about the student to be understood" (27).

It follows, then, that when students enter the discipline's scholarship as critical writers, their voices can complicate, potently, how teachers read pedagogy scholarship, how they read themselves as teachers, and how they read their students. For this reason, if for no other, students require room within professional publications to articulate their viewpoints. For as much as classroom practices inform our discipline's scholarship, scholarship shapes our classrooms, and if English teachers want to interact dialogically with students in the classroom, students should be speaking subjects in English scholarship. With Joseph Harris, we agree that teachers and writers on teaching "need to find ways . . . to represent not only our own view of what is going on in the classroom but those of students as well" (1993, 789). The discipline needs "a view of students staking out positions as intellectuals, working and arguing through issues" (790). In this regard, *Sharing Pedagogies* aims toward increasing students' participation in the discursive transactions that shape English classrooms and, in turn, their culture.

4

Harris is just one of many teacher-researchers who have called for more student involvement in the dialogues shaping English studies. Among others who have identified such a need, Gerald Graff, for example, states,

> The most neglected facet about the culture war is that its issues are clearer and more meaningful to the contending parties than they are to [the] student. It is not the conflicts dividing the university that should worry us but the fact that students are not playing a more active role in them. (1992, 11).

And in "Students' Stories and the Variable Gaze of Composition Research," Wendy Bishop writes, "When teachers become researchers and students' stories, interpretations, and contributions count, then knowledge making and professionalization come into a better balance" (1993, 210). These observations follow the assumptions of educators like Paulo Freire, Ira Shor, and Henry Giroux, whose work represents important articulations of the political and professional implications of dialogic practices. Students, they suggest, need to become critically aware of the ideological forces that shape them, their teachers, their classrooms, and society at large so that they can act with and upon those forces knowledgeably and responsibly. We believe that students engage those forces as they stake out positions within the very scholarship that informs their classrooms.

Sharing Pedagogies represents such an engagement, and in doing so, joins a list of works that privilege students' involvement in our discipline. Among these publications are at least two works in which students do represent themselves as critical agents. David B. Downing's collection *Changing Classroom Practices: Resources for Literary and Cultural Studies* (1994) includes an article by C. Mark Hurlbert, an associate professor at Indiana University of Pennsylvania, and Ann Marie Bodnar, an undergraduate there. Authors of what Downing, Harkin, and Sosnoski call "the most postdisciplinary writing" in the volume (25), Hurlbert and Bodnar sometimes collectively, sometimes in alternating narratives, examine the tensions they felt between the collectivist-like aims of their introductory literature classroom and their moral feelings of outrage over the class's general support of the Persian Gulf War. In the process of composing their paper, Hurlbert and Bodnar generated nearly 400 pages of prose as they worked through their collective and disparate memories of their classroom experiences. The result is a piece that represents the complexity of their experiences at the same time that it demonstrates the challenges that depicting a classroom poses for students and teachers who write together (230 n2).

Another piece that reflects the aims of *Sharing Pedagogies* is Nancy Welch's "Resisting the Faith: Conversion, Resistance, and the Training of Teachers" (1993), which appeared in *College English*. Welch's first-person account of her experiences as a teaching assistant in a doctoral program offers insights into the ways graduate students respond to the often subtle forces of indoctrination they face within the profession. Welch explains the manner in which pedagogies that are liberatory in intent can, within the context of students' position along the academic hierarchy, produce converts rather than critical thinkers. Although our search has favored collaborative projects, we include individually composed essays like Welch's that provide a student's perspective on pedagogical practices.

In three other texts we have reviewed, all in composition, students find a relatively large space in which to articulate their concerns. Although these works do not display students' involvement to the same extent as *Sharing Pedagogies*, they do invite students' direct participation in pedagogy scholarship. One particular work published in the *English Leadership Quarterly* deserves mention. In "A Tale of Two Writing Teachers" (1993), Wendy Bishop and Sandra Gail Teichmann describe their efforts in respective classes they were teaching to fulfill each of their course's writing assignments along with their students. At the time the article was written, Teichmann, a graduate teaching assistant, was also a student in Bishop's course. In the concluding paragraphs of the work, she offers a vivid account of Bishop, who has failed to meet the class's deadline for a final writing assignment. Teichmann expresses her sympathy for her instructor, but she hesitates to ask Bishop to join her peer writing group "because [Bishop] would not have been joining the group as an equal but as a teacher, maybe even as a judge" (7). Such insights as Teichmann's into students' perceptions of power relations in classrooms do reflect the goals of *Sharing Pedagogies*, and the article as a whole is a telling account of the personal and institutional demands that often divide the classroom experiences of teachers and students.

Another notable text, *The Subject Is Writing: Essays by Teachers and Students* (1993), addresses students whom teacher-researchers are trying to "convince . . . to stay willingly" in composition classrooms (vii). Written predominantly by teachers, this collection, edited by Bishop, includes literacy autobiographies and pieces on writing and writing instruction. These essays were reviewed before their publication by students in writing classes around the country. The authors revised their papers in light of students' suggestions, so they stem from a dialogue with their audience, although the dialogue itself is not made literal. Nonetheless, four essays in *The Subject Is Writing* are written by students. Two of these essays tell the writers' stories of coming to writing. The third student essay, co-written, describes the processes the writers go through in fulfilling essay assignments, and the fourth essay is a third-person narrative that briefly and objectively describes a peer workshop in a writing classroom. Although the student writers do not bring the English curriculum itself under scrutiny, as do the articles in *Sharing Pedagogies*, these four works in *The Subject Is Writing* offer readers rare personal accounts of the feelings, attitudes, beliefs, and perceptions that students bring to composition.

In line with the attention to student voices displayed in Bishop's collection, the expressed aim of Sheryl I. Fontaine and Susan Hunter, the editors of *Writing Ourselves into the Story: Unheard Voices from Composition Studies* (1993), is to

> celebrate the true potential of our discipline's multivocal, heteroglossic, nonhierarchical nature [by creating] an occasion for teachers and researchers . . . who do not feel included in the story of our evolving discipline . . . to voice unheard perspectives—expressing views that are not represented in the prevailing central description of the field, calling critical attention to issues that have been overlooked, writing in genres often deserted for the sake of academic discourse. (9–10)

Accordingly, an entire section of this collection examines how composition teachers increased their understanding of their classrooms and professions once they began asking students what they think about writing. The first essay in this section, Bishop's "Students' Stories and the Variable Gaze of Composition Research," reflects many of our own sentiments. The remaining three essays in this section follow Bishop's cue: Teachers relate their students' concerns and revise their practices and theories according to students' reactions. While none of these pieces makes explicit students' participation in the revisions, the writers acknowledge and highly regard their students' contributions.

5

Following the examples of teacher- and student-researchers like Hurlbert and Bodnar, Welch, and Bishop and Teichmann, *Sharing Pedagogies* engages students and student/teacher collaborators as active participants in the scholarship shaping English classrooms.

We realize, however, that with its capacity to draw distances to scale, to engage students and teachers at the levels at which they perceive reality (Freire [1970] 1990, 52), dialogics is also potentially mystifying, and crucially evocative. Gaps, ruptures, and silences in language exist always (Yaeger 1991, 239–41). In dialogue those gaps, ruptures, and silences do not necessarily vanish. In dialogue, they can appear. Students and teachers can go only so far in representing the nuances of their exchanges.

As editors we know this to be true, as we perceived ruptures, gaps, and silences in the works of our contributors. For instance, we sometimes noted inconsistencies in the ways contributors described themselves and each other. And at other times, we felt certain writers' status as students might be restricting the degree to which they could be honest about their responses to their teachers' practices. Most often, we brought these *signs* to their attention, asking them to respond to what in fact was absent, or at least to what *we felt* was absent.[1] Sometimes writers addressed these absences, interested in what insights they might develop. At other times they would not address them. In these cases writers were either confident they had said what they meant to say or unwilling to rely on memories of classes they had taken two or more years earlier. There were also times when writers simply chose not to address issues we raised for reasons of their own, for reasons, we gather, they would rather keep to themselves.

Are co-writers still in dialogue if one or both writers stop responding to their text? Given the gaps in and ambiguity of language, just how much of students and teachers can be brought into dialogue? Or brought into representations of dialogue? As Iris Marion Young writes,

> [S]haring is never *complete* mutual understanding and reciprocity [our emphasis]. Sharing, moreover, is fragile. The other person may at the next moment understand my words differently from the way I meant them or carry my actions to consequences I do not intend. The same difference that makes sharing between us possible also makes misunderstanding, rejection, withdrawal, and conflict always possible conditions of social being.

> The notion that each person can understand the other as he or she under-
> stands himself or herself, moreover, that persons can know other subjects in
> their concrete needs and desires, presupposes that a subject can know him-
> self or herself and express that knowledge accurately and unambiguously to
> others. ([1986] 1990, 310).

With this in mind, we do not claim dialogics as a tool easily applicable to pedagogy and scholarship. Nor do we claim that those who share pedagogies can
fully represent the complexity of their interactions. Rather, we present the
concept of dialogic pedagogies, of sharing pedagogies, as a method of learning, teaching, and rereading/rewriting the discipline's scholarship. It is a concept in which the *willingness* to talk and listen, to negotiate meaning, values,
and differences among participants, is central.

For as long as time permitted, we worked with our contributors to explore
their pieces' insights, contradictions, and inconsistencies. We proceeded self-
consciously, keeping in mind that pedagogy scholarship involves transactions
between editors and writers as well as those between teachers and students. In
other words, although our position as editors differed considerably from that
of our contributors, who had firsthand experience with the events they depict,
we hoped to make our editing process as dialogic as possible. We hoped that
students' and teachers' and our own pedagogies would be enriched throughout this project, as we and our contributors scrutinized the memories of and
feelings about classroom practices we all brought to this work.

In fact, perceptions did change. Contributors often referred to the process
of writing their articles as an integral element of their learning experience, and
as editors and as teachers we, John and Gail, were affected by our conversations with these writers. In light of stories students were sending us about their
struggles to develop and maintain ownership of their writing, we grew more
cautious about how we asked contributors to make changes in their drafts. We
also found ourselves more careful to notice the risk involved in our contributors' shaping of these articles, and more open to interpretations that conflicted
with our own. In writing this introduction, we also became increasingly self-
conscious about contextualizing student voices, wishing we had both the time
and space to construct even more of a "talking book" (as Ira Shor at one point
suggested to us) in which we, our contributors, and Shor could literalize our
responses (and our responses to responses) to each other's work. And, although
we've always considered ourselves sensitive to the needs of students as individuals, we began to see more clearly students in our own classes who resisted our
criticisms, felt ignored, sought our praise, wanted our intervention, suppressed
their own wishes, enjoyed our personal revelations and private conversations.
In other words, it became impossible to interact with writers, to refer to our
classes, or to hear other classes referred to as homogenized groups of students.
Sharing Pedagogies helped us, as teachers and editors, to see better the complexity of the interests and concerns that inform our interactions with students.

6

Because these articles represent complex interactions between students and teachers, students and other students, and students and curricula, they do not *sound* or *feel* like typical academic articles, and they do not necessarily act as blueprints for course designs. Selections such as "Telling Secrets, Telling Lies, Telling Lives," "Writing Cincinnati," and "At Home with Multiculturalism in Kansas" do offer extensive descriptions of curricula in the areas of autobiography, advanced composition, and multiculturalism, and should provide ideas and expectations for anyone thinking about enrolling in or teaching such courses. And other articles such as "Creating Dialogue," "Between Student and Teacher Roles," and "Out of Control" make concrete suggestions for improving undergraduate instruction and teacher training. But in other cases writers do not advocate pedagogical practices; instead, they foreground their emotional responses to and personal revelations about educational experiences. So that while articles like "Voices of a Student and a Teacher," "Lezlie and Brian's Excellent Academic Adventure," "Dinner in the Classroom Restaurant," "When Pedagogy Gets Personal," and "I'll Have to Help Some of You More Than I Want To" may suggest useful ways of thinking about sequenced writing assignments, protocols, open syllabi, teacher-centered hierarchies, and student-centered classrooms, these pieces emphasize more the feelings of anger, delight, anxiety, and vulnerability brought forth through dialogic practices. Every article in this book focuses to some degree on the responses of individual students and teachers to particular educational experiences, and it is this individuality and particularity that make tenuous any function these articles might serve as prescriptions for curricular designs.

It is, however, through these portrayals of the particular and individual, the personal and the emotional, that articles in *Sharing Pedagogies* enter the lore of teaching practices and accrue considerable theoretical value. With Patricia Harkin, we understand lore—which takes the form of personal stories, syllabi, departmental memos, student papers, and the like—as a way for teachers to use classroom narratives to explain and to solve local and cultural problems (1991, 125). And as Downing, Harkin, and Sosnoski might say about the lore-ic pieces collected here, these narratives have "an outstanding advantage over concepts" in that they "retain the complexity of the human relationships under investigation." Against the "thin generalities of abstract theories" and the flattened characterizations that too often constitute scholarship in English pedagogy (1994, 20), *Sharing Pedagogies* provides what Clifford Geertz (1973) would call "thick descriptions" (quoted in Downing et al. 20). Such descriptions make the depicted situations more recognizable to the practitioners of the pedagogies under consideration.

With this understanding, we organize the articles in *Sharing Pedagogies* in the form of an academic narrative—arranged, roughly, accordingly to grade levels—as a way of tracing not only the impressions students and teachers form about dialogic practices throughout postsecondary education, but also as a way of tracing the different academic experiences, different types of courses, teachers, and classmates, and different university settings—that affect dialogue. In this sense, *Sharing Pedagogies* is not a narrative with a single viewpoint; no single definition of dialogic pedagogy or response to dialogic pedagogy reigns. Rather, the voices printed here can be read against, as well as alongside, one another; for this reason, we feel *Sharing Pedagogies* needs to be read as a whole—its voices weighed, aligned, brought into conflict. As in most complex narrativizations, the reader should take an active role in locating and reflecting upon the personal, social, and institutional factors that affect the individuals depicted here.

So, for instance, readers considering the place of personal revelation in English classrooms will need to weigh the rewarding interpersonal relationships among students and teachers portrayed in articles like Lezlie Laws Couch and Brian Arbogast de Hubert-Miller's, and Ott, Hurlbert, and Elizabeth Boquet's against the guarded approach to student/teacher interaction discussed by Katharine M. Wilson and the discomfort in such relationships that Rosemarie Lewandowski and Roland Cooper, and Mary Anne Browder Brock and Janet Ellerby, express at various points in their narratives. This collection as a whole leaves much for readers to decide about what pedagogical practices might be appropriate for them, about what kinds of responses these practices might incur given readers' own situations, and even about the feasibility of such practices to begin with. At the same time, we hope that the voices of these students and teachers will bear heavily against any tendency to read the practices discussed here as prescriptions, any tendency to overlook the complex motives, histories, and perceptions that attend interactions among students and teachers. In other words, *Sharing Pedagogies* is a narrative that many students, teachers, and teachers-to-be should find applicable to their own situations, but like their own situations, this book is a narrative already peopled.[2]

Among these articles, readers will find people experiencing in different ways the affects of academic hierarchies and the struggle for student empowerment (e.g., "When Pedagogy Gets Personal, "Out of Control," "I'll Have to Help Some of You More Than I Want To," "Creating Dialogue," "Lezlie and Brian's Excellent Academic Adventure," "Writing Cincinnati," "Voices of a Student and a Teacher"). Readers can examine the ways these issues drive many of the pedagogical practices treated here, such as open syllabi and the willingness to revise syllabi in midcourse (e.g., "Dinner in the Classroom Restaurant," "At Home with Multiculturalism in Kansas," "Telling Secrets, Telling Lies, Telling Lives," "Between Student and Teacher Roles," "Voices of a Student and a Teacher"), the development of alternative sites to establish cooperative and collaborative classrooms (e.g., "Between Student and Teacher Roles," "Dinner in the Classroom Restaurant," "At Home with Multiculturalism in Kansas, "Lezlie and Brian's Excellent Academic Adventure"), the willingness of teachers to share their writings with their students (e.g., "Telling Secrets, Telling Lies, Telling Lives," "Dinner in the Classroom Restaurant," "Lezlie and Brian's Excellent Academic Adventure," "Creating Dialogue"). Throughout this collection—this narrative—issues and practices occur and recur. Together, these articles narrate the attitudes, beliefs, expectations, and tribulations that can at any given moment constitute a classroom. They are attitudes, beliefs, expectations, and tribulations that dialogic pedagogies bring into play.

Notes

1. We emphasize our own perceptions here. After all, *Sharing Pedagogies* rests on the premise that readers' interpretations of the classroom descriptions can never capture the reality of the classroom experiences as well as the teachers and students who participated in those classes.

2. However, like most narratives, the organization of this volume implies exclusions, for no narrative can accommodate each and every approach and perspective constituting postsecondary education. *Sharing Pedagogies*, for instance, contains—unfortunately—no responses to computer-assisted education, no accounts from minority or gay and lesbian students responding to courses devoted to canon revisions, no reflections on cultural studies approaches to composition courses, no pieces by white students describing their experiences among nonwhite classmates studying nonwhite literature, no articles by men who have taken women's studies or other courses with predominantly feminist bents, and even no article in which a male student shares views with a male teacher. In our drawing to scale the distances in this narrative, an inch off has indeed meant someone absent.

Through various stages of our work, we had the opportunity to consider proposals for and drafts of articles in such areas, but for various reasons could not include them in this collection. In these cases, the hindrances we describe above were quite evident: Teachers' and students' courseloads led several potential contributors to withdraw their proposals; one student writing alone felt he should not be completely honest about a professor who would be on his dissertation committee (even though his memories about the professor were predominantly positive); and in the absence of models, other teacher- and student-researchers struggled through several revisions without ever meeting the generic standards that changed for us more often than we care to admit.

One

Voices of a Student and a Teacher

Freedom vs. Forced Education

Roland Cooper
and Rosemarie Lewandowski

Roland: I was brought up on a small farm in New York State. I played with the animals on the farm and my younger brother. Like most kids, the first day in school was hard for me because I was shy and didn't like myself; I thought other kids wouldn't like me either. If it wasn't for me liking this young girl in my kindergarten class, I would have fought my mother harder to stay home. I was always getting into trouble—daydreaming, not paying attention, and not following directions.

In first grade I tried hard to understand what my teacher said in the classroom, but couldn't concentrate on my work. She gave us a little book to read. She would yell at me to pay attention. I didn't understand what we were reading in class, but was too ashamed to tell her I didn't understand. I thought the other kids would laugh at me.

Nothing happened that I can remember that made me interested in school until I got to fifth grade. In this grade, I loved to write poetry, and was amazed at how I could make words rhyme. The stories were fun too, but I hated that dreaded red marker. My English teacher used it like a gunfighter. Every red mark shot down the grade of my papers. I became so frustrated when I wrote because of the spelling, punctuation, and grammar mistakes, that for a while I went back to daydreaming and getting into trouble in class.

To graduate from high school I made a deal with the principal to join the Marine Corps. After being out of the service for seventeen years, I decided to apply to Union County College to become a Physical Therapist. To my surprise I was accepted into the college even though I had had a bad record in high school. I was so enthusiastic about going to school.

I was placed in English 098, a writing course at a nearby town campus. I had mixed feelings about this course. My ego was bent out of shape at first; I didn't realize it was a developmental course. Our first essay was to pick a personal experience that we had and write about it. The following is part of the essay I wrote, "In God's Time Not Mine":

> I was about four years old, and my brother was three. We went down to the pond, even though Mom said not to. I picked up some rocks and started throwing them into the water to watch the frogs jump. I picked up the rock and raised it to my chest, it was so heavy that I couldn't hold it, and besides, it hurt my hands. When I let go of it, I just kept going with it right into the pond. My brother started yelling, "My Brother, My Brother, My Brother" but no one was around.
>
> I was so scared at first, I tried to reach the dock. I thought if only I could stretch long enough. I was so cold. I kept going down, and down, and down. I was so tired, that I just wanted to rest. Everything got black, but I wasn't cold or tired anymore. Where was I? There was no light anywhere. Suddenly, there was a pin-head of light. I started rushing toward it. It was so bright it hurt me to look. All of a sudden, it was all around me, so warm and I felt totally free. Even though I couldn't speak and the light didn't talk I knew it wasn't my time yet.
>
> "Please don't let me go back, it feels too good!" In another second my father was turning my head and pushing my arms up and down. It was like feeling all the pain and suffering in all the world, at one time.

Rosemarie: Roland was a student who enrolled in a section of my developmental writing course, which had been opened up for late registrants after our suburban community college's semester had already begun. In addition to registering late, he also missed the first few class sessions, so I spent some time filling him in on what he had missed. Our conversation singled his face out of the total of over one hundred students in my teaching schedule. He was also unique because he was the only student in his mid-thirties in that class.

Early that semester I asked students to write about an important or dramatic experience from their past. Roland's drowning topic was unusual, since most of the other students were writing about their proms, high-school graduations, or vacations. For the next writing, I asked students to look over their work and add as much description as possible to enrich the settings for their narrations.

Roland sat in class, uncomfortable. All the other students were writing or looking over their drafts, brainstorming a list of details they were able to remember about their experiences. When I asked if he needed some help, he said he couldn't recall any descriptive details about the drowning incident—the location or the people—it was too long ago. When I suggested he make up some detail to complete the assignment, he said he did not want to change anything he had written, because it was true, and he had spent a lot of time on it.

Roland: Mrs. Lewandowski was trying to tell me what to write. Instead of helping me to be a better writer, she was teaching me to write like someone else. To add something that didn't happen in that experience would be a lie. I wouldn't be able to accept that. I've thought about making corrections on the paper, about including things that *I* remembered that would add more description to it. But still, I wouldn't be adding something that wasn't true. I wouldn't be just trying to color the paper with sensory detail.

Rosemarie: Roland's resistance to my suggestions was very challenging for me. I could not understand why he would not trust my judgment about his writing. I looked upon my students' experiences as material for good stories, but for Roland the story was his life, his truth. As a full-time adjunct that semester, I was teaching five developmental courses, each four credit-hours. My way of coping with such a large number of students was to be well organized. This was my strength, and Roland was interfering with that. I felt too hard-pressed to think of an individualized solution to this disagreement.

I had recently attended a conference on teaching English in the two-year college and had seen a presentation by an instructor from another community college. She had brought samples of her developmental students' writing, together with the writing prompts she had handed out in her class. I was impressed by the sequencing of writings—from narrating a personal experience, to adding detail, to making a statement about its personal significance. It seemed to provide for various modes of writing within one personal essay, even bridging the gap toward analysis and academic writing—something that many developmental writers, and even college freshmen, struggle with.

Convinced that my goals in this assignment were valuable, I resented Roland's unwillingness to try. After discussions with several colleagues, the fundamental question for me became, Why was Roland so resistant? I wondered if this act displayed his reluctance to attempt new and unfamiliar types of writing, explore new ideas. Was he emotionally attached to the work, which surely reflected a large investment of his time and effort? Was he afraid that he might change his mind, and then need to challenge his sense of closure on what the drowning had meant, how it had changed his life?

Roland: I was so excited. I couldn't wait to break into our small groups so the others could experience my story. I couldn't see how it could be written better. My classmates confirmed my feelings when no one could tell me how to change it to make it better. I was astonished at my ability to make the reader identify with the feelings of a four year old.

The only one who wasn't satisfied with my work was Mrs. Lewandowski. I felt she resented me because I wouldn't write like I was someone else just to fit into her idea of how to teach this writing course. I was mad at her and all the other teachers in my life for helping me to feel that I wasn't important as a person, just someone to justify their existence as teachers.

Rosemarie: After thinking about my problem with Roland for several days, I realized the situation highlighted a conflict between the concept of sequenced assignments and my long-term goal of empowering students to take control of their own writing. How could I ask students to write about a personal experience, yet still think I was in control of the handling of that knowledge? In the case of Roland's essay on the drowning, it didn't seem possible to separate technique and meaning in a text, to ask him to change the treatment of the experience, without altering its meaning. How could I encourage students to take control of their writing if I forced an assignment on all students, even one who found it impossible—no matter what the reason? There had to be a way to negotiate the situation.

Before the next class, Roland and I spoke in the library. I apologized for trying to force him to add detail to his paper. I said that he must ultimately choose what and how to write. I could see in his face that he was obviously shocked to hear this, and he told me he had planned to see me about dropping out of the class. I explained to him that I saw myself torn between my enthusiasm for a wonderful, intellectually challenging assignment, and my long-term goal for students to express their own ideas, develop their own voices. I had never discussed my teaching goals with my students, and wondered if all this—my apology, my admission of the pull of two separate goals—would overwhelm and confuse Roland, leaving him with no confidence in my position.

My own student experiences combined with my professional training had pushed me toward privileging the intellect over people's feelings. Roland was helping me to adjust my thinking about his learning in a writing classroom: My staying text-based denied the reality of the person behind the writing, as well as the social aspect of writing in a classroom. By telling Roland to make up sensory details if he could not remember them, I was neither encouraging him to explore his reality nor allowing for real meaning-making. Logically, it seemed that the best way to accommodate a class with a variety of individual voices, each exploring a unique story through writing, was through conferences and my individual responses to their work. I decided that I needed to forget about the sequenced assignments.

Roland: Mrs. Lewandowski and I agreed that I could leave the paper the way it was, or I could make corrections on the paper at a later time. I was satisfied with the paper, especially with the acceptance of my peers. Mrs. Lewandowski asked me if I would add more detail. I said that I would if I could remember anything more, but I wouldn't write something that was a lie.

I don't know if it was me or what this experience did, but I felt more relaxed and freer to write. After our talk, I noticed a change in the other students as well. Everyone seemed to be more at ease. I think it's because the experience changed her. She started asking us, as students, what we thought we should do to our papers to make them better. I felt that she started to give us more control over our writing, and by doing so helped us to become more critical writers, helped us to put the responsibility for our work where it belongs: in our hands.

Rosemarie: I must admit I was not completely comfortable with the change in my teaching style. I felt strongly that I could no longer return to my sequenced assignments, yet it was not exactly clear to me how to encourage development in the writings of so many individual voices. It was impossible to manage private conferences for the several drafts of each paper of approximately one hundred students. Without the aid of sequenced assignments, I found it difficult to assess how much of a student's writing I should suggest be revised. I still have not reached closure on this issue. Since this was a touchy subject with Roland, I imagined other students felt this way as well. We were all getting to know one another much better, and Roland and many other students were comfortable working with their groups and in our private conferences, yet it was not clear that their writings were consistently improving. This type of instruction looked like it was going to require longer than the sixteen weeks of the semester.

At Roland's insistence that he needed to conserve money, I allowed him and several others to take the state test for entrance into Freshman Composition at the end of this mid-level class, even though they had not completed the developmental sequence of writing requirements. My concern for the students was coming into conflict with institutional ideas about assessment and effectiveness. While the college believed that a competent writer should be able to pass this test, I hesitated to tell a student who worked so hard on his writing, who was so motivated as a student, that he was not ready for Freshman Composition. These decisions about competency seemed more complicated than a single standardized test result indicated or even allowed for. When Roland failed the test, which required him to enroll in the highest-level developmental course, he signed up for my class.

During that following semester, I decided to use *Ways of Reading* as the course text. A fellow adjunct instructor had lent me her copy of the book, and the preface by editors Bartholomae and Petrosky had struck me immediately: "We wanted to acknowledge that re-reading is a natural way of carrying out the work of the reader, just as re-writing is a natural way of completing the work of a writer" (1990, vii). This seemed essential in my top-level developmental writing class, since students often look upon my suggestions for revision as severe criticism, a corrective for "bad work." And as a result of my experiences with Roland's class, I had come to feel strongly that "students can, with care and assistance, learn to speak for themselves" (ix), even in a developmental English class at a community college.

We began the semester reading Freire's "The Banking Concept of Education." For several years I had been asking students to write about their goals, why they were in college—a topic of apparent interest to them. I had been trying to encourage students to take control of their writing, and Freire's idea of empowering students to control the conditions of their lives struck me as taking that effort to a more important level. I felt excited about the prospect of sharing educational experiences. For years, I had listened to students complain about the large quantities of material they needed to "study," i.e., memorize, for lecture courses such as Psychology or History. They were sometimes frustrated and bitter about their inability to understand what they studied and their professors' apparent unwillingness to explain it sufficiently. I expected Freire's essay to open up these complaints to a broader perspective on the ways of teaching and learning in our educational systems, so that the students would take part in discussions that reflected larger questions about the academic world.

To my surprise, Roland saw a connection between Freire's ideas and our own previous disagreement over his paper about the drowning incident. "What an original and interesting interpretation of the 'banking concept,'" I thought. He wanted to write about this. Although I knew that we had resolved our conflict, now it was being opened up to *the entire group of new students.* Roland and I seemed on the verge of moving from teacher-as-authority and teacher-as-object to teacher-as-person and teacher-as-peer, and I was uncomfortable with that. This was the first time I would be the subject of a student essay, and I felt more and more that my role as teacher was shifting from a professional, more distant stance to something much more personal. I feared that I might lose authority, so that students would challenge every suggestion for revision, perhaps even balk at the lengthy and challenging reading assignments in the textbook. Instead, something unexpected and exciting happened: Roland's paper, together with the class discussions of Freire, led the class to suggest that we apply the "problem-posing" concept to our writing class. Now that I'd actually come to know the students a little, I felt more comfortable discussing the semester's plans and modifying them to go along with their enthusiasm for Freire. We decided to set aside one hour of each week for students to focus on their own interests and concerns: newspaper and magazine articles, poetry, photographs. Since this was a writing course, I suggested that part of that time be put to writing about what they found most valuable and interesting in each session. Some students went on to use these selections as ways into paper topics.

Roland: I was still in shock that this English professor had apologized to me. I felt that we'd bridged the gap between teacher and student. As soon as the class did the reading of Freire, Mrs. Lewandowski and I had a conversation about using the experience with "In God's Time Not Mine" during my previous writing class. I felt so compelled and excited to share this experience with the class. I think this story about Mrs. Lewandowski and me had to be written. The following is the final draft of my paper showing a direct correlation between Freire's "Banking Concept of Education" and the way the beginning of my first writing class was taught:

> The difference between the "Banking" concept of education and the "Problem Posing" concept of education in my opinion are as plain as night and day. In the following examples I try to show how Freire would explain "Learning from one's Mistakes." Utilizing Freire's "Problem Posing" concept of education.

Learning from One's Mistakes
Being that human beings are creatures of habit, in order to want to change or "learn" a person must first experience some form of discomfort. Example: Personal disapproval of the results of ones actions. In spite of the rationalization process that first takes place, and if the person is capable of being honest, intolerance towards ones self may come next. Being frustrated by the realization and the identification of ones shortcomings the student through courage and positive motivation of self interest is moved to acceptance, the action of being humble, the student changes or "learns."

Freire's example of the "banking" concept of education, is stated on page 208, second paragraph, "Instead of communicating, the teacher issues communiques and makes deposits which the students patiently receive, memorize, and repeat." This next section is dedicated to the contradiction in terms, and is this students attempt to show an experience were by the "Teacher Makes the Transition", from teaching Freire's "banking" concept to her students, to teaching using Freire's "problem posing" concept of education.

I have been taught as soon as I was old enough to go to school, to see everything in relation to the properties of a subject that I know it possess. Therefore I have excepted what a teacher has to teach, and have experienced being taught in the same way.

Freire talks about a "specialized" form of the banking concept, between the teacher and the student in the educational system, example: p. 208 "Narration (with the teacher as narrator) leads the student to memorize mechanically the narrated content. Worse yet, it turns them into "containers," into "receptacles" to be "filled" by the teacher."

This next section is dedicated to this students personal account of a teacher, last semester, using the "banking" concept of education.

Banking Concept in the First Semester
I'm in my first English class, Introduction to College Writing, 098. We are working out of the book Student Writers at Work: The Bedford Prizes, Second Series. The teacher seems to bounce across the floor filled with so much enthusiasm about teaching the class.

She says, "We are going to do the exercise on page 272, The two Drafts by Jonathan Schilk. After reading the exercise answer the questions on page 277. There are five questions, the first one is, "Schilk's second draft provided him with a good place to begin developing his ideas. Describe the strengths and weakness of this draft, and ends with, "Could you suggest ways of revising it?" I read Schilk's second draft, "The Sea and Me" and answer the questions along with the rest of the class.

"What do you think about Schilk's Second Draft?" She asks as she starts to pace across the floor of the class room. Most of the students don't like it and think it's boring, but I say, "I don't particularly like it but, I like the way we get to revise it."

The teacher seems a little annoyed with me but doesn't address the statement I made. She stops in the middle of the room in the front of the class and says, "Schilk wrote three more drafts, before he wrote his final prize-winning essay!"

I say to myself, "What the hell's the sense in answering her questions if she doesn't want to hear the answers!"

She says, "Your next assignment is to read Schilk's Final Draft, '57 Degrees.' What page is it on? I don't have my book open to the page." Someone says page 278. I start to feel even more apprehensive about taking this class, but I say to myself, "Maybe after reading the second story things will be different."

The class time is up, before we all leave the teacher says, "Bring your computer disks with you on Friday. We will be in the Academic Learning Center, in the library on the second floor. During the second period you are going to start writing your first paper on the computer. How many of you have used computers before?" A couple of people raise their hands, then she says, "There will be someone there to give you a seminar on how to use the computer. See you on Wednesday!"

I had to go to court on Wednesday so I couldn't get to class, but I called the college and left a message for the teacher in the voice mail box.

Friday is the next day that I have class in English. I get to class after my Algebra class, although I'm tired I'm glad to be in my English writing class.

The teacher says, "Open your books to Schilk's Final Draft, on page 278." We open our books to the story she asks for and then the teacher asks, "Did everyone do the questions on page 284?" Some people including me say yes. She remarks about the difference in Schilk's two drafts, how Schilk's final draft is polished, interesting and highly readable.

The teacher is so forceful and enthusiastic about us learning to write like Schilk that she doesn't take into account that we aren't "containers, or receptacles, to be filled by the teacher" (Ways of Reading, p. 208).

Then after answering the questions the teacher asks, "What do you think about Schilk's Final Draft? Isn't it a lot easier to read?" Most of the class agreed except me, I say, "I liked the second draft better, because we got a chance to make corrections on the story. I didn't like the final draft because the writer explains everything in too much detail. It became boring to me."

The teacher has a very stern look on her face as she walks around picking up the homework. She starts to the front of the class and as she gets near me she says, "Everyone didn't like Schilk's second draft, but liked Schilk's final draft except you! Let's see, you liked the second draft, because you could make some revisions on it, but you didn't like Schilk's final draft."

I start to say yes, she takes my paper out of my hand and walks to the front of the class. I feel so embarrassed. I say to myself, "I'm so pissed off I could scream!"

We break into groups and the teacher tells us to read the stories we wrote in our journals and critique each other's work. I read my story, "In God's Time Not Mine", to my group. No one in my group can answer my question, "What can I add to my story?" The teacher says, "I think you could have added more dialogue, between your brother and yourself. You could be more descriptive about where the story takes place." I think to myself, I'm really pissed off now.

"If I add more dialogue, the story will be a lie! That's not what happened in the story, and I don't think I was that interested in what kind of day it was. I was only four years old." That doesn't please her. I say to myself, "She's determined to make me write my story like Schilk, but I'm not Schilk! I'm not an 'empty vessel' that the teacher 'fills' to change me." I left the class room so angry. I wanted to scream. I don't think I can stand this anymore. I'm going to have to quit. I was so disgusted that I just went home and threw my book bag with my English books on my bed. I didn't look at them till the next morning just before school.

The next day I met my teacher in the library. She called me into her office, said she had something to say to me. I thought. . . she was going to tell me to drop the course. She had a discomfort look on her face.

Teacher Makes the Transition

I assumed by looking at her face, that the Teacher makes the Transition, from teaching the "banking" concept to the "problem posing" concept of education, as the student, is Learning from one's Mistakes.

She said, "I apologize for trying to force you to add more detail to your paper. You must ultimately choose what and how to write." I was so shocked I almost fell over. . . .

I never have had a teacher apologize me for anything, let alone for forcing me to do what they wanted. I think this is the first time I ever thought of a teacher as a person with feelings and problems. She explained to me how bad she felt when she thought she had hurt my feelings. I was almost moved to tears. "I really like this English class I told her. I never did well in school before. I always got C's D's and F's."

She went on to say, "I'm really glad that you're not going to drop this course."

Rosemarie: By bringing in Freire, and discussing goals and methods for education, I opened myself to this criticism. It is not flattering to consider myself as an example of a teacher using the "banking concept" of education. I'm still not comfortable with it, although it was a natural outcome of our class discussions of various student experiences with education. The exercise with the Schilk essay had been a failure, something unpleasant to share with a new class of students. But Roland's paper showed me that intellectual work is powerful for students when ideas speak to their personal experiences. Also,

Roland's closing paragraphs show that I, too, am a learner. It is almost as if our roles are reversed, and he delights in his Freirean analysis of my words.

Roland: What I think Rosemarie learned from this experience was that students aren't receptacles to be filled. In my opinion, this should be taught to all students who are going into teaching today. Because Rosemarie's the kind of person who's more concerned with the person she's teaching as opposed to the "stuff" she's teaching, she's been able to change her attitude and outlook on instruction, and her teaching technique.

In the back of my mind, I know Rosemarie's a teacher, but I don't see her that way. I need to see her as one of my peers; I am more comfortable seeing her as learning from this situation. I look forward to working with a teacher, knowing that we're in collaboration in the learning process.

Rosemarie: Although Roland did not pass one half of the state test, I passed him on to Freshman Composition. He was so willing to work on his essays, get help, that I believed he could handle the demands. Still, I wondered how he would fare in the class. During that subsequent semester, he came to see me about a paper he'd written. It had been returned with a small red "C" at the top, a few red circles around commas, and no comments. (This is a concern as I weigh final grading: knowing what comes next, wondering if the student is well prepared.) I advised him to discuss the grade and the writing with the professor. Afterwards, Roland told me he'd felt the professor would not listen to him, so he transferred into a different section, with a different professor, and with a former group-mate from one of the courses he had taken with me. At the end of that semester, Roland told me that he had to take a grade of Incomplete and try to make up two papers before the first six weeks of the following semester were over. I wished him well.

Roland: I used to have a great fear of teachers. They are always so forceful. If you didn't do what they said, then you weren't a good student, which made you a bad person. By Rosemarie apologizing to me, and changing her technique in teaching, that made her more of a human being to me, someone that I could learn from and benefit.

Before I took Rosemarie's class, I'd never experienced a class where I could sit down and critique someone else's work, give my opinion about their work and be compassionate about subjects, without fear of retaliation on anyone's part. That is something that I had early as a child, and it was taken from me. But now I'm starting to feel that enthusiasm for learning again. I get caught up in it. I'll sit down at a computer and write a story—I'll forget where I'm at. It's like when I draw or paint, I'll lose myself totally in what I'm doing.

Mrs. Lewandowski showed me that anybody can learn from anybody. When I first started in the class, I thought of myself as having a lot more experiences than the other students. Yet another student, Fred, was one of the people who totally amazed me in his ability to write. The kid sits down and in two seconds he will write something. I'm fascinated with his abilities. I needed guys like Fred to keep me down, so that I could say, well, see, I'm not that great. So I still have room to learn. I could learn something from this kid.

I think one of the hardest lessons a writer can learn is to be true to one-self, and still accept and learn from someone else. I thought that I was a good writer, but sitting in Mrs. Lewandowski's class and watching those kids write as well as they do made me a little embarrassed. But I used the difference in our ages to see where I needed to work. To me, that's fascinating because I could never do that before. I was either above somebody or below them. I could never come straight across and learn directly from someone. That was what this experience changed in me. Because of my respect for Rosemarie and my willingness to learn, I hang on almost every word she says to me. I want this knowledge that she has, even though I'm not going to get it just by listening to her. It doesn't work that way—just like the banking concept of education didn't work for me.

Now, if I have a problem with another teacher, I can identify what the problem is. If it's my problem, then I can work on it. If it's their problem, as it was in my first Freshman Composition class, and I can't work on it, then I know that the only thing I can do is change the situation, do what I have to do: Find a professor who's enthusiastic about teaching the student, not just trying to force education down their throat.

Roland and Rosemarie: At the beginning of this project, Roland had a fear that he was not "good enough" to be able to write this essay. He also could not remember any details of specific experiences in learning before en-tering the community college; he was overcome by fear. He didn't believe he had the discipline to complete this task. He felt the pressure of the editors' request for him to write the introduction to the essay. He also feared he would not be able to write with someone else. No one had ever touched his work; it was his, not someone else's. This experience not only has given him the abil-ity to loosen his possessiveness of his writing, but also has allowed him to accept and adapt another's opinions.

It has not been easy. The three-way pull among Rosemarie's, Roland's, and the editors' ideas generated much discussion and negotiation, even to the extent of wondering why this essay needed to be written. One thing that trans-formed for Roland was his trust in Rosemarie's faith in his writing ability. That trust began to grow when we resolved our conflict in the classroom. Even more recast was Rosemarie's compassion, her fear that she had hurt Roland by trying to force him to write more—initially in their first writing class together, and now with the writing of this essay. We have accepted the fact that we are not going to reconstruct each other's personalities or writing styles, but that our voices do complement each other. We are now more open to each other's suggestions, and our willingness to change is greater. Our working together side-by-side on dual computers in the community college computer lab has been a novel experience for both of us. It has been very challenging, to find the time in two complex lives, and to mesh two unique ways of thinking. This is a far cry from a teacher teaching the "banking concept" of education.

Rosemarie is no longer the-one-who-teaches, but the one herself taught in dialogue with Roland, who while being taught also teaches. We become jointly responsible for a process in which both grow. What Roland once again found strange was that Rosemarie had fear herself, that even teachers are human beings. When Rosemarie had anxieties about how we would be able to write together—that there might not be enough time to polish the writing, that we wouldn't be able to co-write the passages that needed to be done together, that Roland might want to change what Rosemarie had already written about him, that the editors might reject our paper for its length, that our disagreements over structure seemed unmanageable—Roland's faith in our ability to complete this project nurtured the confidence that she needed to continue working.

This is the first time that either one of us has allowed another writer side-by-side with us. We are completing each other's sentences.

Two

"I'll Have to Help Some of You More Than I Want To"

Teacher Involvement and Student-Centered Pedagogy

Chris Zawodniak

Teachers always have power in a class. They hold the grades, and usually, students perceive them as holding the knowledge, too. The way teachers use this power is perhaps the defining characteristic of their pedagogy. Some teachers may work with students to create the class environment; others may force a class environment upon students. Regardless of one's approach to students or intent in designing a syllabus, teachers have the power even before they step into the class.

This power is no easy burden for teachers: Those who ignore lines of power within the class often reinforce them, and those who meet power issues by being too controlling often narrow the space for student creativity. A careful balance is hard to achieve, and no one knows how the power issues will play out until class starts.

I write this essay to give you a student perspective on the issues of power in the classroom. But it is only one perspective, and I guess I'm not an ordinary junior—I don't think most students my age (twenty) are concerned with critical pedagogy. (Maybe many are, and they just don't have the words for it.) Anyway, I learned a lot about teaching styles and writing and conducting classes in my first year of college. And because of this exposure and my awareness of it, I have come to focus on my own ideas about teaching.

English teachers often have the same goals—teaching students how to read a text critically or how to write well; but the means and methods of achieving those goals are what count in the classroom—in practice. In Freshman Composition, I experienced the complications of achieving a sense of empowerment through what my teacher, whom I'll call Jeff, considered a student-centered pedagogy.[1] I still am gaining an understanding of what happened in the course. Throughout this paper, I give snapshots of the class structure and the day-to-day activities.[2] I also reflect on what has puzzled me most throughout this writing: my affection for Jeff and my shifting views of his attempts at a student-centered pedagogy.

It is important for undergraduates to write about teaching because it is what happens to us as college students. The significance of a student perspective becomes clearer in the light of scholarship I'm reading on student-centered classrooms and literacy.[3] One thing that has seemed remarkably absent in the discussions about the teaching of English is the voice of students. I have read articles by educators, but few show direct student perspectives. The student perspectives shown are used for the teacher's ends. Though the students are the subjects, the students' views about teaching are used by teacher-researchers to make their own points. While academic writing by academics cannot be any other way—certainly professors cannot claim to have a student voice—I write this article for self-understanding. The writing has helped me to understand my Freshman English experience and my role in that experience. In addition, one of the most important things students can do is write down their ideas, for in that writing lies the beginning of narratives that aren't usually regarded in professional discourse, narratives that extend beyond end-of-the-quarter questionnaires. So I write this essay with the hope that it will be a strong student voice, with the recognition that it is only one student's voice, and with the hope that many others will follow.

It is the first day of class in my first quarter of Freshman English. Jeff has already passed out the syllabus. Some words are spoken, but I don't remember them. Then, from my teacher I hear, "I'll have to help some of you more than I want to." And I'm thinking, "This is radical—*not* what I expected." I don't quite understand what Jeff's comment means. It seems rebellious, yet official. Perhaps Jeff is admitting that teachers, like everyone, get tired. Teachers aren't machines that never run out of energy, but sometimes they have to help students even more than they want to, even when they have been working with students all day. Jeff's directness was giving him validity as a person (like us students), not a teacher who could do everything. I'm thinking that Jeff won't fit into some teacher mold; he won't pretend that teachers can just go through a routine. Rather, he seems like one who will shake things up, break that mold.

The course description, paraphrased from the syllabus, is as follows:

> Learning-by-doing in this course will make you become more aware of yourself and of what your other options could be. Writing isn't a subject, but

an activity, and in this class you'll be doing activities rather than listening to lectures. Even more than in other courses, you should come to every class and keep up with your work.

Reading this syllabus now, I would say that student awareness of "options" (a word that still means little to me in the syllabus) is the course goal. But Jeff's description seemed so vague to me that I couldn't grasp what the course plan or his vision was. From the syllabus, I didn't know what Jeff wanted, but that only intensified his mysterious character to me. He was like a puzzle with dazzling pieces, but not a whole picture could be made from them. Syllabi are not as revealing as a teacher's day-to-day instruction, so I don't expect too much from a syllabus. The syllabus does, however, show the ideology at work in this case: that students should be left to work by themselves. When teachers leave us students alone, Jeff's syllabus suggests, we have the best chances for freedom to find our own voices, and, perhaps, creativity. Students' independence allows students to make the class, was Jeff's silent motto; and it matched perfectly with what he had said that first day: "I'll have to help some of you more than I want to."

During the first week of class, I wrote at the top of the syllabus another thing Jeff said: "The five-paragraph essay is not only old and silly; it's a rule for rule's sake." Who couldn't love that? It says, "Break the rules," and it went against most of what I had been taught in high school. I also liked Jeff because he wore sneakers and jeans. In addition, he was an inconsistent shaver. I guess I saw him as not being a snobby academic—he seemed to fit in with us students. His style seemed to refute the formal power teachers usually show by dressing up or standing behind a podium to give a lecture.

As the quarter progressed, however, my admiration for Jeff was joined with frustration. Jeff's pedagogy, as I experienced it, was that the teacher should interfere as little as possible with class activities, leaving the students to run the class. As a result, he did give prompts, but once conversation among students started, he rarely spoke. Jeff would sit looking at us or into space, and we would talk and then look at him, waiting for some kind of guidance. There was a lot of silence, but I don't think it was usually good silence. It was usually the silence of our uncertainty and intimidation. It wasn't what Jeff did that bothered me—all teachers give prompts and all want student participation—it was how he did it that was bad. He perhaps thought that in that room, we, students and teacher, could be equal and have an ideal class. However, to achieve the ideal class I think Jeff wanted, students would have had to leave their assumptions about teaching and about the power of teachers at the door. As David Bartholomae suggests, when we students get to college we invent the university—we try meeting the freshman English course with what we know, which is most usually the ways of high-school composition (1988, passim). We students play off our accumulated experiences, just as teachers teach from their accumulated teaching experiences. Instead of looking at one another, teachers and students alike can easily be a day or moment behind, responding to yesterday's teachers, or long-ingrained ways of teaching, writing, and teaching writing: We are reflections of our past experiences. In Jeff's class we students were, after all, inventing the university with our former experiences, with our memories of high-school classes where few, if any, teachers sat on their desks and refused to tell us what to do next.

One of the themes of Jeff's method as I saw it was that we can't comment on what we do not know and we don't know what we cannot prove. This often meant that Jeff didn't speak much in class, because when we speak we usually make some sort of claim or assertion. Jeff said that once, a student asserted that the Bible's story of creation was correct, and Jeff said he couldn't prove the student wrong. I took Jeff to mean that we cannot comment on that which we do not know; we can only move to higher levels of probability. With these examples, Jeff's silence in class discussions wasn't too surprising. Perhaps for Jeff, silence was an occasion to investigate. I think that's how he saw it for us, and he didn't want to do the investigating for us. He didn't want to do our job as thinkers, but it was difficult for me and many of my classmates to understand what he wanted.

I initially thought Jeff was radical when he said, "I'll probably have to help some of you more than I want to." But today I question his motive for that statement. Shouldn't he have helped us to be as good as we could be? Perhaps, I thought, all teachers sometimes have to help some of us more than they want to, and as I said at the beginning, all teachers get tired. But I now realize how much his statement could have reflected not only an actual fatigue in, but also a dispassion for his teaching. Jeff's method didn't allow for enough constructive guidance during class or through the quarter. As a result, I often felt alone and mean-spirited in the class. I felt alone because of the mean-spiritedness, which I felt because we students were, despite the lack of constructive guidance, always subject to Jeff's judgment, to his power.

This feeling of judgment was intensified by the fact that Jeff rarely participated in discussions except to qualify a student's comment or to rein in the conversation if absolutely necessary. In many class sessions, he seemed to present knowledge or ask questions of us while preserving his role as judge of our ideas. Usually we could speak our minds, but Jeff was still the guard of knowledge in that he evaluated our responses rather than encouraged further dialogue. One day, Jeff brought in a newspaper article about the Pope's rewriting of the Church laws. The students got off to a good start, talking about and criticizing the conservative laws. The abortion issue entered the conversation, and the class was discussing it in relation to the time of the founding fathers. I said, "Abortion is more common now than it was 200 years ago." Then, Jeff said, in a flat tone, that it wasn't more common, just more public, out in the open. I felt like he was judging even the smallest parts of our conversations. I thought Jeff was being too picky, but part of me then still just wanted to figure him out and follow his rules.

As much as Jeff might have tried to leave his power outside the class by speaking only when necessary, the students didn't want him to. We expected him to do things that he didn't do, like give strong, constructive guidance, not just critical comments. To some extent, I think my classmates and I wanted to *obey* Jeff. As my Critical Writing teacher said on the first day of class last week, "I know that part of acclimating yourself to a new class is trying to figure out what a professor wants." We wanted to know what Jeff wanted, but he wouldn't let us. Not confining us to his directions, Jeff tried to relieve us of some of the pressures of molding papers into what he wanted. This idea is not totally bad. Students need to risk their own thoughts, and some can only do this if they don't have the safety net of the teacher telling them what to do. But I felt I had to do too much guessing in Jeff's class. Paradoxically, he gave me nothing to obey yet forced me to obey him.

It's a nice idea for students to be self-motivated, but sometimes we aren't. Jeff tried to guide us, but his guidance was paradoxically too formal and too informal for me. He wanted to follow a plan, which most teachers do, but Jeff's plan revealed itself by his simply not telling students what to do—at all. He seemed unable to respond when the look on a student's face or the silence in the classroom meant he needed to be more inviting and explain himself more. Even in his written responses to our papers, Jeff's comments rarely extended beyond "more," "unclear," or "good." Our subject was personal essays, but his aloofness didn't encourage our emotions to come out. It was very difficult for him to help us get to *our* good writing. He showed us good writing, but passion and concern for our writing seemed lacking.

One day Jeff started class by saying something like, "How are your papers going?" The question isn't threatening, but he spoke in a dispassionate and distant tone. His delivery supported what he had said on the first day of class: "I'll probably have to help some of you more than I want to." For a moment, no one spoke. Then I complained that I was having trouble with my "explaining a concept" paper. I was having trouble showing my thesis, that football was an outlet for violence (a subject I later abandoned). My classmates asked me questions: "What are you trying to show?" "What do you have down already?" "Is that exactly what you mean?" I tried to respond productively. Then another classmate spoke: "That's my problem, too. I know what I mean to say, but don't know how to say it." Then another spoke, and so on. Soon many of us were talking about one another's papers, trying to help each other.

Then Jeff spoke. The class got silent. He said to me, "Do you want an extension?" in a serious tone. "Yes," I said. He gave another person who spoke up early in the discussion an extension, too. I felt like I had risked Jeff's judgment, and I felt great anxiety doing so. I think the extension had the effect of punishing the other students, just because I spoke up in a moment of boldness and no one else did. Even here, when Jeff's pedagogy appeared student-centered (when we students ran the discussion ourselves) it had the effect of rewarding a few instead of helping everyone in their writing.

Jeff fulfilled his position of power in two ways: by being rigid and by being laid back. Jeff was laid back when he tried to bond with us by telling us he had to clean up his kid's "shit" or telling us that he played basketball with friends. When he did tell us about the basketball, he kind of smiled. I don't know why this sort of communication wasn't greater. One day when we students were talking about our personal experience papers, Jeff mentioned that once he found a human carcass, but, he said, "It's too early in the morning for that story." And it was, but at that time I felt like the class was together—Jeff was just one of us. This intimate, relaxed approach brought out the best in him. Yet, I think the class was a little suspicious of these times, for we never knew what the next day would be like. We never knew when rigid Jeff would return.

My most vivid memory of Jeff's rigidness was the day he responded to our criticisms of the class. Students were given a chance to anonymously write their biggest criticisms one Monday, and the following Wednesday Jeff responded to them. He staunchly defended all criticisms against his teaching: "Some of you complained that I didn't come to class prepared. It took me five years to learn all of this." Then he pointed to the blackboard on which, sometime before the day's session began, he had written all the concepts we had discussed that quarter. He didn't seem interested in improving his teaching or helping us students understand him. He thought he was always right in his instruction. Jeff's position gave him responsibilities that he officially met, as in this case, but he didn't meet the power position he had in my eyes.

Jeff didn't give the impression that he wanted to hear what we had to say. I felt like we were often guessing his meaning—his truth?—and we were trying to figure out what he wanted to hear us say. I certainly mastered this, but I was obeying and being manipulative, not learning to think for myself. I don't feel that I grew a lot in my writing abilities—although, at the time, I felt I had grown a lot. (I did get an "A" and earned the respect of the teacher.) Because Jeff didn't make us do things in any encouraging sort of way, his pedagogy was like a rugged individualism, divisive and negatively competitive. I wonder if he was trying to get us to adapt to what he considered the real world.

Jeff, however, wanted students to be observers of the world from his isolated class. He implied this once when he said that to understand a system you have to get outside of it. But his pedagogy didn't work for the class theme, which was *personal* essays. In writing personal essays, we go into the world, as observers and participants. For example, in my profile paper I wrote about the lady who worked at the cafeteria because I already had experiences with her, impressions of her, even if I didn't meet her until later. I couldn't understand the nuances of preparing for the morning cafeteria rush or of being the lady who runs the meal cards through the machine and does a lot more, if I were outside that system. For my personal experience paper, I revisited an experience about moving from New Jersey to Ohio just before the start of third grade. By getting inside that experience, not outside it, I could give rich details. Good personal writing takes us into a place, and we can't create it by trying to remain outside our surroundings.

One thing that has become so clear to me and frightened me during the writing of this article is how much I liked Jeff and how much sympathy I have for him because of his misguided approach. Throughout the quarter, I was almost as caught up in Jeff's ideas as he himself was. During that quarter, I had horrible roommates, and Jeff's class was an escape from the chaos of my own dormitory. His rigid teaching became a spot where I (almost) knew the rules. But the rules just didn't work. Even late in the quarter, I felt like I was asking Jeff's permission for something—approval, perhaps?—when I would show him my rough drafts. I was always checking with Jeff to make sure my writing and reasoning were right, and that constant, nervous checking now shows itself to me as a sign that something in his student-centered pedagogy *wasn't* right.

Since my class with Jeff, I have taken classes with several teachers who have had different approaches to writing instruction. The ways of writing that they taught me have lasted longer and proven more beneficial than the fear of judgment I experienced in Jeff's class, which had the effect of constraining my writing. In Freshman Composition—and in all writing courses—we students need to create our own identities, and it is through our voices that our identities emerge. Students cannot fake a discourse and have it contribute to long-term writing growth, if only because faking discourse robs us of our voices.

Moreover, we students know when teachers are lying. It sometimes takes us a long time—I am an example—but we do find out. Then the unlearning of poor instruction can be difficult, but we do unlearn and relearn. Rather than Jeff's tricky compositional hoop-jumping, teachers should help students find their own voices from the start. This can be dangerous, and is probably always difficult (for teachers as well as students), but not more so than overcoming another teacher's poor instruction.

Despite Jeff's belief that he could vacate the class in order to bring out student voices, this paradox remains: We students must have active teacher involvement at the core of any student-centered classroom. We need to be welcomed —not left to attempt masterpieces with post–high-school hands. Teacher involvement is the key not only to starting conversations, but also to guiding them along their meandering paths. When the teacher's power acts as a welcoming embrace, rather than a vacuum, students can develop their own ideas and feel comfortable that they are in an environment in which their ideas can flourish.

Teachers and students in composition courses like the one I describe here have to get personal: We have to get into the personal to write about it, and teachers have to talk about the personal to help us talk about it. Teacher and student must work and continue conversations together because, as Paulo Freire says, "Men [sic] are not built in silence, but in word, in work, in action-reflection" ([1970] 1990, 76). When we realize the classroom implications of Freire's wisdom, we can overcome the isolation that often exists between teacher and students. When we recognize the necessity of mutual involvement, students and teacher both can work together to achieve a pedagogy that is student-centered.

Notes

Thanks to Brenda Brueggemann for her guidance throughout the writing of this essay.

1. Since my freshman year, I've transferred to Ohio State University. This article is about a course I took at a previous college, which, for reasons of anonymity, I do not name.

2. The theme for this composition course was personal essays. Students wrote various types of essays, such as personal experience, profile, problem solution, concept explanation, and an in-class essay, but all were to come from students' own experiences. The essays were to be reflective of or have some relevance to each individual student.

3. These works include Mike Rose's *Lives on the Boundary* (1989), Glynda Hull and Mike Rose's "This Wooden Shack Place: The Logic of an Unconventional Reading" (1990), and Mina P. Shaugnessy's *Errors and Expectations: A Guide for the Teacher of Basic Writing* (1977).

Three

Lezlie and Brian's Excellent Academic Adventure

Lezlie Laws Couch
and Brian Arbogast de Hubert-Miller

Brian: What happened? After months of writing and talking about it, Lezlie and I still have different opinions about which events are significant in our relationship as teacher and student. Consequently, this article is a failure. Although the failure is not utter and absolute, it is a failure nonetheless because we cannot fully frame the reality of our success.

Lezlie and I have a relationship marked by small nuanced exchanges too rich and contextual to communicate accurately. Some events seem quite casual to one of us and yet consequential for the other. This difference of emphasis is telling, and it should be kept in mind for anyone seeking to understand a teacher's power to guide and stimulate, and a student's need to grasp the humanity and limitations of teachers. As researchers we would like to have given you a prescription for your personal application. Such a prescription, however, is unrealistic because serendipity played a large role in our relationship. We can only hope that tales from our excellent academic adventure will encourage you to be bold in response to opportunities, to remember that boundaries might be only where you set them.

You should know something about us. After a long career as an artist, I decided, in August of 1993, to return to college to complete a degree abandoned almost twenty years ago. My goal is to find a new outlet for my creative energy as a writer-researcher-teacher. Shunning tradition, I have designed my interdisciplinary studies major to focus on rhetoric, ethics, and social criticism.

Being a novice student is disconcerting after operating at a high level of professionalism for decades, so respect for my past status is exceptionally important to me. I wanted to find a kindred spirit in the academy who could help me negotiate this transition to a new career, and Lezlie turned out to be that all-important person. Our small town, midwestern roots, and baby boomer ages provide us some cultural and generational familiarity.

Lezlie has been teaching writing courses at several grade levels for the past twenty-five years. Her interest in students and energy for teaching remain abundant. Her writing reflects an interest in popular genres, like the personal essay, to which she has turned with vigor in the last four years. This shift in genre and audience, away from traditional academic writing, has an impact on her teaching. She creates an interactive writing experience with her students as a way of identifying more closely with their struggle to become better writers.

Lezlie protests every time I wax eloquent about her teaching skills. The events we are about to recount will vindicate my high admiration for her as a teacher, but even more importantly as a creative person. Our nontraditional interactions might be seen as threatening by the faint of pedagogical heart, but not by the rugged individualists in the teacher-researcher corps. Although every course begins with the first day, even that was atypical for me.

First Class

Brian: In the 1970s I would have said Lezlie gave off "good vibrations." She radiates knowledge, though knowledge alone does not make a good teacher. What does is an empathic personality and stimulating creativity. Her teaching method embraces two distinct roles: the no-nonsense assessor and the playful collaborator. The former is represented by her syllabus, which was clearly constructed to intimidate with its excessive length and thorough detail. Her classroom demeanor, by contrast, is warm, funny, humane, and thoroughly engaging. This "split personality" felt comfortable to me because it was much like my own. I am a no-nonsense person, except when I am being totally silly.

On the first day of class, I released myself into Lezlie's care because I thought of myself as a novice writer. The course, Expository Writing, is the second of two writing courses required of all majors. I wanted to learn how to write, and my impression of her power to grant that wish mesmerized me. I let her take control.

Her purposes for writing became my own. "Writing is an act of discovery, a way of taking one's place in the 'great conversation' of humanity," she said. This attitude was a new but sensible perspective to me. My filing cabinets, a treasure of intellectual chaos, were already full of bits and pieces of that conversation. Finding my place in the conversation was clearly what I was looking for. Then she made an empowering statement, one that touches the core of creative identity: "Writing is highly idiosyncratic; we all set about creating texts in ways unique to our capabilities, tastes, and habits." Well, that is pretty much common sense, but it was news to me. I thought writing was like chemistry or calculus, with rules to decipher, master, and then elegantly mix and match. She liberated me from that notion. Then she appealed to my businessman side by making the class a guarantee: If we would hit the ground running and work extra hard in these first few weeks, she guaranteed that we would see a big payoff by week twelve. I was determined to press her claim. What could I lose? There were witnesses. If it didn't work, at least I had grounds to sue for a tuition refund.

Lezlie: For me, this first session of Expository Writing was unremark- able. I was relishing yet another chance to teach writing right, but having taught this course often, I was also well aware of the difficult days that lay before me and my students. I moved through the syllabus in my usual me- thodical fashion and did my spiel on my beliefs about writing and its place in the liberal arts curriculum: Writing is discovery; Writing is generative; Writ- ing is power, yeah, yeah, yeah. After twenty-five years, I've got this act down fairly well: Show them your empathy for their concerns and fears; show them a demanding but supportive instructor. Any writing teacher would find this first day typical.

I do offer a guarantee, which evidently impressed Brian. "Follow my guidelines, faithfully perform the tasks I ask you to perform, and I guarantee that you will see dramatic improvements in your writing by week twelve of this course. I guarantee it."

And so, for this one student, at least, such a guarantee elicited its desired effect. As for me, I was clueless about the adventure Brian was about to in- stigate.

"Claiming an Education"

Brian: By about the third week, class was intellectually satisfying, but I was eager for a bit more action. I was on a zesty, baroque, academic adventure and was seeking, as with all things baroque, an adventure suitably elaborate and layered. So, in keeping with my silly side, I composed a letter to my teacher. I can honestly blame it on Adrienne Rich. Though to be scrupulously fair, Lezlie's open classroom attitude did invite writing mischief.

Adrienne Rich made a speech at Rutgers that has been widely circulated in essay form under the title "Claiming an Education." We read it in class, and it seemed as if she was speaking directly to me when she said, "Refuse to sell your talents and aspirations short, simply to avoid conflict and confrontation. . . . You have the right to expect your faculty to take you seriously" (1993, 659–660). Rich contends that a student is not a vessel into which education is poured, but a claimant of an education, someone with expectations asserted "in the face of possible contradiction" (657). There is a proper role between teacher and student according to Rich, and it involves collaborators engaged in learning.

Spurred on by Rich's deliciously inflammatory rhetoric, I wrote a clever letter full of humor and all the creativity I could muster. I asked Lezlie to make me a special case, in deference to my "rights" as a student. I asked her to be my "academic friend." By that I meant the collaborative learning partner Rich suggested, one that would help me negotiate my midlife transition. The letter would really determine whether or not Lezlie was a kindred spirit. In the event I had misjudged her progressive nature, the letter ended by giving her an out: "Either you will be polite and keep your distance, or you'll want to come out and play."

I did massive amounts of rationalizing as I waited for her reply and confessed my daring to some other students, who were either horrified or deeply amused at what I had done. Without a hint of emotion, Lezlie entered class the next week and casually handed me her reply, a sheet folded neatly into thirds for privacy. Apprehensively, I opened it and read: "Wow . . . I welcome it. Although, I truly think you have endowed me with more gifts than I possess. . . . Nevertheless, I am here to serve your needs. . . . Let's talk."

One of my friends in the administrative offices said Lezlie had called around checking up on me, probably to be sure I was not in need of a psychiatric evaluation. When we met a few days later, she kept the conversation focused on me. By meeting's end she had managed to draw out an abstract of my life story without telling me anything about herself except that she loved her dog, Ginger. I left her office reassured that "learning is an open process" and that she would be "mindful of my creative needs." This type of extra-class interaction is very important to me, and by her disposition Lezlie demonstrated she was the very model of Adrienne Rich's ideal. With my letter, I claimed my education, and with our first conversation outside of class she began the wonderful process of honoring that claim.

Lezlie: Since I teach in Rollins' evening degree program, I work with students who are returning to school by virtue of their willingness to make fairly significant sacrifices in their lives. These people are incredibly serious about their education. But Brian was soon to set a new standard in academic seriousness—as well as audacity. His letter appeared on the clipboard attached to my office door in the fashion that I have since become accustomed to receiving his voluminous communications—beautifully typed, and printed (with footnotes and a works-cited page no less!) and inserted in a clean white eight-by-ten-inch envelope. This letter was the most arresting piece of writing I think I've ever received from a student. It was engagingly passionate, painfully frank, and highly idiosyncratic. In the first paragraph, he saucily informs me that he does not address me as "teacher" because "you are not my teacher yet. We have not bonded and I am angry about it—make that very angry." Slow to ruffle, I was amused, but definitely on guard. I read on.

He continued, in what has become Brian's familiar and straightforward writing style, with a series of demands: *demanding* to be noticed, *demanding* recognition for his previous accomplishments, *demanding* my best instruction, *demanding* to be fully challenged, and, on top of all this, *demanding* my friendship. "I need you to be my academic friend," he wrote. I was overwhelmed.

It was apparent that Brian had been listening very, very closely to every single word I had been saying in class. His writing was rich, detailed, filled with liveliness and texture, amazing in its use of ideas from both his previous course readings and our class discussions. Any teacher of writing would have been pleased to see a student demonstrating so many of the skills that she praises in her lessons. But since this was only week three of the semester, it was quite obvious that this student came to me with well-developed writing skills. What could I possibly teach a student who writes with such verve, such confidence, such power? The feeling I had verged on intimidation.

And there were reasons other than this developed style about which to be intimidated. This was a pushy student, indeed. Barely into the second page of his five-page letter, he gives me a list of his needs:

> I need an emotional contract. I am too old for the 18–22 year old formal distance of undergraduate instruction; it is too "us and them," too adversarial. I need new friends who recognize me, like someone from their past who they had only known by sight, but now see an opportunity to connect with, who are susceptible to my creative charms, who respect my accomplishments and are not put off by my clumsy, passionate attempts to extend my dreams.

"Oh gad," I thought. "What do I have on my hands this semester?!" Many adult students are eager to share their professional and personal successes with their professors. This is certainly not unusual or even unwelcomed. But this man wanted more than just letting me know he has lived a vital and creative life before he walked into my classroom. He wants *me* to engage with him in his new creative endeavor.

For five pages, Brian describes his need for creative stimulation and his intuition that I could be the "locus of his [new] creative life." He made it clear that, at forty-three, he does not have time to be coy, self-deprecating, distant, or even patient. He approaches every project full throttle, and it soon became evident to me that this semester, *I* was his project.

I wasn't quite sure exactly what Brian was asking of me through this letter, and though committed to transformative education, I was ever so slightly leery about the prospect of becoming the "locus" of someone's attempts at transformation. Whatever it entailed, a relationship with Brian was sure to be exhausting. I thought a long time about how to respond, for response was absolutely called for. I could decide to pass up the ride that he was offering me by being, as he says in his letter, "polite" and keeping my professional "distance." Or, I could hop on the hog of an academic machine he was riding and see just how this kind of creative spirit maneuvers his way through the academic labyrinth. My brief note responding to his plea ended, "I am here to serve your needs. Let's talk."

Three days later Brian came to my office to make his first "claim" of me as a colleague in learning. He regaled me with stories of his previous life as a merchant, a concept designer, and a professional sculptor. I was truly fascinated with the twists and turns his life had taken and very interested in his work as an artist, creating large works for public spaces in corporate headquarters of companies like BellSouth and Johnson & Johnson. His presence inundated my office: a loud uproarious laugh, eyes sparkling with intellectual greediness, arms and elbows punctuating his emphatic monologue. He talked and he talked and he talked, delightedly and unabashedly, goaded only slightly by my curiosity.

Two hours later, I knew I had a fascinating case before me—a man at the precipice of a major change in his life, a student driven to engage fully his academic experience, a learner seeking guidance as he makes his way from one world to another. So brash and self-assured was he about one version of himself, yet so nervous and bemused about his own emerging academic identity. I was intrigued—and not a little uneasy about my ability to assist him in the acts of reconstruction I sensed lay ahead of us.

Turning the Tables: "Florida Time"

Lezlie: A key notion that weaves its way in and out of the course activities is what educator Robert Hutchins calls "the great conversation" (1952, xi), that ongoing dialogue about ideas that lively minds have been enjoying for centuries. Typically, essay assignments in my expository writing course ask students to draw upon course readings, to respond to them, to use them to build or defeat arguments, in essence to enter into the ongoing conversation that has shaped our culture as well as our selves.

But there's another kind of "conversation" that takes place in writing classes, and that has to do with the dialogue we have with each other about the process of writing. Unlike the "great conversation," this conversation is a highly private one, one that takes place between teacher and student or between two students, traversing fragile and sometimes intimate terrain and allowing a reader to constructively respond to the rough cuts of a writer's thoughts. One way we do this is through written protocols to draft writing. These protocols are simply written transactions of how a reader is being affected by or is understanding a piece of writing, section by section, paragraph by paragraph, even line by line.

Protocols become a predominant "conversation" in my classroom, for they emphasize how writing a text really is much like carrying on a conversation. A writer has to pay attention to the emerging response that his words elicit. A good protocol response shows the writer where this attentive reader was moved, where a notion came to life, where meaning was imposed onto experience. It also shows where the language becomes convoluted or vague, where references or commentary don't seem to connect with the idea being explored. It makes painfully clear those points in the conversation when the listener might say, "What do you mean by that?" A good protocol drives home the dialogic nature of much good writing by showing how one reader was pulled into or pushed out of the conversation.

Brian: Three days after learning how to do written protocols, I was leafing through the course materials and stumbled onto an essay called "Florida Time" that Lezlie had written. I began to read her essay and felt the urge to make some notes in the margins. Although I didn't put the notes on a separate sheet of paper, what I was really doing was practicing a protocol. It never even occurred to me that it might be inappropriate to do a written response to my professor's work. The whole enterprise began somewhat as a playful joke, but by the time I was finished, my reading demonstrated that I had learned to apply Lezlie's protocol writing guidelines.

And during my reading, something extraordinary began to happen. In her carefully crafted words, I saw a fellow artist struggling to create her world. The pages were alive with her personality, and I sensed a parallel with my own struggle as an artist. She was carefully dealing with images and details as I had dealt with colors and lines. Ever since that reading, I have seen her as an artist first and a teacher second.

My silly side possessed me once again. I rushed off to school and left the protocol on her office door. I can't remember any other teacher having the guts to share a draft of her work with students, so she asked for it. What transpired in those next few days transformed our perception of each other and pushed our relationship to a place I am sure Adrienne Rich would want it to go.

Lezlie: Before I even reached the top of the stairs of Orlando Hall, I could see a large white envelope attached to the clipboard on my office door. Expecting to find minutes from a recent Professional Standards meeting, I hurriedly opened the envelope before I entered, so I could pitch the stuff into the trash even before sitting at my desk and depositing my armload of books, mail, and student papers. Instead I found a copy of an essay I had written, a copy that had been marked, highlighted, underlined, edited, and commented upon copiously. Lines and arrows zigzagged the pages of my text.

"What on earth is this?" I thought. Reading quickly through the attached note, I saw that Brian had taken up my call to conversation more thoroughly and more animatedly than I had expected from even the typically good students I find in my classes. I think my very first reaction was that this would be entertaining—and that Brian was having a bit of "back-at-you" fun with me. This playfulness was borne out by his first two protocol comments, both of which make nit-picking criticisms about spacing and margins.

But as I scanned the numbered comments on the text, I could see that Brian was taking his reading task seriously; he was indeed reading critically and commenting honestly on everything that caught his eye. He pointed out awkward phrases, contradictions, good ideas, words he liked, humor he enjoyed. The hubbub of Orlando Hall completely disappeared for me; I closed my door, pushed the clutter from my desk, and gave my full attention to this experience. I knew something unusual was happening.

I was amused, I was pleased, I was nervous, I was touched, I was annoyed. My eyes searched greedily over the margin comments for one thing— approval. Joke or no joke, I wanted first and foremost to know what he thought, and I hoped desperately that his reactions would be positive. Without really reading for meaning, I scanned for positive words and phrases: two "goods," one "funny," an "I like this." My heart raced. I'm sure this sounds ridiculous, but I have to emphasize how powerful my need for positive reinforcement was at this point, and it is this feeling that has been most powerfully instructive for me. I wondered if my reaction was typical or if I was experiencing some sort of emotional arc that caused such a need for approval. Do my students do this same thing when they receive my responses to their papers? Do all writers seek approval first, need verification before they can receive critical comment?

Peter Elbow has an answer to this question. In his article "Ranking, Evaluating, and Liking: Sorting Out Three Forms of Judgment," he maintains that "liking is perhaps the most important evaluative response for writers and teachers to think about" (1993, 199). He says we become better writers by learning to like our own writing and also by knowing an attentive reader has liked it too.

I suddenly realized that I rarely know how my students actually feel about my protocol responses to their writing. When I return drafts to them, I always ask if they have any questions or comments, but I have no way of knowing if they are mad, pleased, grateful, annoyed, frustrated. Are they understanding how I liked their writing? In Brian, I had a conduit through which I could acquire information about my methodology's effects on students' learning. At that moment, I was being taught what it feels like to have someone talk back to your writing. I became acutely aware of how response can assist or deter an insecure writer.

After having overcome the initial flush of emotions generated by the intrusion of his marking, I looked next to see what he was actually saying about my essay. What exactly were the strengths of this piece? And the weaknesses? I genuinely wanted to know. And I trusted Brian to tell me these things, in an honest, constructive, and friendly manner. Elbow says, "If I like some-one's writing it's easier to criticize it" (1993, 200). But the reverse holds too. It's easier to receive criticism from a reader when I know that he likes what I've written.

In all, Brian makes forty-nine separate comments on the draft and con-cludes with four endnotes. These forty-nine comments include praise, correc-tions, suggestions, empathic engagement, and each one I found instructive and useful. In one comment, though, I thought Brian had misread my essay. I have a fairly long paragraph that makes brief character sketches of several of my high-school girlfriends whom I am seeing at a high-school reunion.

Brian comments, "I am getting the feeling these females are representing a once-removed self-characterization." Several days later, when we finally talked at length about his comments, I was quick to point out how interesting his observation was, but incorrect. My intention was simply to give a picture of the people who were attending the reunion. Brian insisted that his observa-tion was correct in that the whole piece is, in effect, a reflective essay in which a writer attempts to characterize shifting images of herself. The quick descriptions of friends run the gamut of emotional and personal achievement and depict women at various levels of self-understanding as well as an author intrigued with the shifting image she herself seems to be presenting to the world. Could it be possible that these attempts to depict my impressions of friendships renewed at a class reunion were attempts, in fact, to depict my own shape-shifting self in middle age? I was amazed. And really impressed.

How many times have I urged students to listen, accept feedback, remain open to possibilities of the text? And here I was doing exactly what I warn my students not to do when they receive feedback from their workshop members: being defensive, making excuses, denying the reader's response, resisting the new and expanded reading that was being offered to me. Incredible.

What, I wondered, does my own response tell me about the way writers typically respond to feedback? How often do they resist my suggestions? Or deny my responses? Suddenly, this one student's playful encounter with a classroom exercise had catapulted me to a new level of understanding about my role as a respondent. I could hardly wait to talk to Brian again.

Brian: Shortly after class began the next week, Lezlie moved to the end of the table where I was sitting, looked me in the eye, and launched into a viv-id description of what I had done to her essay, telling the class in great theat-rical detail what she has just related to you. My private comments became a public performance. She had come out to play. I had set the tenor for *our* con-versation, and she was joining right in. All I could do was blush profusely and cover my head with my hands. The room was focused on us. I continued to be the brunt of her pedagogical joke until she told the class that our experience would make a good journal article. One of the students who sat next to me whispered in my ear, "brown nose," but all I cared about was that Lezlie was making me a special case. She could have responded to my second overture by maintaining a professional distance, but she took the opportunity to go further. She had turned the tables on me and was enjoying it thoroughly. She was definitely a kindred spirit.

From that point on, Lezlie and I began to have conversations filled with a new enthusiasm. Her public proposal of a joint creative venture about what and how we were learning from each other evolved into a presentation for the Conference on College Composition and Communication. Preparing that presentation and writing this article for *Sharing Pedagogies* were ways of focusing the flurry of insights that accompanied our lively conversations about our experiences as writers. We undertook these projects in the *real* world outside the classroom, and I was thrilled. She initiated me as a student-researcher. She fed me scholarly articles and asked me to interview students about protocols. She was willing to teach me about an academic's life, to create an experience not usually available to undergraduates. She was becoming my academic friend. What is amazing is that all this happened within the first month and a half of class.

Lezlie: Well, I thought class was pretty interesting that day. I had been eager to get to class and tell everyone about this new and humbling experience. My students are accustomed to my beginning-of-the-class stories, but they must have recognized fairly quickly that on this day I was unusually excited about something I had learned. I relayed the events of reading the protocol to them, presenting in great and humorous detail the excruciating array of emotions that accompanied my reading of Brian's critique. They chuckled, some in sympathy, some in glee that I was getting a bit of my own medicine. I wanted them to know that I would never be able to think about protocols in quite the same manner as before. I knew now, more profoundly than before, the complex and often contradictory feelings my own written responses must engender in my students.

Suddenly, as I was telling the class my story, I realized that a unique opportunity lay before me. I had the interest and attention of a bright and articulate student. It was within his means to help me read myself as a writer so that I could better read my students as writers. This was an imminently worthy research topic. And so, like Mickey Rooney entreating his friends to "put on a show," I blurted, "Hey Brian. Wanna write an article?"

Protocol Denied: "Onward Christian Soldiers"

Brian: During the course's tenth week, something extraordinary happened in our academic adventure: an emotional conflagration. The incident I am about to recount is as powerful for me and loaded with meaning as my analysis of "Florida Time" was for Lezlie. At the beginning of class, she handed me a protocol on my fourth essay, "Onward Christian Soldiers," which is about gay Christians who are being persecuted in Colorado. The protocol reads as follows:

> This opening page is excellent. Very well written, very engaging, very dramatic. I love it! . . . Clear, focused, to the point. This whole essay is well done, Brian. I don't know that I have any serious suggestions for revision . . . I'd just leave it alone.

What more in the way of a glowing response could any student hope for? But something was wrong. I felt cheated and confused. "Onward Christian Soldiers" had only taken me about ten days to write and fifty pages of drafts to polish. My previous essay, "Passing," required about three times as much draft material and to this day remains a frustrating disaster. As a matter of fact, I was making another failed draft of it at the same time I sailed through "Onward Christian Soldiers." How did I mix disaster and glory? Why was my work all of a sudden good when the week before it had been oh so very bad? Was she paying attention, or was her response just fluffy teacher boilerplate? I wanted to know.

Gradually, a physical response built up, leaving my stomach churning and my skin flushed. I was disoriented, dissatisfied, and growing angry. As class drew to an end and almost all the students had cleared the room, I moved part way around the table, shook the protocol in the air, and confronted Lezlie. "What does this mean?" I shouted.

Behind that remark was an array of bewildering emotions that Lezlie and I are still discovering. I wanted something from her, but didn't have a clue what it was. I knew, however, that I had overstepped a boundary, crossed a line as both student and friend when I confronted her. As best as I can remember, Lezlie responded to my question in a calm but bewildered way. How could she productively engage me? I barely registered what few comments she was able to make. I went home and became filled with remorse and immediately composed a letter of apology. After two rounds of correspondence that still bring tears to my eyes when I read them, we came to class the next week with the relationship fully repaired. But what had happened?

If you recall, on the first day of the term I had more or less decided that if Lezlie said my writing was bad, then it was bad, period! I thought I had no basis for making an independent value judgment. What the hell did I know about writing? The best strategy seemed to be blind faith because in my eyes she was the absolute authority, and I was there to absorb as much knowledge as possible. Doing that allowed me to fully immerse myself in the possibilities Lezlie would present. But this frame of reference for my novice-writer self had unforeseen consequences, one of which involved discounting Lezlie's praise of my writing but elevating her advice as faultless wisdom. Thus, I read the praise she gave me in the "Onward Christian Soldiers" protocol as no response at all.

The intricacies of why I elevated her advice and discounted her praise are a subject fit for another paper. Suffice it to say that I had come to writing class with a strong creative value system, a system I had checked at the door when I entered a new creative arena—language. By resorting to blind faith, I did not need to reach into the confrontational, rebellious aspect of my creative currency. Her advice became a mysterious revelation of fact. But I suppressed her praise since it would require an assessment of her competence. To do this I would have had to bring my own creative judgments, based on my past creative experiences, to bear on her evaluations. I felt that this would have put me at odds with her, and I didn't want this to happen. I didn't want to end up contesting every point she made in class; I believe this would have created a very monologic situation, one in which no one learned anything. Although this rather compliant approach does not work for everyone, I felt—at least through the first months of classes—I needed to be a sponge. Thus, instead of regarding Lezlie as a critic, with positive and negative opinions, I saw her more as a doctor focused on healing my sickly writing. There was nothing threatening in that attitude. Every time Lezlie criticized me, not only did my writing condition improve, but my esteem of her grew ever larger. So long as Lezlie was spoon-feeding me advice about my writing, my frame of reference was safe.

Although that explains, as best I can, what I thought happened at the time, it doesn't tell you what I learned. That is a difficult task since it is ongoing, but I'll give it my best shot. Lezlie had made me a guarantee at the beginning of the term, and I had certainly worked hard enough to earn the reward. However, the reward I received was not the one either of us anticipated (namely, that my writing would improve, which it did). My more important reward involved two basic lessons about my status as a writer.

I was thriving on her faultfinding. As a masochist might say, "It hurt so good." Therefore, my first lesson required me to step out of the role I was playing and admit that I was not a novice writer. My filing cabinets are full of proof that, at the very least, I had been practicing the craft for a long time. Although I had entered Lezlie's class profoundly believing that I was a terrible writer and that any facility I had was a mysterious fluke, the class helped me to understand the process of writing so that I could manage it better and feel safer about taking creative intellectual risks. It heightened my awareness of the nebulous verities of the writer's craft and the writer's life. Lezlie helped me (and continues to help me) figure out who I am as a writer and how I can fit into the great conversation. She helped me put a "trade" vocabulary to my experience, which is a necessary precursor to working as comfortably with words as I have with other media.

The second lesson was my accepting the *responsibility* for my academic friendship with Lezlie. As with any new friendship, there was an intensive period of interaction. But she had other responsibilities, not only to my fellow students, but to people outside of school, and of course to her fabulous dog,

Ginger. I could only demand so much special attention before I would burn her out. A friend must also be a good steward, so I wanted to become less needy.

In retrospect, my letter of apology to her marked my shift to a more responsible friend and a more self-directed writer. From the confrontation, I realized that I could no longer have blind faith in her as I had at the beginning of the course. Instead, I now chose to see her as a critic, albeit a privileged one. I was claiming an active role in my own education. I accepted responsibility for the writer I was and hoped to become by establishing my own critical standards based on a recognition and acceptance of my strengths and shortcomings as a writer.

Would I have begun my transition to this new frame of mind had I not denied my literacy at the beginning of the course? Lezlie thinks I would have found another way, but my temperament tells me I would not have. My well-honed creative ego needed to be set aside in those early days so that I could absorb the greatest amount of knowledge. It eventually surfaced again to take charge during my disoriented anger on that ironically rewarding afternoon. My critical standards now blend what I've learned in Lezlie's course with *my* artistic standards and modes of expression.

Lezlie: A journey that takes only the high road can be called no adventure. The very word *adventure* implies a descent into the unexpected, perhaps even the disturbing. Brian's anger at my response to his fourth essay propelled us into uncharted territory, leaving us both a bit disoriented and somewhat shaken.

From my point of view, Brian was progressing exceptionally well. He was, in fact, an ideal student. He wrote down everything I said in class; he read and highlighted every handout I gave him; he marked and annotated every response sheet he received on draft essays. He wrote and he wrote and he wrote; and I tried to carefully observe and explicate each move he was making toward mastery of the informal essay, as well as his shaping of a new professional identity. Since his first letter to me, we had written letters back and forth, had innumerable conferences, talked on the phone, gabbed after class, corresponded through e-mail. In fact, these long and frank conversations about writing and teaching had led us to exactly the academic friendship he had demanded of me some seven weeks earlier. He was getting exactly what he had demanded of me: *lots* and *lots* of attention.

And now, in the homestretch of the course, what do I get for all this attention? A spit-fire temper tantrum from a precocious child. It took me a while to sort out the meaning of this little tantrum, so let me backtrack a bit.

For the fourth assignment of the course Brian produced a beautiful essay, as my very short and yet complimentary response to his draft shows. And yet Brian was furious with me. Since I was oblivious to his growing pique, his remarks to me after class really caught me off guard. I don't really remember the specifics of the interchange, but he was challenging me, prodding me, goading me to say something (but I didn't know what) about his paper. He was really mad. From his perspective, those short but glowing comments were "stingy," and he was not going to let me get away with slighting him. Too much was at stake. Hearing that he had successfully accomplished the requirements of the assignment—and the course for that matter—was just not enough.

There are several interesting permutations of this particular moment in our adventure. On one level, to be perfectly honest, I was just plain annoyed with Brian. I thought he was being incredibly pushy—a spoiled brat demanding full-out response to his every move. I had guaranteed a breakthrough, and this essay certainly marked a shift in Brian's command of both the process and the product of his writing. But oddly enough, after having reaped the benefits of our mutual effort, he was mad because I gave him a glowing but short response. I really didn't understand what was going on.

Nevertheless, I was intrigued to observe a learner so incredibly disturbed with my efforts on his behalf. In a letter of apology that followed, he was quick to reiterate his complaints about my response and to yet again delineate his weaknesses: "I have serious problems with organization and topic control in my compositions." And yet he admitted that the lessons we were doing in class were incredibly helpful to him. He said he wanted to be validated by me, but pure validation is "still not what I need."

Then what do you need, Brian?

I remembered my first reading of his comments on my essay and my own particular neediness at that moment. It's probably safe to say that all serious writers are needy—in all sorts of different ways. My concern was, How does one teacher best attend to the various needs of her developing writers? How can I possibly adjust my responses to each of my students and serve their needs as individual learners—and maintain my own sanity? Most definitely a difficult task, but not insurmountable, especially if opportunities for *real* conversation exist between teacher and student.

When I went back to his letter of apology, I found the problem. He wrote:

"Onward Christian Soldiers" was very well organized. I felt it in my bones. I needed you to recognize that. I needed to be praised for skillfully if accidentally and momentarily overcoming a problem that tormented me in the 150 pages of draft material in my previous essay "Passing." I needed you to remark on the interesting way I took the three newspaper articles and used them as the core of my third section and let them be surrogate support, as the museum director did in the Mapplethorpe essay we read in class. I needed to know how skillful I had been, specifically in that risk. I needed you to notice the risk and to unfold it. I needed you to tweak it in your praise. You did not do that. "Clear, focused, to the point." How sterile. I felt cheated.

Note how many times Brian uses the word *needed* in this paragraph. Good or bad writing aside, he wanted to know that I had *noticed* what he had accomplished.

"[N]otice the risk and . . . unfold it," he says. I can't imagine any better advice for a teacher of writing. And I can't imagine any advice more threatening either. *Notice the risk, and unfold it.* That means articulate it, point it out, talk about it, challenge it, admire it. In spite of the research that says students don't pay any attention to teachers' written comments on their papers, I'm convinced to the contrary. Students may ignore margin notes about comma splices and run-on sentences, but they don't ignore honest, attentive conversation about their ideas. They are hungry for it, in fact. In my end-of-the-semester weariness, I had let wane the intense conversation about writing that Brian and I had been having. I thought I could get by with a pat on the head to this good student. How wrong I had been.

But there was something else happening here too. James Baldwin once said that a young person doesn't really want you to answer his question, he wants you to hear it. Maybe Brian wanted to talk to *me* as much as (maybe more than) he wanted me to talk to *him*. Knowing we were going to try to document some of what we were learning from each other, I was constantly asking him to write out his responses to what was happening to him in class. In fact, some of our most fascinating and illuminating conversations grew out of the written documents he was making of his own literacy. I encouraged him to analyze his frustrations and successes, and in so doing he performed a kind of self-therapy. On more than one occasion I have been uneasy with Brian's assertions about my skill as a teacher; I have really done nothing more than allow him to chronicle his own learning, to actually give voice to his side of the conversation that invariably goes on unvoiced in traditional classroom settings. However, my response to his fine essay failed to create a framework within which his newly minted skills could be articulated. His explosion after class revealed a student in the throes of reclaiming his own artistic authority, for in my failure to explicate his learning for him, he was faced with doing it himself.

The letter he wrote to me after our confrontation is a clear and insightful analysis not only of his own writing but also of how my pedagogy has affected his writing. He had, in essence, given himself the critique that he wanted from me; he had unfolded the nuances of his essay that he thought only I could give him. I am reminded of the saying, "When the student is ready, the teacher will appear." It came as a surprise to both of us that the teacher who appeared was Brian himself. Although my short response to his paper was without pedagogical intention, in effect this response catapulted Brian to a more sophisticated level of conversation about his writing and learning, a conversation in which he became coequal conversant, rather than dutiful apprentice.

So what happened to us? In the final analysis, our adventure has taught me this: As much as his long hours of drafting and my work in the classroom, it was our various insistent, hard-nosed, and *real* conversations with each other that fostered our reciprocal discoveries about the acts of writing and teaching writing.

Epilogue

Brian: The tale itself is not anywhere near an end; we haven't said all we could say about how our writing voices have merged as we prepared this paper, or how our lessons came into better focus when we collaborated on a conference presentation, or just how much goofball fun we have had creating and nurturing our academic friendship. We have developed a shared openness and mutual personal regard that allows us to trade off being student to one another's teacher.

Our story demonstrates that certain conditions are necessary for some students to find a place in the academy. I would have left school again, frustrated that the institution was completely hostile to someone like me, had Lezlie not taken the tack she did. She put a humane face on the gargoyle of academic bureaucracy. If progressive pedagogy is to prosper, teachers like Lezlie must accept greater responsibility to do that. They must pass along their values not just by modeling them in the classroom, or writing papers for colleagues, but with extra-class interactions.

Lezlie's progressive pedagogy is not just philosophical theorizing about education. For me, it is a reality. My own career as a professor will be forever colored and enriched by our exchanges. Such a gift can only be given by an academic friend. We are having a great conversation and an excellent academic adventure.

Four

Creating Dialogue
What the English Curriculum Doesn't Teach

Denise Stephenson, Michelle N. Pierce, and Bob Mayberry

This article began as a series of conversations about what we found lacking in the curriculum of undergraduate English majors. Collectively we've attended or taught at twenty-two colleges over three decades. In some ways, we are at very different stages of the academic journey. Michelle recently finished her B.A. in English and is teaching English in Japan. Denise recently completed a dissertation about academic writing for an American Studies doctorate while directing a university writing center. Bob has a Ph.D. in English and an M.F.A. in playwriting and teaches composition and literature. Having decided to collaborate on this project, we began sending notes through the mail; when we got together, we taped our discussions; we made the final revisions to the article via e-mail. We felt it was important to preserve our individual voices, so this article is both a blending of our insights and a series of anecdotes that led to those insights. We also offer suggestions that we believe might improve the curriculum.

What brought us together to write this article, and what connects our otherwise disparate experiences, is our sense that undergraduate English majors have a conflicted relationship with the demands of their own discipline. They learn to fear writing, distrust their talents, doubt their successes, and see themselves as impostors. Our own experiences suggest that those lessons are implicit in the English curriculum and the way it is taught.

The Impostor Syndrome

Lying is an important academic issue that is not limited to the question of what constitutes plagiarism. Lying creates barriers between faculty and students. Perhaps too often, faculty assume students lie.

The director of Freshman Composition came to speak with the writing tutors. He said repeatedly, "Students lie." He wanted us to realize that in tutoring sessions, students might bad-mouth his program and TAs. He didn't want us to believe students. He assured us that when students said bad things about our tutoring, he didn't believe them. What he didn't seem to realize was that we were all students. Was he calling us liars? He never tried to exclude us from his accusations. *(Denise)*

At the same time, students learn they must tell lies in order to fulfill assignments, to make the grade. The most significant lies undergraduates learn to tell are the ones that pass for truth in the classroom. These lies are at the heart of the impostor syndrome that we discuss here.

I had an assignment to write an in-class essay on a bilingual experience. My previous papers had received D's. I wrote that I moved from Japan to the States during the fourth grade. Because my English-speaking skills were inadequate, I had to repeat the third grade and was no longer allowed to speak Japanese at home. I made it all up. My grades improved; I continued to write lies for that instructor. *(Michelle)*

Michelle's story demonstrates the impostor syndrome perfectly. Though she was not bilingual, pretending that she was facilitated not only a better grade but also a new persona, one that the instructor accepted as true. For Michelle, the knowledge that she had lied, had made up this imaginative past, meant she was an impostor in that classroom. She was not the person that her teacher thought she was. The grade didn't belong to Michelle but to her fictional representation of herself.

When writing academically, I guess I lie. *(Michelle)*

But the impostor syndrome is not limited to fictionalized personal stories. In fact, we use the term because several friends and relatives, Michelle among them, were graduating with BAs and pronouncing that it meant nothing; they were frauds. Maybe, they thought, they'd gone to the wrong schools or just weren't very bright. Maybe another degree would help. But Bob and Denise, both with advanced degrees, thought these people were among the best and the brightest; their grades supported this conclusion. So why did these bright students believe that their undergraduate educations had taught them nothing?

> Unfortunately, as a learner I feel I am a teacher pleaser: I attempt to figure out what teachers want me to learn. And I learn it so I can make the grade. I am left feeling I haven't learned much. *(Michelle)*

Students respond to faculty expectations of what constitutes acceptable academic behavior—in writing, in speech—by putting on *masks* to hide their embarrassment or sense of inadequacy. All performances become lies, no matter how successful their grades indicate they've been. By such means do we all—undergraduate, M.A., and Ph.D. students—learn that academic lying can get us A's.

When I applied to my Ph.D. program, I had to write a seven-page letter of intent. I tried not only to be creative and thorough, but to tell the truth. At the time, there were two ideas I imagined pursuing as dissertation topics. I included both in the letter. I was admitted to the program as an M.A. instead of Ph.D. candidate because, the faculty advisor told me, my letter of intent was "not clearly focused." Honesty had cost me. Several of my cohorts had *told lies*; they weren't pursuing anything that vaguely resembled their letters of intent. They'd learned long ago that being an impostor was the way to meet faculty expectations. *(Denise)*

The primary way we construct ourselves in the academy is through language, so it's not surprising that students often feel pressured to invent new personas in their writing. But while more experienced writers often feel empowered by the opportunity to construct a self in language, a mask of their own making so to speak, students often feel alienated and disempowered by what they think teachers expect.

> *Denise:* Writing is always donning a mask, but it's not always clear to students that to some degree writers choose a mask. The question is, Who chooses?
> *Bob:* Each time I write, I construct an image of myself through the choices I make. Writers never stop making masks; rather, we learn to influence how the images we construct are perceived by others.
> *Michelle:* I was hoping there would be an end to wearing masks. I want to believe in various

> paths for storytelling. I want to find the Yellow
> Brick Road that doesn't lead to that strange
> man hiding behind the curtain.

Students acquire an academic style, an academic mask, primarily through exposure and experience. They try it on like clothing borrowed from their parents' closets. And since status is afforded to looking the part, or sounding the part, it is appearance that is rewarded. When the clothes or masks don't fit, those who wear them to win their teachers' approval feel like impostors.

This impostor syndrome is fostered by a lack of clarity regarding what constitutes an acceptable appearance or acceptable behavior. What is good in one class may not pass in another. Bob recalls his first semester as a graduate student and his complete ignorance of what was expected of graduate students in a seminar:

> The prof assigned a paper on Joyce's *Ulysses*: Trace the journey of an object in the novel. "That's all?" I asked. The prof, whom I'd gotten A's from as an undergraduate, smiled mysteriously. I wrote about a bar of soap that travels in Bloom's pocket. I described everywhere it went. When I read the paper aloud, the class laughed. The prof asked if I wrote all my papers like that. High praise, I thought. None of the other papers were funny like mine. None of the other students had traced their objects' journeys; they'd *commented* on them. Several students referred to critical interpretations of their objects' journeys. My undergraduate profs had frowned on using critical sources.
>
> "Don't you get it?" a classmate asked me after class. "Didn't you notice how different everyone else's paper was?" He told me that in grad school you were *expected* to refer to the scholars. No one had explained that to me before. And in seven years of grad school, no one mentioned it again. *(Bob)*

Bob had not intuited the professor's expectations; he hadn't assimilated the appropriate academic behavior. Instead, he'd written papers the same way he'd written them for this professor as an undergraduate. Those papers had been rewarded with A's, but the seminar paper was laughed at because it didn't bear the vaguest resemblance to the class's or professor's expectations for academic writing. Bob was still wearing his undergraduate mask.

Expectations of writing vary, yet many instructors seem unaware of this or unwilling to make it explicit to their students. What constitutes acceptable academic behavior—in this case, what constitutes good academic writing—is simply assumed. In the final English course of Michelle's B.A. program, she was still encountering this lack of specificity about what constitutes "good *writing*."

When I wrote what I thought was academic, I got "good" as my evaluation. When I said, "Fuck it," and wrote what I wanted, I got "excellent." My expectations of academic writing came from my thirty-six hours of English and from the teacher's example paragraphs, which were very academic. But no one in class wrote anything resembling the examples. One woman wrote about her piano teacher in response to an assigned story. The class and teacher praised her. It wasn't what I thought I was supposed to do. It didn't fit my model of academic writing. I was confused about what the teacher wanted and how I was going to be graded. *(Michelle)*

Bob wondered if Michelle had assimilated a model of academic writing not so much from her critical reading as from years of teachers telling students what was unacceptable. Michelle called her model "imaginary." Denise noted that Michelle measured herself against both her imaginary, ideal model of academic writing and against other students' creativity. It's no wonder she felt like she failed in spite of the high grades she received.

Classroom Suggestion 1

Students need to be told explicitly what faculty perceive as appropriate academic behavior, especially their expectations for writing assignments. Teachers can put their own grading criteria into writing, emphasizing that there is no single, perfect model of academic writing that students will be measured against, but that in certain areas, like use of scholarship, there is general agreement.

Both Michelle and Denise recall the frustration of trying to write for professors, trying to intuit their criteria or anticipate their expectations. Writing to please a teacher becomes little more than a game and eventually, inevitably, leads students to perceive themselves as impostors. Our experience suggests, paradoxically, that the less faculty articulate their expectations the more they encourage students to try to psych them out and intuit what they want. As proponents of dialogic pedagogies have suggested, opening the issues of grading criteria and teacher expectations to discussion, perhaps even to negotiation and revision, empowers students, increasing the likelihood that they understand the purpose behind previously obscure assignments. Students and teachers exploring together varied approaches to a writing assignment can be a potent antidote to the impostor syndrome.

> *Michelle:* If we could observe the writing processes of teachers and other students, then we could learn to combine, cut, paste, and add to create our own structures, to tell our own our stories. We wouldn't feel like impostors because we could tailor our own processes.
>
> *Bob:* You're calling for open dialogue between students and teachers, between students and students, on the idiosyncratic processes by which we compose.
>
> *Michelle:* No teacher has ever sat down and gone through the motions of writing or rewriting with me. Why haven't they? We wouldn't expect someone to build a house by just giving them a hammer, nails, and wood, and saying, "Okay, it's your turn."

The best way we know to teach *the act* of writing is to have students write in class and for teachers to write with them, talk with them as they write, help them when they get stuck, suggest a trick or three when they need it, and when they've finished something, ask them all to share with each other how they got through it. Also, it's essential that teachers share their writing, their processes, their choices, along with students. Such dialogue is the only way to assure that students will not feel a set of secret, arbitrary expectations is being imposed on them. When teachers, in particular, articulate the choices they made in their writing, students learn about their own processes, the only ones valuable to them.

Classroom Suggestion 2

To demystify the writing process, teachers can demonstrate revision by rewriting a paragraph of their own in front of the class. By explaining their choices, they make their own writing processes visible to students.

We have found such teaching to be rare because teachers know they become vulnerable when they expose their own writing processes.

> Though I've been teaching and publishing for twenty years, I still get a knot in my gut when I stand in front of my students and compose sentences and paragraphs as they watch. As often as I've done it, it's still unnerving. *(Bob)*

Teachers seem fearful of such vulnerability. In Japan a colleague of Michelle's asked her a question about grammar that had arisen in the colleague's ESL class. Michelle pointed out that the teacher's manual was in error. Her colleague was troubled: She'd told the class the wrong answer and now had to admit her mistake. Michelle suggested she tell the class there had been a mistake in the teacher's manual. The colleague was appalled at Michelle's suggestion. She said she didn't want her students to know she used a teacher's manual.

Faculty fear being exposed as impostors just as students do. Some, like Michelle's colleague, imagine their authority will evaporate the moment students realize teachers don't have all the answers. Others, having internalized the poisoned curriculum of their own educations, believe their writing is as unworthy as that of their students and, consequently, hide it from their students and their colleagues. Faculty wear masks too.

> *Michelle:* If teachers let students know some of their secrets, maybe students wouldn't feel so inferior— maybe teachers wouldn't feel like such frauds.
>
> *Denise:* So there are frauds on both sides of the fence. The masks some teachers wear prevent students from understanding mask-wearing because it is invisible to most students.
>
> *Bob:* Students feel like impostors, fear being unmasked, and use language to please teachers and avoid being humiliated by them. Teachers, similarly, use language and academic conventions to maintain their power over students, to protect themselves from being revealed as impostors too, that is, as human beings who do not always have the answer or whose writing is not perfect or whose knowledge of writing conventions needs shoring up from teacher manuals.
>
> *Denise:* Faculty often play the great and mighty Oz, hiding their humanity behind masks.

Though we all use language to hide behind from time to time, the writing class should be the one place where we can discuss *all* the functions of language, even how we use it to mask our intentions. In the writing class we can put the entire process on the table and examine it, without being defensive about our own motives or critical of those of others. Such dialogue should be initiated by teachers.

For years, composition specialists have advocated writing workshops. Michelle and Bob are familiar with such workshops, particularly through their work in creative writing courses, and they believe the workshop is a useful model for what we're advocating here. In the typical workshop, students read their work aloud and everyone is invited to respond. The ensuing dialogue makes evident to the writer, if it wasn't before, how various the expectations of different readers are. In the best of workshops, no set of expectations, no opinion of the writer's work, is privileged over any other. The teacher is just one more reader, one more respondent, often the most experienced or articulate, but never the final authority. Workshop participants rarely complain of feeling like impostors because they acquire from the workshop a clear sense of audience. They are not writing for a teacher, whose expectations are very often invisible to students, but for peers who articulate those expectations each time they discuss a new work by another writer.

Classroom Suggestion 3

Asking students to read their papers aloud in class and then discussing the consequences of their writing choices minimizes the impostor syndrome because students compare their writings with those of other students, rather than with the unspoken expectations of their teacher or the professional writing models in most textbooks. Student writing itself should be the focus of discussion, the primary location of learning.

Even in conventional classes, teachers can discourage students from seeing writing merely as the fulfillment of empty requirements of form and style (the arbitrary and reductive structure of the five-paragraph essay comes to mind) by asking students to read their work aloud to each other and discussing how their choices as writers affect their audience. At the same time, by demonstrating their own writing processes, teachers can serve as mentors to their apprentice-students and demonstrate that no piece of writing is ever perfect or finished, so there is no reason for students to measure themselves against some ideal paper in the teacher's head (Knoblauch and Brannon 1984, 120). Such open discussion and sharing of writing are the essence of classroom dialogue and the antithesis of the impostor syndrome.

Marginalia vs. Dialogue

All three of us have been troubled by how frequently correction is the focus of writing in English classes, whether composition or literature. Michelle realized that no one had ever demonstrated how she might revise a paper. Instead, she'd been given many years' worth of contradictory marginalia, different kinds of advice from very different teachers. In most literature classes, and in a frightening number of composition classes, revision is limited to the reductive act of correcting whatever the teacher marks or annotates. In some courses, no dialogue whatsoever takes place between students and teachers about written work.

> *Michelle:* A few years ago I took a literature course during which I had to write five or six papers. I never had to rewrite, nor was I given the option. Each time I sat down to begin a paper, I tried to make sense of the comments written on the last.
> *Denise:* Because every assignment is different, instructors' comments don't necessarily help students with other papers.
> *Michelle:* I kept repeating to myself that I must do better next time. I thought if I just wrote six pages instead of four, my papers would somehow improve. They did not.
> *Bob:* We've all had Michelle's experience. I'm guilty of replicating it with my students. To ask students to rewrite in a serious way means engaging in at least two dialogues with them in the place of the usual marginalia: I suggest how they might revise and then evaluate that revision. That's at least double the work. So mostly teachers talk about revision but write comments on finished products. That's not the same as teaching the process of revision.

Marginalia cannot address problems that arise for students *during* the composing process because marginalia responds to the written product, rather than to the writing process itself. By its nature, marginalia is separate from, rather than part of, writing; it comes after the fact. Michelle repeatedly returned to her previous papers in hopes that earlier comments would improve the paper she was currently working on. Unfortunately, marginalia only addresses the problems of a given paper. It does not help students develop writing processes that will serve them over the course of their lives, or even their undergraduate educations.

The only thing I remember learning from comments written in the margin was not to summarize the plot in analytical papers, but I never got explicit directions on what to put in place of the summary. I took this single suggestion; beyond that I just quickly read through the markings until I got to my grade. Paper graded, paper dismissed—along with its advice. *(Michelle)*

Marginalia is one-way discourse, not dialogue. The chances for miscommunication are increased when the conversation is one-sided. The exception to that, of course, is when marginalia invites dialogue, when students make a habit of discussing the comments with their teachers, asking them to clarify their comments and what alternative writing choices exist.

Conferencing is the most direct means for teachers to communicate with students about their writings and creates fewer misunderstandings than do written comments. Conferences can initiate students into the ongoing discussions within the discipline and reduce their sense of being impostors.

> I never had an instructor who gave conferences; I'm not sure what happens during one. Maybe we would discuss my ideas and my content. We'd behave like humans—speaking to one another. Conferences might be a way for the student to feel less intimidated to ask questions. *(Michelle)*

Classroom Suggestion 4

Conferencing provides an alternative to marginalia that explicitly encourages dialogue between teachers and students. Conferences allow students to ask teachers about the intent behind marginal comments, give teachers the chance to explain in more depth than a marginal comment does, and reduce the possibility that comments and markings will be misunderstood.

Typically marginalia is the final word on a given assignment. When those comments are misunderstood, students not only don't learn what the teacher intended but often form bad habits based on their misunderstandings.

> I live in a fast-food society where I've learned to write single-draft papers with minimal recursiveness that receive good grades:
>> Drop off one paper.
>> Instructor writes two to three comments per page.
>> Student reads grade.
>> Trash.
> But what have I learned? To stay up all night? *(Michelle)*

Furthermore, since most marginalia focus on identifying errors or weaknesses, students may recognize they've done something wrong without having any idea how to change it. When written comments are the sole response to a paper, the burden of understanding is left to students. They have the task of interpreting the comments, and a tricky act of interpretation it is. Marginalia cannot substitute for discussion of criteria and expectations. In fact, without a common context for understanding marginal comments, students are left in the untenable position of trying to decipher the professor's often cryptic commentary.

> *Bob:* I once described a student's prose as a mixture of complex sentences and simple assertions. I meant it as a compliment. The student read it as a statement of what was wrong with the paper. I only found out because she later asked me how she could avoid simple sentences.
>
> *Michelle:* I don't see teacher comments as dialogue. I see them as statements of what's wrong with my paper.
>
> *Denise:* So students see marginalia as criticism while teachers see it as an opportunity to communicate with students about how to improve their papers. Those are very different perspectives.
>
> *Bob:* That's the chief reason I use written comments so rarely. I wonder how many of them have been misinterpreted over the years.

Dialogue creates opportunities for students to check their perceptions of comments against those of their peers or against the intentions of the teacher. Had Bob's student not asked him how to avoid simple sentences in her paper, she would never have realized that she misunderstood the intent of his written comment. Nor would Bob have ever discovered his comments were being misunderstood. Without dialogue, there is no chance for revision. Apprentices learn from mentors both by watching them at work as well as by asking questions about the meaning of what they see.

Classroom Suggestion 5

One alternative to extensive reliance on marginalia is teaching students to rely on their peers for commentary on drafts. Students learn to respond constructively when given the opportunity. Peer responses are much more likely than teacher marginalia to initiate further revision.

Criticism vs. Praise

A professor railed on my midterm exam. There was no introduction! No conclusion! She said I couldn't write! I'd show her. For the final paper, I decided to write the most *academic* paper I'd ever written. I struggled and struggled with it. I wanted it structurally perfect. When I got it back, the last page was filled with large scribbles criticizing my content. It wasn't the paper she would have written on this subject— no comments about my paper. And then she wrote, "But at least it's well written." Meant no doubt as a compliment, albeit a backhanded one, but I didn't find it satisfying, gratifying, or helpful. *(Denise)*

Teacher commentary on student papers is mostly critical, sometimes downright insulting or sarcastic. Such commentary is not surprising in a discipline that values criticism above praise. Teachers reenact the kinds of comments they received as students, and the cycle is perpetuated. Michelle's undergraduate experience made her feel she was an inferior writer in spite of the many A's she received. As she points out, every A was accompanied by notes saying,

"You did this, and this, and this wrong." This kept me feeling insecure about my writing. I thought that showing this to anyone except a prof would expose me as a fraud—an illiterate masquerading as an English major. *(Michelle)*

Teacher criticism undermines any sense of accomplishment; it reinforces students' doubts about their writing abilities; and it makes them feel like impostors. At the same time that teachers gave Michelle high grades, their written comments criticized or corrected her writing. What are students to make of such double-edged messages?

My favorite paper received an A. The cover page was filled with praising commentary saying that I "did a lot in a very short space." But the marginalia inside the paper was primarily critical. The instructor wrote, "I don't follow this line of reasoning," "This is a different argument," and "I don't see the connection." How do the comments inside the paper equal the grade and praise on the cover? It appears he was attempting a dialogue with me, but these messages are incredibly contradictory. If the paper is so good, why so much negativity? If the paper is so bad, why the good grade? *(Denise)*

As Denise's experience suggests, students rarely feel as though they've succeeded because they're always made to feel inadequate in some way. The criticism undermines the achievement.

The same was true for Michelle. As she progressed in her undergraduate career, the A's on her papers persuaded her less and less of her writing skill, while the criticisms that accumulated one atop another from a series of teachers, each focusing on a different aspect of her writing, made her feel less and less confident. Worst of all for many students are the grades without commentary, the A-minuses and B-pluses that imply students aren't quite up to par while offering no explanations.

As criticism continues unabated, students reason that their A's are not deserved. They are, as Michelle put it, masquerading as English majors, and with each new assignment they fear being exposed.

If teacher criticism can be so damaging to the self-confidence of a successful student like Michelle, what must the impact be on less successful students? Imagine how discouraging a B-minus or C paper must feel when accompanied by a plethora of red-ink criticisms and corrections. Professors may see the corrections as merely technical, but students, Michelle reminds us, read such commentary as critiques of their persona and ideas.

If I write a lie and the prof criticizes it, he's not attacking me,
but some fictional me I've allowed him to criticize. (*Michelle*)

Writing is so intensely personal that students create masks to protect themselves from criticism. If the writer has no investment in what is being criticized—if the paper doesn't reflect her ideas or image of herself—then the criticism can be ignored. Curricula that emphasize criticism and correction encourage such masquerading and in so doing undermine the very confidence of those they are purported to serve, English majors.

It was during my first comp class as a college freshman when I discovered that I couldn't write—at least not academically. I had received two or three D's on the first few writing assignments, all with "frag" branded in the margins. I remember my instructor spending one class period chastising us about sentence fragments, but he didn't teach me how to *fix* one. (*Michelle*)

What does the English curriculum teach majors? Is it preparing them to confidently use their talents as writers and readers in their chosen careers? It seems to us that all too often the result is quite the opposite, as it was for Michelle when she fabricated a bilingual experience for a paper.

Magically my grades improved, not by focusing on fragments
but by fabricating experiences. I continued to write lies for
Freshman Comp. I learned not to be myself but to write an analytical paper without believing in my argument. I wrote what
they wanted me to write. (*Michelle*)

No student paper is so good it escapes the trained critical eye of the professor. As a result, English majors learn to fear writing, distrust their own talents, doubt their own successes, and eventually see themselves as impostors.

I'm amazed I gained any confidence in my writing. The confidence I do have comes from my creative writing classes where praise is a huge part of the curriculum. Suggestions are offered orally rather than mistakes pointed out in marginalia. I don't have red ink all over my words. In the end, the changes I make are my own. (*Michelle*)

Classroom Suggestion 6

Teachers can encourage dialogue by praising student work. Oral suggestions increase student confidence and enthusiasm, while marginal criticism undermines learning.

In spite of the curriculum, it seems, many of us do develop a certain confidence about our writing. What confidence the three of us have in our writing can be directly traced to teachers more concerned with offering praise and support than criticizing our efforts.

My Shakespeare prof filled student papers with glowing comments about our ideas, insights and understandings. As a result, students flocked to his classes and produced their best work for him. I learned more about teaching writing from him than from anyone else. *(Bob)*

Praise survives in courses like writing workshops and creative writing classes and in the literature and composition classes of teachers we remember fondly. The English curriculum is neither uniform nor consistent; teachers are capable of great surprises.

Assimilation

The day we received our history papers, the instructor lectured us. "You should have a friend read your paper aloud to you so you know what gibberish it is." And then he said, "I thought Freshman English was a prerequisite for this course, but none of you know how to write. Maybe there isn't a prerequisite, maybe I should get one." After he badgered us for fifteen minutes, he returned our papers. I felt just horrible in spite of my A-minus. *(Michelle)*

Bob: What happened the next time you wrote a paper for him?
Michelle: I didn't have to.
Bob: What's the point of his badgering everyone if this was the only paper assigned?
Michelle: I never thought about that. We didn't have another paper to turn in. I don't understand the reason for him screaming at us and telling us we were stupid. We weren't going to learn anything from his lecturing us. I'm angry now that I realize that. I was angry then, but I'm really angry now.

Michelle's history instructor's behavior was irresponsible. It is unfair to blame students when the curriculum and the system are at fault. Unfortunately, such behavior is not that unusual. Rather than offer constructive criticism, he assumed—as many professors do—that students in his classes should already "know how to write."

> My English instructors at the 300 and 400 level didn't teach writing. Maybe they thought I should have learned to write in my comp classes. I don't remember my comp instructors teaching me to write. I do remember getting papers back with "CS," "frag," or "awk," which weren't the abbreviations in my writing handbook. But learning such abbreviations doesn't foster dialogue. Why aren't we continuously taught new things about writing throughout our education? Having received a B.A. in English, is that the end of that? I can't improve? I have nothing else to learn? *(Michelle)*

Teachers often assume that there is a necessary sequence to the courses in their fields and that all students experience the curriculum in the same way. But students do not. The only place a sequential curriculum exists is in the catalog.

Much of the knowledge expected of students by instructors is knowledge that is never directly taught in the classroom. Most education is actually a process of assimilation. Undergraduates are expected to look up esoteric codes like "frag" and "awk" to discover what they mean and how to correct them. Graduate students are expected to learn jargon and the structure of academic writing by reading academic journals, even though journal reading is not often assigned for this purpose. Faculty assume that osmosis will occur. From the pages of academic texts through the porous membranes of students' eyes, academic conventions are supposed to be assimilated. But it doesn't always work that way.

For example, undergraduate literature students are rarely told that there are competing theories of literary criticism, and they almost never know which theory is privileged in a particular class. Bob had never heard the term "New Criticism" mentioned in his undergraduate classes, much less any discussion of alternative methods of analysis. Yet his teachers assumed that he would assimilate their critical approach sufficiently to reproduce it in assigned papers. But as his anecdote about the seminar on *Ulysses* makes evident, it wasn't until well into grad school that he *got it*.

Assimilation is a hit-or-miss process. It fails at least as often as it succeeds. And when it fails, students are penalized. The result is that even the brightest students, like Michelle, blame themselves. They believe they are intellectual impostors.

> In the classroom I'm busy trying to pass or be accepted—to assimilate. In several of my lit courses, I tried to write the papers

my instructors wanted. Of course there's no way to know what they wanted, and I was left feeling I hadn't learned much. *(Michelle)*

The best antidote to the impostor syndrome is a healthy dose of dialogue. We hear a good deal of talk among our colleagues about students "entering the conversation," but how often are they allowed to participate fully? It's important that students be allowed to both listen and speak and that they be included in larger meetings where both students and faculty discuss the curriculum. Collections like this one, inviting students to author articles about their own educations, are important not only because they give students a forum, but because faculty will realize how much they can learn about the curriculum by listening to students. Both Bob and Denise have had their eyes opened by Michelle's experiences.

The most important conversations will inevitably take place in the classroom. Teachers need to be explicit about what they expect of students, especially on exams and papers, and why those expectations will vary from one class or department to another. By listening more carefully to students, faculty might learn how inappropriate some of their expectations are, how naïve the notion is that all students come to a class similarly prepared, or how woefully inadequate marginal comments are as the primary mode of communication between teachers and students.

The whole notion of assimilation should be opened to critical examination and discussion. Students should be encouraged to question the value of their assimilating into academia: What am I being assimilated into? What might I have to give up? Who will I become? Do I want to be assimilated or not? Making visible the process by which students are assimilated into the university or into a discipline can help diminish their sense of being impostors and may empower them to contribute a fresh perspective to the continuing dialogue about the role of the university.

Finally, we might all reassess how well the curriculum of English programs serves undergraduate students, how it has fostered an *impostor syndrome,* and how we can change that.

Coda

Between the time this article began and the time we submitted our final draft to the editors, Michelle moved to Japan and taught English in a high school for two years, and Denise wrote much of her dissertation and was hired to run a writing center. Along with these external changes, we recognized some internal ones as well.

Even though I still have a couple of chapters of my dissertation to write, and therefore am still a student, I've been away from that institution for a year and a half and I feel more confident. Getting some chapters accepted by my committee helped, but the change in status when I became director of the writing center worked miracles. I'm treated like a colleague. It's obvious when faculty request things of me that they expect I can accomplish them. When the chair asks for a few pages for a curriculum proposal, he's not looking over my shoulder. No one questions my ability to write well; it's expected. (*Denise*)

Moving out of the role of student empowered Denise and Michelle. They felt less like impostors. When the three of us began rewriting this article a year and a half after our first draft, Michelle was the one to start our e-mail conversation. Her prose was less hesitant than it had been.

At the beginning of our collaboration, I was a student while Bob and Denise were teachers. I was terrified to participate. I didn't want to write anything first; I wanted to see what the two of them had written before I shared. I procrastinated. A year or so later I'm thrilled that I began the drafting this time around. This feels like a huge step for me. I feel more confident. I feel I have more autonomy to write what I would like. I'm less afraid to share because no one has the power to denigrate my writing. (*Michelle*)

But moving beyond the role of student is only a partial explanation of why Michelle and Denise have more confidence in their writing.

Confidence comes from praise and acceptance, the kind of support and recognition I got while in grad school, first in my Ph.D. program from my mentor who for three years praised my writing so much I began to believe him, and later when I returned to school to get an M.F.A. and received that kind of recognition from playwrights, directors, and actors. When I finish a draft these days, I decide who will give me not just useful comments but, more importantly, praise. I share drafts with people who will appreciate what I am trying to do, who will encourage, not discourage, me to write more. (*Bob*)

We also received encouraging responses from the editors of this collection, Gail Tayko and John Tassoni. Their delight in our writing, along with the challenging questions they asked, helped us focus our revisions. At times we borrowed their language (with their permission, of course) for passages we struggled with. They provided another voice for the kind of dialogue we advocate.

Not all students have the kinds of opportunities we've enjoyed to move from student into teacher roles, nor can they easily find audiences that will appreciate their work. How can we foster this kind of support *within* academe? By praising student writing. By persuading faculty to praise student writing. By subverting the critical atmosphere of English departments with enthusiasm. And by encouraging, rather than discouraging, writers to write more—to acquire the experience necessary to become confident in their skills. Through our conversations we became aware of how the English curriculum itself undermines the confidence of even the most successful students. Creating dialogue—especially discussions between teachers and students about the curriculum itself—is the best way we know to diminish the alienating effects of the impostor syndrome.

Five

At Home with Multiculturalism in Kansas

Sandy Feinstein, Amanda Folck,
Carman Costello, and Jennifer Muret Bate

Introduction

Sandy: I was not surprised that I was asked to teach the multicultural class required of students seeking secondary-school certification in English at Southwestern College in Winfield, Kansas. The other members of the English department are white Anglo-Saxon Protestants from Kansas, Oklahoma, and Kentucky. And in the self-study report sent to the North Central Accreditation Board, only three of our school's faculty were listed under the category of "diversity": a Caucasian woman who teaches French and was born in Strasbourg, France; a Caucasian Moslem mathematician from Iran; and myself, identified in the report as from New York and Jewish.

Having been educated in the metropolitan areas of New York and Los Angeles, I am particularly sensitive to the problems of minority representation in the classroom and the curriculum, but even more conscious of the difficult task of finding a means to educate students in other cultures while not speaking for any ethnicity—including my own. When I learned I would be teaching multicultural literature in Kansas, therefore, I knew I wanted to find a means by which my students would feel invested in the course and define for themselves what multiculturalism means in their cultural context; more importantly, I wanted them to discover themselves within the context of multiculturalism and, as Kenneth Bruffee puts it in advocating for collaborative learning, I wanted them to "try to discover what distinguishes beliefs of their own communities from those of other communities and in what respects, if any, the beliefs of most of those communities are nearly identical" (1993, 193).

The class had only eight students, six superficially homogeneous. Only one of the students was African American. She was from St. Louis, as was one of the Caucasian woman students. There were six women and two men, one of the men a nontraditional student in his forties. The class was to prove, however, the truth of Suzanne Miller's observation that "Individuals are rarely monolithic in their cultural makeup, but rather are simultaneously members of several cultures and subcultures. Thus, diversity is likely even in classes that are superficially homogeneous" (1992, 12). In a way, it might be said that the class was structured to demonstrate both Bruffee's and Miller's observations, except at that time I was unfamiliar with their work.

The assignments were created to reflect the intention that (1) our class reflected diversity, despite its "homogeneity," and (2) the students shared the beliefs of communities other than their own. Two of the assigned projects reflected this intention. The first project, which Amanda touches upon, was what I called a "creative construction." It asked the students to "write a story, collection of poems, songs, cartoons, etc. The project should give a sense of who you are culturally—i.e., in relation to family, region, heritage, religion, etc." The second project, on which Carman and Jenny will focus, asked the students to "Locate a text that you feel reflects your cultural background. We shall order or make copies of the text and read it together as a class. Then write a short paper on a particular image or theme in that text that is particularly meaningful to you." Even as I retype the assignment from the syllabus, I am conscious of how little I knew of what was likely to happen, what texts would be chosen, what directions the class might take.

I knew, however, that I would have help in whatever direction we found ourselves going. The person in charge of inter-library loans rarely takes more than a day to process a request; consequently, I knew we would always be able to get whatever works we needed in timely fashion, and that's exactly what happened. In addition, one of the students, Jenny, worked at the local bookstore, so book orders also arrived in record time—invariably within a week of our order. With the luxury of knowing that my book orders would be processed efficiently, I didn't have to worry about the logistics of acquiring the necessary reading materials in the middle of a semester. Knowing I can get a book in a week's time has necessarily affected the way I put together a syllabus. I distribute a syllabus at two- to four-week intervals in order to be as flexible as possible and respond to what is actually happening in the classroom. Over the years, I have grown accustomed to changing direction midcourse. In one sense, these changes and my willingness to alter the direction of a class reflect my understanding of dialogic pedagogy. It is my course only until I come to know the students in the class. Then it becomes their class and, together, we construct a course that makes the most sense to all of us.

Before I knew the students, I had decided on four texts I would use. We began with Toni Morrison's theoretical text *Playing in the Dark* (1993) and a packet of poems representing a range of voices.[1] The first week I tried to make the Morrison text accessible and to personalize it by giving two different journal assignments: For 8/29, I asked the students to choose one poem from among those I had handed out and "Discuss how one of the poems supports or contradicts Morrison's thesis"; for 8/31, I asked the students to "Identify what or who you think has served as the 'other' in your life. How does your experience support or modify Morrison's thesis?" I also assigned three fictional texts, Henry Roth's *Call It Sleep* ([1934] 1991), Jean Toomer's *Cane* ([1923] 1969), and Sandra Cisneros's *The House on Mango Street* ([1984] 1989). By the time we finished with "my" texts, I would know the students, they would know me, and I knew they would be ready to take over ownership of the class.

On the first day, I had begun the process by which we would come to know one another. I asked them to do two freewrites: five minutes to define multiculturalism, after which we discussed their definitions and mine; the second freewrite to define the term again by writing about their cultural backgrounds. Discussion resulting from this second question was lively. A few students weren't sure where their ancestors had come from, and so they talked about their hometowns, their families, and their faith; others knew their ethnic makeup precisely and reeled off exotic combinations that surprised the others. I was among the exotics with grandparents from Mesopotamia, Romania, Poland, and Ukraine.

After we had shared who we are, it became impossible to teach the assigned texts in any conventional way—that is, with the teacher armed with piles of scholarly works and ready to lecture punctiliously on each text. I found myself explaining why I had assigned the texts, revealing my concerns that they might not like them, and mentioning what I found personally familiar in the texts. *Call It Sleep* was a kind of homage to my immigrant background; *Cane* was the salute to growing up in the sixties when Jean Toomer's lyrical evocations were a favorite among my friends; Cisneros I discovered while on sabbatical in Miami (1992–1993)—she had given a reading at the local bookstore. These tidbits were part of our group's conversations about what multiculturalism might mean to each of us; I controlled the discourse only insofar as I had chosen the initial topics. What follows, then, is a discussion from those who helped create the class by sharing who they are and, in so doing, discovered multiculturalism in their own lives.

Learning from Others, Learning to Be a Student

Amanda: Throughout the first few days of my multicultural literature class, I would have been considered by a previous instructor to be an "enrollee." Larry Wilgers, a professor of History at Southwestern College, once explained the difference between "students" and "enrollees." Students become enthusiastically involved in their education, enjoying homework assignments and doing extra research and experiments to enhance their learning experience. A student wants challenges and enjoys new and creative experiences. Functioning as an enrollee, I had presumed that the class would not be a success for me because (1) I did not consider myself multicultural and (2) the class makeup was not a good balance of ethnic backgrounds. Having been familiar with the instructor, I *enrolled* in this course *only* to fulfill a requirement for my English major.

After a few class sessions, having soon discovered that I, too—a white, Methodist midwesterner—was multicultural, a spark of interest altered my attitude about the ways I could benefit from studying multicultural literature. What followed next was my rapid transformation from enrollee to student that happened naturally without much conscious awareness on my part. I escaped previous ways of learning as an enrollee and became a student because of two key elements: a comfortable learning environment well-suited to the class and the diversity of resources used to improve my ability to learn. In order to create a mutual environment, everyone, the instructor too, orally shared his or her cultural background by discussing ancestry, region, religion, immediate family, and employment. I told the class my background: I am from Lyons, Kansas, a rural community of approximately 4,500 people; my upbringing is conservative Methodist; my family origins include German, Irish, French, and English; and my parents were born and raised in Lyons and reside there still. I listened to and learned about the other students' backgrounds in much the same manner. This approach enabled me to become familiar with and to better understand where each person came from.

Another way we became comfortable with each other was through a wide variety of class activities. The exercises from the class were mostly interactive: group discussions, interchanging the roles of teacher and student, and role playing scenes from studied texts. Role-playing required creativity and self-confidence. Students had ten minutes to rehearse a selected topic with their partner. From Roth's *Call It Sleep*, examples of our situations to act out included meeting a new kid in the neighborhood girl-to-boy and boy-to-boy, a man befriending another man while one is trying to seduce the other's wife, and a stranger trying to understand the questions of a child whose native language is not English. In a group with two other members I acted out a scene from the book in which a father chastens his son when others are present. Jenny was the father, I was the son, and another student was an adult who was a guest in the home. Although we were only role-playing, I felt embarrassed and angry when Jenny was scolding me. This exercise helped me to identify with the young boy in *Call It Sleep* who experiences this ordeal. The improvisational acting also created common feelings of nervousness and excitement for each of us when it was our turn to perform. I felt that the shared experience brought my classmates, the instructor, and me closer together, making the atmosphere conducive to learning.

Another technique that helped to shape the shared learning environment occurred when we each took a turn to teach the class. I had help in choosing a text that represented my own individual cultural influences. I asked my professor for a suggestion as to what text she thought represented what she knew about my background and culture. Other classmates chose their texts through different means. For example, one student chose her book after having seen a blurb review in the *Hungry Mind Review*. Another student had originally purchased *African-American Folktales* (1993) for her daughter and decided that it would work for this class. Jenny, who worked at a bookstore, picked her book from a catalog. Knowing that my personal cultural influences varied greatly from my classmates, despite the seeming similarities of race, region, and religion, it was a challenge for me to teach my text, "Old Mrs. Harris" from Willa Cather's *Obscure Destinies* (1932). I think each of us shared in the anxiety when teaching, but like role-playing, this experience helped me to feel comfortable in the class, and I was able to talk freely and avoid potentially tense situations while discussing sensitive issues such as personal beliefs, prejudices, and racism.

In addition to group exercises, I benefited from a variety of individual activities. Writing in a journal over assigned multicultural topics and the construction of a multicultural portfolio are two examples of individual assignments. Journals allowed me a chance to reflect privately upon the required reading materials. One example of a journal assignment while studying Toni Morrison's *Playing in the Dark* was to identify people or things that have served as "others" in our lives and show how our experience modified or supported Morrison's thesis. I enjoyed this journal exercise because I had to confront what had been the others in my life. In a journal entry dated 8/31/94, I wrote:

> Right now the "other" in my life pertains to my Christian faith, temptation, and making responsible moral decisions. Basically, my "other" is my own self. I feel as if my home environment and college lifestyle have crashed together, causing me to make choices that conflict and compete with one another. I fear I lack the self-discipline to raise myself to full potential. Whether I'm aware of it or not, my "other" is always present.

Although confronting opposing elements in one's life can be an unpleasant situation at times, I found I needed the time for reflection and felt that I gained in my personal and spiritual growth. Journals allowed time for thought, which added to the rewards of reading the various texts and drew out the deeper differences among us, providing the basis for our Kansas multicultural experience.

Through the multicultural portfolio project, a personal construction put into some sort of container, students could choose the means by which to make a creation pertain to their individual cultural influences. I felt apprehensive pulling together concrete items that represented my personal cultural influences. The idea of having my own personal culture was exciting, yet still a new and awkward idea. I was worried that I would not be able to provide very many cultural influences, unlike my classmates, who, I thought, would have no problem with this project. But once I got started, I realized just how many personal influences I had and felt comfortable in sharing them with the class. I used a wicker basket filled with my favorite works by multicultural authors and art pieces. I shared my mother's art with the class: a portrait of an African-American woman, sketches of war-torn and impoverished children from the Biafra civil war, and a pointillism picture of Nelson Mandela, which has hung for the past five years in my family's living room. Before this project, I did not realize how many cultures affected me. Before this exercise, I thought I came from a small white rural community where there is little multiculturalism or appreciation for the arts. I felt foolish for not recognizing the artistic and multicultural factors in my own home while I was living there.

The experience of being educated individually and by the group was an incredible one. This course empowered me to abandon being an enrollee and thoroughly enjoy being a student, the ideal for education.

The Carnival Is a Culture

Carman: The first night of Multicultural Literature, Sandy handed out a syllabus that described each of the major papers and projects we, the class, would have to do. The assignment that caught my eye was as follows: "Locate a text that you feel reflects your cultural background. We shall make copies of the text and read it together. Then write a short paper on an image or theme in that text that is particularly meaningful to you. Presentation dates will vary." As it turned out, I was not the only one who wanted a bit more information about the presentation part of the project. Sandy explained to us that we would be teaching our text to the class for our presentations. She told us to use her as an example when she taught Henry Roth's *Call It Sleep* using her cultural background to approach the book. Still, most of the class was a little wary of teaching our cultures.

For this project, I chose the only text I could think of that was unique to my culture. I grew up in a culture different from most of modern America, but I'm not African American, Native American, Hispanic American, or Asian American: I am a Caucasian female from a middle-class family, a family that owns and operates its own carnival throughout the spring, summer, and fall. Therefore, I planned to give the other students a taste of carnival culture. I assigned the first half of Dean Koontz's *Twilight Eyes* (1987) for the class to read. The book is rich with explanations of carny slang terms, ideas that reflect the morality of the carnies, and passages that reflect carny culture. This novel combined with my experiences working and living on a carnival to form my sources for the project.

With the help of *Twilight Eyes*, I set out to provide others with insight into carnival life, which many know little or nothing about. I was, however, worried about the teaching process. First of all, I did not want to assign all the reading, around 250 pages, on Monday and have it due on Wednesday, but in the end the reading was assigned in one chunk. As I walked into class the Wednesday night that I was to teach, I figured no one in the class would have finished the reading. I also began to worry that the other students would not understand why I had chosen the text I did. I was suddenly afraid I had made a bad choice for my text. Hoping for the best, I reluctantly entered class, not as a student, but as a scared teacher.

My tension began to subside as soon as I entered the classroom. I overheard one student remark to another about how interesting my choice of text had been. Finally, I was able to put a smile on my face and begin my class period as a teacher. I read passages from the book that explained how I perceived the carnival culture, and I told stories about incidents from my own background with a carnival. The class seemed amazed when I pointed out how many of Koontz's descriptions were very close to real carnival life.

One such example of the carny culture that Koontz used quite often and accurately was slang—carny terms. Many of the people in my class, I was amazed to discover, did not know what Koontz was talking about when he used these terms, so I went through the text, stopping at each carny slang word I came across, and offered an explanation. One example of this slang would be *marks*, the word carnies use to refer to everyone who is not a carny. Another slang term used often by Koontz is *slough night*. Slough night is the last night the carnival spends in a certain town. It is the night the carnies must disassemble all the rides and games and fun, and load it all onto or into trucks and semi-trailers. I also told the students to stop me if they found a term they did not understand. To me, an inhabitant of the carnival world, it seemed silly that they did not understand the terms. For example, Sandy asked me what *pitching the tip* meant. I laughed for a moment and then explained that a carny's pitch is the lines he or she delivers to the marks to try to get them to spend their money at the carny's stand; the tip refers to when one carny has a large group of people, marks, listening to the pitch. So *pitching the tip* means a carny is giving his or her spiel to a large crowd. All of a sudden the entire class seemed to understand one part of my culture that had been more than a mystery to them: It had been nonexistent.

Another part of my culture that I shared with the class is carny talk. Carny talk was not explained in Koontz's book, but it is something that has always been important in my culture. It is a way of speaking, similar to pig Latin, where certain letters are placed within a word to alter the word's sound. Carny talk uses the sound "iz" after or inside every syllable to accomplish the change.

An example of carny talk would be, "Hizow iizs yizour cizousizon, Eizd?" meaning, "How is your cousin, Ed?" I explained why carnies use this code language: to speak to each other about a mark in front of other marks, or, as my parents did, to say something one does not want the children to understand.

One of the class's biggest questions was whether or not Gibsontown is a real place. In *Twilight Eyes*, Koontz talks about Gibsontown, actually known as Gibtown, being the center that many carnies call home during the winter months. I told them that, yes, Gibtown does exist, and it is known as winter quarters for many carnies. At first they did not seem to believe me, or at best, I was really pushing their belief. Luckily, my parents, who make a trip to Gibtown every February, had supplied me with a map of Gibtown and brochures they had from last year's "Carny Convention," as they call it. Everyone wanted to look at the handouts I had brought, and as each person looked at them they seemed to be saying, "Wow! I guess Carman knows what she's talking about!" I feel that part of the reason I was successful in my teaching was that I brought extra aids to show to the class.

As I offered explanations for different carny slang terms, explained carny talk, and told stories of my own cultural experiences on the carnival, I was surprised by how well I seemed to be holding the class's interest. I was actually teaching, and the class was learning from me. Later, I asked some of my class members how they thought I did as a teacher for a day; I was pleased to hear positive comments about my work. Many of them mentioned the map and brochures I had brought. They said that these items did add credibility to what I was trying to tell them. One student said she especially liked learning about carny talk. She said she had never imagined that a culture like the carnival would have its own language. Many agreed that choosing the carnival as a culture was a great idea because it provided an example of how we, the students, were different, even though we might look very similar on the outside. All in all, the comments I received from my classmates gave me some much needed confidence in my teaching abilities.

Looking back on the project now, I feel I did a decent job of sharing part of the history and life of a little-known and rarely talked-about culture. Most of my classmates had been to a carnival at least once; however, none of them had ever imagined that there could be a separate culture contained within the carnival. Yet the carnival is a culture so different that it is often mocked: My grandfather was laughed at when he started our carnival fifty years ago, and I still hear hurtful remarks today. Despite these remarks, the people of this culture are not ashamed. They are proud, caring, respectful people who believe in what my mother calls "carny power." It was this power that I wanted to share with my classmates. By sharing my chosen text and incidents from my culturally rich life, I was able to accomplish what I had hoped to do, and at the same time I also helped to broaden our class's definition of multiculturalism.

The project not only helped me understand my culture and build confidence in my teaching ability, but it also enabled me to be more attentive and learn more about the other students in my class and their individual cultures. I realized how attentive the other students had been for me, and I wanted to be at least as attentive, if not more, for their presentations. So, in the process of paying attention and being a model student, I was able to learn and absorb information from each student. As I learned about my classmates' cultural experiences with cooking, Christianity, and education, they learned about my culture, the carnival. We learned about the cultures that literally live right next door to us.

Feeling Culture, Cooking Culture

Jenny: Sowell and Bernstein notwithstanding,[2] there is little doubt in academe today that the study of multiculturalism is important. In such a highly globalized society, one dares not perpetrate intellectual isolationism. As a double major in Elementary Education and English, I am keenly aware of the need to be well-versed in multicultural literature. As middle class, Caucasian, and Protestant, I have been painfully aware of what I determined to be a total lack of cultural diversity in my own personal life. Bearing all this in mind, I enrolled in a multicultural literature course offered at my school. I expected to spend the semester reading works by recognized pillars of multicultural literature, such as Toni Morrison, Amy Tan, and Ralph Ellison. My feeling was that this would be an impersonal look at the abstract concept of multiculturalism. Instead, I found that the class took a rather unorthodox approach to the study of multicultural literature. As a result of this approach, I learned that multiculturalism is important personally as the manifestation of many cultural influences apparent in my life and the lives of my classmates. In addition, I discovered that culture could not merely be confined to pages within books and esoteric academic discussions. Culture is a rich influence that permeates our lives and expresses itself in our daily activities. In particular, I found that my exploration and presentation of my own culture expanded far beyond the boundaries of the traditional classroom and bubbled over into the kitchen. In order to share my culture with my classmates, I had to bring them home and make them dinner.

As this paper's introduction suggests, the class itself was unusual in its seeming lack of diversity in composition: This group of eight sprang entirely from midwestern roots. Almost entirely Caucasian, the class's homogeneity was striking. In fact, two of the eight are direct descendants of original Mayflower crew members. Though the class was tremendously enriched by the experiences of our urban African-American student and Jewish professor, we did not fit the profile I hoped for in a multicultural class. The lack of diversity seemed especially limiting when I learned that we, the students, would be responsible for choosing and teaching texts representative of our own cultures. I did not expect this group to undertake the task of defining and exploring multiculturalism through our own experiences. Yet it was precisely our experiences that provided the framework that shaped this course and allowed us to explore the literature more creatively.

Through our reading and discussion of our first texts—those chosen by our professor—I encountered sophisticated and subtle examples of multiculturalism in literature. For example, I learned that the author of *Cane*, Jean Toomer, identifies seven different "blood mixtures" as significant cultural influences upon his work: French, Dutch, Welsh, Negro [sic], German, Jewish, and Indian (Bontemps 1969, vii).

We were then instructed to choose works that represented a broad sense of our own cultures, if not as explicitly as *Cane*, then implicitly. Knowing the background of our class, I didn't expect to find much diversity in the literature chosen, yet the works turned out to be surprisingly diverse. Student-assigned texts included, among others, *The Other World* (1994) by short story writer John Wynne, *Twilight Eyes* by thriller novelist Dean Koontz, *Vibration Cooking* (1992) by actress and National Public Radio columnist Vertamae Smart-Grosvenor, and *The Four Quartets* (1943) by T.S. Eliot. These texts provided an unconventional curriculum for a class in multicultural literature, for Wynne, Koontz, and Eliot are (or were, in Eliot's case) Caucasian men. What made these texts so fascinating, however, was not specifically the authors' ethnic origins, but rather how each student connected with the culture represented in his or her chosen text.

In another part of this chapter, my classmate Carman Costello discusses why she chose Koontz's novel to portray her family's long history of operating a carnival. Through discussion, this third-generation carny introduced us to the unique culture of the carnival. In hearing stories of her heritage and experiences, I came to know a culture I had previously overlooked; in short, I discovered a new facet of multiculturalism. As Carman explained various aspects of the carnival, I could imagine what it might feel like to live there. I found myself entranced with the book and its depiction of the carnival, and I felt enriched by Carman's sharing and teaching. I began to understand how integral her family's carnival work was to her own sense of cultural identity.

Another student chose Eliot's poetry because its theme represented his own conversion experience. He shared with us his connection to Eliot's middle-American cultural roots; and having recently spent a semester studying abroad in Bulgaria, he also shared his identification with the author's disillusionment and expatriation. In these ways, the student portrayed a genuinely felt cultural connection to Eliot's work. In class he discussed his feelings about the time he spent out of the country and how he sought to express what he felt through poetry. During the discussions, he also noted numerous multicultural images and references in the poem—for example, how the Mississippi River figures as an evocation of the Civil War and how allusions to Krishna counterpointed the Western tradition and its spiritual assumptions. In addition, he noted that Eliot employed languages other than English, including Greek, French, German, and Italian. Interestingly, Sandy pointed out some unexpected connections between Eliot's poem and the more obviously multicultural writings of Toomer and Roth. In comparing the texts, she noted Eliot's unmistakable modernist influence on Roth's *Call It Sleep*, and we gained a deeper appreciation of Toomer's experimental style in *Cane*. Although I was originally skeptical of Eliot's relevance to a study of multiculturalism, I appreciated the student's personal connection to the work. I also learned to look carefully for cultural influences. They are not always easily found on the surface of a book or individual.

As the other students shared their intensely personal connections to the texts and the cultures they represented, I became more aware of the personal and down-to-earth nature of my own text. I chose Smart-Grosvenor's autobiography/travelogue *Vibration Cooking* from a bookstore catalog because it seemed too interesting to pass by. Its brief summary suggested an author of varied cultural makeup who defined herself primarily by what she cooked. I was intrigued by the idea of culinary culture, as it seemed an appropriate description of my own family. As it turned out, the book far surpassed my expectations, and I grew more and more excited about the possibilities of sharing my book and my culture with my classmates.

Some of the class were no doubt surprised that I, not the class's African-American student, chose a cookbook by an African-American woman to represent myself. I am from the fourth generation of a white middle-class Protestant farming family. Yet I was easily able to draw parallels between the author's culinary tradition and my own family's history of interacting with and around food. In her book, Smart-Grosvenor associates family members, special occasions, travels, and other events with specific dishes as if her entire frame of reference were completely organized in relation to the preparation, presentation, and consumption of food. Although I was certainly aware of our cultural differences, I identified more closely with the author the more I read of her text. Just as Smart-Grosvenor plans her New Year's celebration around her traditional Hoppin' John, my family centers its Christmas festivities around our annual Christmas Eve oyster stew and vegetable soup buffet. In the same way that Smart-Grosvenor always remembers her favorite family member by the fried chicken that she makes, I will forever remember my grandmother for her potato salad.

As I read on, I was overwhelmed by culinary memories from my childhood such as birthday parties with our traditional birthday cake, anniversary dinners, and holiday travels to meals of Thanksgiving turkeys and cranberry salad. (And, in traveling, the turkey was at least as important as seeing the relatives who had prepared it.) I thought of the many wonderful foods that had been created in our kitchen and of the delightful times I spent there with my parents, sisters, grandparents, and aunts. I knew that the only way I could possibly convey the intimacy and importance of cooking in my culture was to take my classmates home with me. I wanted them not only to gain a sense of my own life and culture, but also to realize the importance of food in *their* lives.

Eight of us spent an evening in my family's kitchen cooking some of Smart-Grosvenor's and my favorite foods. On the kitchen wall, I posted a poem by Smart-Grosvenor that talks about the central role of the kitchen in her family's life. We cooked together and talked about our varied cooking abilities and our memories of our kitchens at home. In our evening of shared cooking, we made Jimmy Carter's barbecue sauce and cornmeal mush—two dishes representative of Grosvenor's southern upbringing. We also made chicken and noodles, which is the epitome of food in the Muret household. Amanda recently reminded me that our dinner together had brought back a favorite food memory of her grandmother, who makes noodles from scratch every year for Thanksgiving and Christmas dinner.

While we waited for the noodles to finish cooking, we sat around the dining room table and talked about our favorite food memories. As we talked, I discovered that many others in the class had strong and varied cultural associations between family and food. As we ate the various dishes we had prepared, we talked about the importance of food as an expression of cultural values and traditions. We discussed Smart-Grosvenor's dedication to the preparation and consumption of food and found that in itself to be a kind of culture. To those whose idea of an old-fashioned meal was boxed macaroni and cheese, this new culture based around the preparation and eating of food was more foreign than any ethnic culture defined by geographic location or skin color. Through cooking together, then, our class experienced something of Smart-Grosvenor's culinary culture and my own family's cultural history.

My semester-long study of multicultural literature was filled with many surprises. Never did I expect that my enrollment in the course would result in inviting the entire class home for dinner, or that a dinner would, in fact, be an appropriate and meaningful way to explore multiculturalism. The course, however, began with the study of noncanonical texts and went on to employ unorthodox pedagogies, such as using student-chosen curricula and personal stories to determine the scope of the study of multicultural literature. These texts and pedagogies encouraged me to look beyond stereotypes and uncover new and subtle expressions of culture. They also gave me the opportunity to teach and be taught by my peers.

Throughout the semester, our class challenged and stretched the definition of *multicultural* to include a vast number of variables ranging far beyond race and origin to include, among others, work, religion, family, and food. The student-chosen curriculum encouraged great personal involvement and creativity among the students. In addition, the works chosen, though they may seem rather an unconventional curriculum for multicultural literature, became important portrayals of culture when examined in light of our personal experiences. As I read poetry, discussed novels, listened to stories, and cooked, I could not avoid being touched and enriched by the personal nature of our studies. Right here in Kansas, I began to comprehend the enormity of cultural diversity present in what had seemed to be a homogeneous midwestern group.

Conclusion

Sandy, Amanda, Carman, and Jenny: In this article, as in the class, the teacher began by identifying the direction and objectives of the course and then proceeded by relinquishing control. We have tried to imitate that approach in the structure of this paper, which was begun by the teacher and developed by the students. Therefore, by agreement, the teacher may conclude only briefly and with that which has already been implied by each of the writers. In other words, the last word may be written down by the teacher, but it represents the shared thoughts of the group: Working together, we discovered the fantastic loom of learning that enabled all of us—teacher and students—to share in the experience of a collaborative education.

Notes

1. This packet included poems by Olga Broumas, Margaret Walker, Claude McKay, Thadious M. Davis, Terri Meyette, Alice Walker, Alice Sadongei, Wendy Rose, Rosario Morales, Dionisio Martinez, Thulani Davis, Albert Goldbarth, Charles Fort, Yusef Komunyakaa, Michael S. Weaver, and Ray A. Young Bear.

2. Thomas Sowell and Richard Bernstein argue that multiculturalism is basically without real educational value and advocate a back-to-basics approach to schooling.

Six

Writing Cincinnati
A Student and a Teacher Design a Course
Michael Gilland and Lucille M. Schultz

Michael and Lucy: In the spring of 1994, the Department of English at the University of Cincinnati offered for the first time a course called Writing Cincinnati. This was an upper-level writing class in which the city of Cincinnati served as both the text and the subject for text for student writing. Sometimes independently, sometimes collaboratively, students studied, investigated, and analyzed various aspects of the city's past and present life and then wrote their papers.

Because of its subject, the course attracted a fair amount of media attention: It was covered twice by the student newspaper and once by the faculty/staff newspaper. Guest speakers included Kathy Doane, the assistant features editor for the Tempo Section of the *Cincinnati Enquirer*; Roxanne Qualls, mayor of Cincinnati; Mary Stanton, director of Bethany House Services, providers of job training and temporary housing for women and children; and Kathleen Ware, director of quality improvement for the Cincinnati public schools. On the last day of class, a reporter for the *Cincinnati Post* interviewed the students. In addition, an all-women's Appalachian folk group talked to us about the music that is part of this region's Appalachian heritage and then entertained us with their rendition of "Boil Them Cabbage Down" and other well-known folk tunes performed on flute, guitar, and mountain lap dulcimer.

Students published their writing from the course in *Cincinnati Magazine*, the city's glossy promotional magazine; *Cincinnati Post,* the city's evening newspaper; *The Downtowner*, a tabloid covering news of downtown businesses; and *CityBeat* and *Everybody's News*, the city's premier arts and entertainment alternative newspapers. Students who were in the course talk about having a reunion to share their current writing with each other; students who have heard anecdotes about the course ask when it will be offered again. Partly because of the innovative design of the course and its town-and-gown connection, the teacher received her department's most prestigious teaching award.

By many external standards, the course was a success. Perhaps the most telling fact about the course, however, is that it was codesigned by a student and a teacher and that now we are writing this essay together. The essay is the story of our work together—and of our reflections on our experience. We tell the story in alternating voices because we believe it may be interesting—and helpful—to readers to hear the same story told from two different perspectives. We hope this shared project might be of interest to other students and teachers and perhaps even spark other creative collaborations.

Stage One: The Background

Michael: I'm not a teacher. I'm not even a student anymore. Due to a twist in my financial aid that took me out of school, I'm writing my part of this essay on a Sunday, my one day off. I'm now a construction service technician and a part-time musician. I drive 200–300 miles a day and put in sixty to seventy-five hours a week to support my family, to pay back student loans, and to save for the college courses I need to finish my degree. Tomorrow, I'll be on the road at 5:30 A.M., but I'll get off early because I need to be at a concrete-pour at 2 A.M. on Tuesday. These days, I don't have the time I want to write and record my music (or to read and write at all).

I attended Cincinnati Public's School for Creative and Performing Arts from the fifth grade until I graduated in 1981. After the next year at the Berkeley College of Music in Boston, I was forced to return home because I ran out of money. After an eight-year tour of duty in wholesale and retail sales, I began my college career at the University of Cincinnati's College Conservatory of Music, where I studied Electronic Media for three years; I then transferred to a five-year, dual-degree course of study called the Cincinnati Initiative for Teacher Education (CITE). The CITE program is a cooperative effort between the College of Education and the McMicken College of Arts and Sciences. I was working toward a B.A. in English and a B.S. in Secondary Education and would add these credits to the 100 I already had toward a B.F.A. I felt this new program would give me a competitive edge in the job market after graduation. In fact, the way it was supposed to work is that in the last year of the program (the fifth year) I would have been teaching in a high school in the Cincinnati area on a part-time basis, making a part-time salary, and going to college half-time to complete my graduation requirements. Then I got a big dose of reality in my second year in the program: Local school tax levies failed, teachers were getting laid off, schools were timid about committing to part-time contracts, and without being aware of it, I had used up my financial aid eligibility.

I first met Professor Schultz in the spring quarter of 1993. She was a guest speaker in my education seminar, telling us how a new course she was planning would go from an idea in her head to the actual classroom. As she solicited ideas for the new course, my hand was up more times than not, and my voice offered every other statement or suggestion. At the end of the class, I approached Professor Schultz in hopes of gaining her sponsorship for an independent study in which I would be her apprentice, so to speak, as she continued to develop the course. As a native Cincinnatian (born, raised, and sustained here), I felt qualified as an idea generator; I knew my way around town, so I'd make a great gofer; and I was excited about getting a jump on my curriculum planning career. She told me to check back with her the following winter quarter when it would be time for the actual preparation of the course. She thought she could use my help in some manner, and I liked the idea of the one-on-one tutelage that comes with an independent study; the fact that I could get three undergraduate credits for being a gopher also caught my attention. I thought it would be fun—and an "easy A."

Lucy: I'm a tenured associate professor in the Department of English at the University of Cincinnati, an urban, comprehensive research institution. My field is composition and rhetoric, and for almost a decade, the focus of my teaching and my research had been grounded in our required writing sequence for first-year students. I was first associate director, then director, of a large first-year writing program (we serve more than two thousand students a quarter) and thus my work was focused on teacher-training and on developing curriculum and assessment strategies for this three-course, first-year sequence.

When I completed my stint at that job in 1992, I suddenly had the possibility of developing writing classes for our upper-level students—and out of that possibility (and time for reflection) came my idea for the course that would be called Writing Cincinnati. I have a deep and long-term interest in city life—and also a conviction that it is important to build town-and-gown bridges, bridges that connect civic life with academic life. Many of our students come from small towns or suburbs and have little hands-on experience with city government or city life; I have taught students who reported never having been downtown for a civic or cultural event. My idea was that investigating and writing about Cincinnati would open up new worlds both for me and for the class.

Serendipitously, as I was drafting the course proposal, I received an invitation from the College of Education to talk to a group of future teachers about how I develop a course. It was during my time with these students, at a meeting sometime in early spring, that I met Michael and learned of his long-time interest in Cincinnati. In fact, he said—with some enthusiasm—he might call me sometime to talk more about the course. As I walked back to my office that afternoon that I met Michael, I smiled to myself about his enthusiasm and felt energized by his interest in the class; his was, after all, a student's voice, and one of the first I heard in response to my ideas for this new course that I had in the works. In spite of Michael's interest, though, I wasn't at all sure I would ever hear from him again. I guess I thought that as so often happens, he would get busy with what I call "the tyranny of the immediate" and that as time passed, his interest would be pulled away by something more pressing.

Stage Two: The Design Process

Lucy: But then, six months later, in the early fall of 1993, true to his word, Michael did call me. And he was persistent. He wanted to know if he could do an independent study with me that would focus on course development, in particular—the development of the city course. It would be a chance for him to see the thinking that goes into creating a course and to help with that process, and, he argued, he could help me with the background work. I had no experience with this kind of project, and I didn't really know Michael. But it was true that I could use some help, and that Michael was willing to provide that help, and so it seemed like an opportunity not to pass up. After I got permission for Michael to do an independent study with me (this would allow him to get academic credit for our work together in course design), we began our collaboration.

Michael and I met every other week during the winter quarter; sometimes we had an extra ad hoc meeting to touch base on the headway we had made or the stumbling blocks we had encountered on a piece of our work. We also got to know each other's answering machine very well. When we started meeting, I had no fixed idea about how we would develop the course: I knew I wanted students to investigate the city and to write a lot, and I knew I wanted them to serve as a writers' group for one another as they drafted and revised. It also seemed important for all of us to do some background reading about cities and, in particular, about Cincinnati. So I started talking to colleagues in urban history and urban architecture about suggestions for readings, and passing those tips on to Michael. I asked if, as his first task on the project, he might compile a bibliography that we would pass out to the students. He set to work on that, and he and I both started imagining ways in which the course might play. We decided to put together a packet of photocopied readings that would provide the class with a shared reading experience—so I asked him if based on his work with the bibliography, he would pick twenty or so readings from which he and I could then choose the dozen or so we would use in the packet. I've lived in this city eleven years; Michael, on the other hand, has lived here his entire life, and his family has called

Cincinnati home for generations. So my thinking was, why not be bold and entrust a student to use his "lived" knowledge in a school setting; that is, why not let Michael have a major voice in picking the Cincinnati texts other students were going to read? Although I don't know that I would have articulated it at the time, I was putting into practice what I have learned about Ira Shor's and Henry Giroux's work in dialogic pedagogy about recognizing and supporting what students already know when they enter our classrooms.

For me, one of the first big payoffs of the early stages of our collaboration is that Michael, spontaneously I think, came up with the name for the course. When my department required me to submit a course description months earlier, I had tentatively called the course what an English professor might call it: The City—As Text and Subject for Text. As Michael and I worked together, he started referring to the course as Writing Cincinnati—and before we knew it, that became its official name. A small thing for a student to name a course? On the one hand, maybe so. On the other hand, it was a first for me. And a first for Michael as well.

As the five-page bibliography took shape, I next asked Michael to start brainstorming an idea list to help students think about areas of the city to investigate. He was back with his list in a few days, suggesting, for example, that students might study some aspect of Cincinnati's public alternative schools, of local businesses and breweries (we have some of both with national reputations), of environmental problems—especially the smell—affecting the Mill Creek Valley, of radiation testing at local hospitals, of all the Cincinnati communities that have Mt., Hill, Hills, Heights, Ridge, or Bank as part of their names. As I saw Michael produce these documents—first a bibliography and then an idea list—I was increasingly aware of his talent and startled at how lucky I was to be working with him. I'm not sure how I would define our relationship at this point; Michael and I were not exactly colleagues, but neither were we in traditional teacher and student roles. Somewhere along the line, I became "Lucy" to him, and I found myself relying increasingly on his judgment and on his ability to do his part of the project while I went off to do mine.

I was beginning to think more about the daily operation of the course. Instead of asking students to write individual papers that I would grade, I asked them to submit a portfolio—at the end of the course—of their Cincinnati-based writing. And instead of asking for specific kinds of papers, I suggested a range of genres (including reflection papers, historical papers, proposals, reviews, interviews) but asked students to choose projects that would be interesting to them. Because the course was open to both undergraduates and graduate students, I decided to vary the page requirements; from the undergraduates, I asked for twenty pages of text, from the graduate students, thirty pages. All the students knew that some pages of the writing could be more finished than other pages; in other words, I was willing to accept a portfolio of projects that were in various stages of completion. (As a writer, I always have several projects going, some closer to being done than others, and I wanted students to have this experience, too.) In addition to asking them to produce portfolios, I also wanted students to keep writer's logs, one several-page entry per week on any aspect of their work they wanted, with a final three-page reflection entry on their experiences with Cincinnati as text and subject for text.

Michael: My background in sales no doubt helped me to wiggle into this project on course designing that was well beyond my expertise, but I was up for the challenge. Early in January, I showed up for an appointment in Lucy's office to get the paperwork squared away for our independent study. Trying to be on top of things, I brought along some ideas about how I thought the course should be designed. I had it all figured out: Students would write three five- to seven-page papers on some aspect(s) of Cincinnati, then a thirty-page paper that would be a culmination and expansion of two of the previous papers. I had a list of topic ideas and a list of possible paper formats. I even had a weekly schedule worked out with tentative guest speakers (other professors) and the idea that we'd hold a contest and try to get the winning paper published in *Cincinnati Magazine*. At the bottom of each square of the lesson plan was the word "readings" (I figured that Lucy had all the reading material picked out already).

Responding to my suggestions, Lucy liked the idea of publication, but she wanted to see many of the manuscripts published, not just one. She also liked the idea of guest speakers, but thought on a bigger scale than I did and said, "Why don't I write to the mayor and see if she'll come visit our class?" She said the topic list and the possible paper formats were a good start, and as far as the readings . . . Wham! . . . she slapped down four or five thick hardbound books that she had already checked out from the library and told me to read through them and come up with what I thought would be good selections for a course packet. She also asked me to track down additional readings on Cincinnati that I thought would be useful and bring them to our next meeting. I remember thinking that Lucy liked my enthusiasm, toned it down, focused it, and explained that we could think up the actual writing assignments pretty easily, but that we needed to get a running start on finding the readings for our packet. At one point Lucy asked me if I thought I had enough work to keep me busy and I thought . . . ssshhheeeuuw . . . all this on top of my other fifteen credit hours should keep me bug-eyed for ten weeks. As it turned out I made the dean's list that quarter.

My role in the design process was to search libraries for possible writing topics and to put together an extensive bibliography that students might use as part of the background reading for their writing about Cincinnati. Any errands the project needed were mine to run as I was promoted to the rank of workhorse (that's a step above a gofer). I made frequent stops at the library on campus and the main public library downtown, but I found the pot of gold at the

Cincinnati Historical Society's library in the refurbished Union Terminal, on the city's west side. There I found a wealth of information: hardbacks, paperbacks, magazines, flyers, old advertisements, photos, blueprints, recordings, handwritten letters—it was all quite captivating. As I sat at the table reading, I could sometimes look out a window and see the trains passing in the rear of the terminal, a great atmosphere for my investigations into the city's past. For a time, I was visiting this library three to four times a week, sometimes researching the project, other times following up on something that had sparked my interest. Lucy told me to look for diversity in finding the best material for our course pack, so I searched out essays that crossed class, gender, and race lines, essays written for the popular press, essays written for a scholarly audience. And I was looking for books about cities in general: How, when, and why did cities come into being? That's what we hoped to talk about in the first couple weeks of the course. I was also looking for books about the history of Cincinnati that we would use in the next part of the course. Finally, I had an eye open for fictional works that used Cincinnati as their setting.

The biggest obstacle I had to overcome in this stage of my work was my own fascination with the material I was reading; sometimes I was unable to put the books down, whether or not I thought they were relevant to my search. For instance, I came across a reference to Bond's Hill. I live in Bond's Hill, so I read further. It turns out that down the street from my house, a guy named Bond built a farmhouse over one hundred years ago. He had the only sawmill in town, so when people needed lumber, they went to Bond's Hill to get it. Where my house sits was once part of his apple orchard. This information fueled my inquisitiveness further, and I began looking up all the hills of Cincinnati, neighborhoods with Hill or Mount or Ridge in them, just to see if they were named after someone and if so, what was that person's claim to fame.

I ended up working on the bibliography throughout the ten weeks of our independent study. I talked with as many professors in as many different disciplines as I could about the project, and they offered many titles for me to check out. When Lucy and I met, I began to realize how much I was learning about Cincinnati—and about course design. Little by little I saw the pieces begin to come together as we made decisions about projects, daily activities, guest speakers. And I was thrilled to be a sounding board and a contributing voice to the deliberations. To be able to make suggestions about the content of the course that were taken seriously was, for me, an honor.

At the same time that I was participating in this independent study supported by the English Department, I was enrolled in Curriculum Decision Making and its co-requisite Curriculum in the Secondary Schools: English Language Arts in the College of Education. In those classes, I studied the history, the trends, and the issues surrounding the secondary English curriculum. On a broad scale, we discussed what curriculum is and why it's important, what students should learn in schools, and who determines what gets taught. By taking all three of these courses at the same time, I think I came close to understanding how curriculum happens. On the small scale, Lucy and I were designing a course filled with various activities and grading criteria. We even had a decision to make about the limitation of the class size and where the class would meet. We wanted the class to function smoothly as a writing, editing, critiquing group, so we selected a conference room with a long oval table for our meeting place and went from eighteen to twelve to ten as the limit on class enrollment. On a bigger scale, our class proposal had to be approved by the English Department and, through the department, by the university as a whole as part of its curriculum.

About halfway into the independent study, I found it was time to register for spring quarter, and I made room in my schedule to take this new course called Writing Cincinnati. Curious thing, though, how my attitude about the number of readings we were planning to ask students to manage, and how my attitude about the number of pages and papers we were asking students to write, suddenly changed. I suggested to Lucy that we trim the readings. I had so many wonderful entries to choose from and use, but I thought it would be better (and I persuaded Lucy) to present a small collection of readings to get the students thinking about cities and about Cincinnati and then to encourage them to move out into the city as quickly as possible to begin their research.

Stage Three: The Working of the Course

Michael: When the class actually got under way in March 1994, I was no longer the person with the authority to pick what the other students would read. Since I was a transfer student from C.C.M. to the College of Arts and Sciences, I was considered a sophomore—and here I was in a class with one other sophomore, but primarily with juniors, seniors, and graduate students, all of whom had much more writing experience than I had. I stepped down from my role as assistant-to-the-professor and assumed the role of student. I couldn't help feeling a cut above, though, as I listened to the ideas and comments of my peers; it was uplifting to see the excitement in the faces of the class on the first day as Lucy talked about the syllabus. When the time came for me to speak as a student, I was just as flushed as a freshman in a public speaking class. But when I was asked to comment on the class preparations or to talk about the resources I'd found, I spoke with confidence and wisdom. At the end of that first day, here's what I wrote in my journal:

> Opening Day of spring writing: At twenty minutes before the first pitch, I found myself rustling through eight pages of bibliography and two pages of my idea list, making up the lineup for ten players. Sorting, stapling, frantic, I

walked onto the field at 11:00, just in time to catch the national anthem. The dugout was full of daring students, sliding headfirst into a course they knew nothing about and unaware of all the work Lucy and I had put into getting up for this game. But late in the ninth inning, at 12:20, they all showed as much enthusiasm as Lucy and I had hoped: We had hit a home run.

It took me a while to shake off the glow of a job well done and get focused on one specific writing topic. During my research for the course packet, I had stumbled on many aspects of Cincinnati life to investigate and found it difficult to pick just one, so I didn't. With Lucy's help, I worked out that my twenty-page portfolio would probably have four five-page stories. One student in the class had the idea to interview Sarah Jessica Parker, the movie star from Cincinnati. I went to school with her; I should have thought about interviewing her, but thinking small again, I chose to have a nice long conversation with my grandfather (to whom I dedicate this, my first published article, for taking me across the country when I was young, and for always bringing me back home to Cincinnati), where I found out about our family's coming to settle in Cincinnati almost 100 years ago and how he made it through the Depression working in Cincinnati. Another topic of mine focused on the history and prominence of a local radio station, WLW, "The Nation's Station." I had trouble setting up interviews with DJs (the receptionist kept transferring me to their answering machines, and they didn't return my calls), but I found plenty of historical information. (Did you know that Doris Day, Rod Serling, and Phil Donahue all got their big start at WLW? It's true.) Yet another topic of mine was an informative piece about the Cincinnati Zoo's Center for the Reproduction of Endangered Wildlife (CREW). I followed up a video clip that I did about CREW a couple of years earlier while at CCM and discussed the history of the project and its goal and progress in cryogenic reproduction. And, finally, even though I knew it wouldn't be completed, I wanted to begin work on a spy thriller set in Cincinnati (still in the "begin work on" stage).

Other class members were writing about such topics as the beer brewing tradition in Cincinnati, the Rookwood Pottery collection of one student's family, the underground jazz scene in and around town, a job training center for women on welfare, and, of course, Cincinnati politics. It was fascinating to hear about the successes and the frustrations of other students as they worked on their projects; I especially liked being able to pitch in with a suggestion or a tidbit that I thought was relevant to someone else's project, and they did the same for me when I shared my progress report. Since I had investigated so many angles of the city, it was hard for me not to say too much. I didn't want to sound like a know-it-all, however, so I observed a lot. I pictured myself in a sort of student-teacher role because of my other curriculum classes. They forced me to look at education not just as something I was getting, but rather as a system made up of many working parts—striving toward a goal with fuzzy outlines. During class, I found myself writing notes on teaching strategies as they occurred to me when I should have been writing critiques of my classmates' works.

The speakers Lucy lined up for the course were the icing on the cake: well-known figures from different aspects of Cincinnati's public life. Their presence in our class stirred conversation throughout McMicken Hall. Students would hang around the door trying to hear or see something, and some would ask members of our class what was going on in our room. They looked on in awe when the mayor of Cincinnati walked down the hallway after talking to our class about the importance of working on behalf of the poorer people of the city and about the stadium issue. (She and I debated and ultimately disagreed about what should happen to Riverfront West. She wanted a park put on the river to bring people down there; I suggested building a stadium for the Bengals to bring 80,000 fans. I'm still glad I voted for her.) Media coverage of our class—cameras and reporters coming and going—also contributed to the buzz about our project. What I heard most was, "What kind of class is this?" and "Is this class going to be offered next quarter?"

Lucy: As this course moved off the syllabus and into the classroom, I experienced a number of surprises. The first one was something of a disappointment, perhaps inevitable, but still a disappointment. Michael and I had worked very closely together in the planning and thinking that went into this course; then suddenly, we were in the more public role of student and teacher. While I wanted the other students to know about—and to celebrate—his work in helping to create the course, I did not want them to feel that he enjoyed a position of privilege in the classroom, a privilege to which they had no access. That meant some pulling back from the collegiality that Michael and I had enjoyed together; we no longer sat shoulder-to-shoulder, talking Cincinnati; we no longer started our work time trading bits and pieces of our lives. I, for example, no longer heard reports about Michael's new puppy (who bites to show affection) or gave him regular updates on the coming-back-to-life of my nectarine tree that had been hit by a heavy winter. I suppose if I had thought ahead, I might have anticipated and prepared for this difference. But the fact is I hadn't, and I didn't. And so one of those universal paradoxes took over: There was something lost (the one-on-one close work with Michael) even as there was something gained (knowing that I was consciously trying to treat all the students in the class fairly).

A second surprise was the degree to which the students claimed their place in the class and worked with each other, even counted on each other for help with their writing. I routinely use writing groups, but they had an impact in this class that I had not previously experienced. In the first few meetings of the course, students situated themselves for and with each other and as part of the larger community: One student spoke of her Appalachian ethnicity, of her attachment to mountain music, and of the costs involved in claiming that heritage as vigorously as she did. One student talked about the challenge of being gay in a city as conservative as Cincinnati. Two other students expressed a dislike for what they called the backward ways of Cincinnati. One woman talked about her jitters about being in a writing class after being out of school for many years. Another student, in a class of self-proclaimed liberals, talked of his attachment to Cincinnati, even to its conservative edge. And I talked a little about having never taught a course like this before and about my hope that together we could create a course that we would all find satisfying. I wish I could take credit for whatever dynamic allowed these students to claim their place as freely and as openly as they did; I still don't know what made that openness possible. I do know that something about our collective vulnerability and about our respect for difference made this class into a viable community of learners and writers, and that student after student talked about the help they received from each other with their writing.

Stage Four: Reflecting on Our Collaboration

Michael: Much as Lucy was for me, I hope to be a mentor to my future students who show a desire to go a little further than the curriculum says they need to go. Looking back, I had that desire. I didn't, after all, really get involved in the project just to get an A; I genuinely wanted some firsthand experience with course design. My thinking was that if I could co-design an interesting upper-level college writing course, I should be able to make a high-school English class interesting. Prior to my independent study, I had the misconception that courses were designed by a school board somewhere in a twelfth-floor conference room with facts and figures, charts and graphs. Now I realize that professors, working within certain frameworks and guidelines and sometimes at the edges, decide what's going to be taught and when and how. My directed research was not a situation in which I would go to the library and bring back some books so Lucy could design the course; it was a true collaboration. The more I saw that she was incorporating my ideas and suggestions, the more involved I wanted to be. As we got more involved in creating the syllabus, she depended on my input to make it as fair and challenging as possible. It's not like she had to, but every facet of the course she cleared with me before putting it in ink. From birthing new ideas and selecting meaningful readings to scheduling guest speakers and determining due dates and how many pages we wanted in portfolios—I helped with it all. And this process has instilled a confidence in me that has carried over to my everyday life. I research things more carefully now than I did before; my schedule is more organized; I'd like to say my writing has improved; and most importantly, I listen better. I learned a lot from listening to and talking with Lucy, and also from our peer editing and critiquing sessions, probably more so than from reading all those books.

Lucy: As teaching situations go, this one was as close to ideal as any I've had or read about: small class, new material, interesting students, and enough collective energy to light up the classroom on a regular basis. I'm still amazed at the way these students formed a writing community and still amazed not only with their writing success (more than half the members of the class published pieces they wrote in the class) but also with the links they forged with the city. One student who began the class by saying "I have never been a big fan of politics, national, or local" wrote this at a later point in the course as she thought about the future of Cincinnati:

> [T]he new multimillion-dollar arts center will be wonderful for the city, but with an already strong arts community, couldn't that money have been put to better use, such as for Over-the-Rhine renovations or other inner city projects that serve the impoverished? And now more money may be poured into a new and bigger stadium (when we can't even fill the seats of the old one) and aquarium. All of these ventures are exciting and certainly may put our city "on the map," but aren't there other matters that are more pressing?

In thinking about this student's question, I don't know if there are more pressing matters or not, but it's very moving to me to hear a college student begin to ask that kind of question.

Another student reported on her experience interviewing women at a community center who were members of a catering group called Power Inspires Progress. The student reported that in her initial interview,

> I assumed that they would be spilling with information to give me, that they would want publicity, and lastly, that they would not need to know who I was. . . . I did not realize that the ladies in the group might be suspicious of my motives, or taken aback by my request for information about their work. I began to feel discouraged and I was afraid to move on. The third interview, though, was like breaking through a brick wall. Sara and Patty (not their real names) and I went out for coffee. They were more than responsive to my questions, and they even showed interest in me. Sara told me to put my seatbelt on, she led me in the right direction, and they were glad to hear that my mom is also an excellent cook.

The student ended by saying, "The West End Community Center has sparked an interest in me . . . and that is working with people toward a community goal."

For me, it was a gift to be able to support these students in the ways they connected with the larger Cincinnati community. It was also a gift to receive Michael's help in setting up the course. I have long told publishers who ask me to review textbook manuscripts, "Sure, I'm happy to look at the text, but why don't you also get feedback from some students who've already taken this course—or who are signed up to take it?" I don't know if publishers do that or not, but I know that I had never before worked with a student in the conceptual stage of a course. Working with Michael was a chance for me to ask for student input not, as I typically do, during and at the end of the course, but in its very design. He had good ideas about the pacing of the due dates, about the readings, about the need to cancel a few classes for students to be able to go into the city to do their research. When I first got the idea for this course, my idea did not include having a student help me design it. And yet, as I look back on the experience, it's the work with Michael that in some way gave this course its energy and its life. In many ways we were working with something bigger than both of us, and that was very satisfying.

Not until I read Michael's account of our work together did I realize how much I was asking of him in the beginning of our work together; and as I reflect on this course, what I, of course, have to recognize is that for all the fun of our working together, we were never really equals. I always had the final authority, the last word, the primary responsibility. But in an educational system that is for the most part constructed in a way that teachers deliver and students receive and the work of the class is confined to what can occur in a college classroom, I think Michael and I made a small but effective subversive move. We took this class downtown—students interviewed, for example, old-time jazz musicians who still make music outside barber shops; the caretaker of a nineteenth-century cemetery; a controversial politician who works out at a downtown health club; the brewmeister of a local brewery; an auctioneer who specializes in Rookwood pottery—and I'm proud of that.

And now Michael's last word: At the end of the independent study, part of my grade was to be based on a paper I would write describing the work I did for the quarter. About the same time I turned that paper in, Lucy showed me the call for manuscripts for the *Sharing Pedagogies* project and wondered if I would like to elaborate on my final paper as a first stage for an essay we might write together. At that time, I was exhausted (this was just after final exams) and wasn't sure whether or not I wanted to write any more. It didn't take long, though, to decide "yes," as the thought of a possible publication overrode my fear of writer's block. Once we started actually writing our essay, I found that my not being on campus made our collaboration a bit more cumbersome. We left messages for each other, faxed drafts back and forth, looked at calendars for meeting times and tried to guess my work schedule so we could plan for times to meet. Nine o'clock on summer Sunday mornings was the best time for a while.

Since we wrote the first draft of this essay, I've returned to school part-time while still working construction forty to fifty hours a week. In fact, I've recently been working at U.C. on a couple of their construction projects: the new home for the College of Design, Architecture, Art and Planning and an administrative building next to the Shoemaker Center. The construction business keeps me on the run. On days that I have class now, I usually have to take off my hard hat and put on my backpack and head straight to class in my steel-toed boots.

And Lucy's last word: I dream about an educational system that will allow students like Michael enough financial aid to finish their education, an educational system that will encourage students and teachers to carve out opportunities to work together in creative ways, and, finally, an educational system that is committed to working on behalf of an ongoing town-and-gown relationship.

Note

We thank the inaugural class of Writing Cincinnati students for our time together: Pamela Allen, Laura Bofinger, Gwyn Casey, Heather Maloney, Tony Peregrin, Julie Perry, Connie Schmitt, Daniel Sotak, and Sherry Cook Stanforth.

Seven

Between Student and Teacher Roles
Negotiating Curricula During Teacher Training

Shannon Siebert, Richelle Dowding, Staci Quigley, Melanie Bills, and Robert Brooke

Shannon, Richelle, Staci, Melanie, and Robert: This article explores teacher development, how emerging teachers work out the roles and curricula they will use in the classroom. We will demonstrate that the development of roles and curricula is a complicated process of negotiation, an ongoing process of give-and-take between student-teachers' own changing ideas for classroom practices, the responses and needs of the different students they work with, pressures from teachers and administrators, and discussions with other precertification teachers. All of these elements influence how students in precertification programs form themselves as teachers.

This negotiation has implications for the way universities and school systems conduct teacher training. We want to critique the program Shannon, Richelle, Staci, and Melanie went through and their initial teaching contexts in local secondary schools because, overall, the view of teacher training these sites promoted was too simple: Almost always, the sense Shannon, Richelle, Staci, and Melanie got from those persons they worked with was that developing teachers were supposed to adopt whatever teaching beliefs and practices their institutional overseer held (whether that overseer was a cooperating teacher in the schools, a university professor, or a school administrator). In the minds of institutional officials, their teacher training program was supposed to be synonymous with conversion: Developing teachers were to see the light and take on their overseer's way of teaching. The reality, however, is that learning to teach doesn't work that way. The available advice about how best to teach is so contradictory, so contentious, that student-teachers recognize significant conflict between the positions of the institutional officials they work for; in response, the process of working out their own teaching roles involves finding their own reasons, beliefs, and consistencies for the practices they will adopt.

As our experiences demonstrate, if teacher-training programs throughout the United States are truly to help prepare teachers for the realities of classroom work, then those programs need to provide far fewer demands for conversion and far more opportunities to engage in the kind of open negotiation that we now see as the heart of the process.

We have been working on the ideas in this article for two years, beginning with a writing group we formed in the second semester of the English/ Language Arts Methods Sequence at the University of Nebraska–Lincoln. Shannon, Staci, Richelle, and Melanie were students in that sequence, and Robert was the instructor. All of us were new to the Methods sequence, four of us as senior Teachers College precertification majors, Robert as an English faculty member on loan to Teachers College for the year.

The Methods sequence is a two-semester set of courses taken by seniors. Students have already completed the equivalent of a full English major and have taken a couple of required courses focusing on future teaching, the most important of which is English 457, Composition Theory and Practice, the course in which dialogic student-centered workshop teaching is presented (for most precertification students, for the first time). This course was the reason Robert was on loan to the Teachers College: He frequently teaches Composition Theory and Practice and wanted to discover firsthand how that course functioned in light of precertification teachers' later Methods work. Given the vagaries of students' progress toward the degree, many students end up taking 457 at the same time they take the first semester of Methods; in our case, Shannon and Melanie had completed 457 before Methods, but Richelle and Staci were enrolled in the two courses simultaneously.

In the first semester of Methods, students each developed an informed position paper (IPP) on the teaching of English, covering at least three areas: writing, language/grammar, and literature. At the start of the second semester of Methods, they revised their IPPs before sending them to their assigned local cooperating teachers. They then, in assigned pairs, went into the local schools to work daily with a cooperating teacher in one specific class (Shannon, Staci, and Richelle worked in regular tenth-grade English classes at Northeast High School; Melanie worked in a computer composition course at Southeast High School). In addition to the daily work in the schools, the

Methods class met Thursday afternoons for two hours of seminar. Also, any interested students met with Robert on Tuesday evenings at a restaurant to set the agenda for each week's seminar. It was during this second semester that our writing group formed, in response to Gail Tayko and John Tassoni's call for papers for this volume.

The following fall semester, three of us did our student teaching: Shannon at Henderson High School (a school in a small town sixty-five miles from Lincoln), Staci at Dawes Middle School, and Melanie at East High in Lincoln. Richelle returned to the university to complete her Psychology Methods sequence. Robert returned to English.

Trying to Negotiate Our Own Practices
While Working Under Competing Models of Education

Traditional vs. Workshop Teaching

Staci: When I look back on my Methods courses, practicum, and student teaching experiences, one word comes to mind: *frustration!* During the past year, I've spent a lot of time pondering various teaching styles, and in retrospect I understand that my frustration primarily stemmed from learning one method of teaching English in English/Language Arts Methods and Composition Theory and Practice while at the same time seeing quite another in use within actual classrooms throughout the Lincoln public schools. In these two college courses, everything I'd ever known about teaching (which, admittedly, was very little) was challenged. I found myself faced with several questions: What exactly is a traditional teacher? What is a workshop teacher? Is one good and the other bad?

I had grown up in traditional English classrooms: I struggled through grammar worksheets, diagraming sentences, reading essays about people I'd never heard of. I pulled an all-nighter before the dreaded term paper was due, hunched over a typewriter with hundreds of note cards scattered about the floor. I read *Beowulf*, not by choice, but because I was told it was worthy literature. Traditional classrooms were the only type of classrooms I had ever experienced, and I thought they worked for me.

I found myself resistant toward the alternative methods taught in the Methods and in the Theories and Practice courses, not because of the methods themselves, but because of the way they were presented. It was obvious that the university had an agenda; I felt that workshop methods were being pushed upon me and that I was supposed to join some sort of bandwagon that bashed the system I grew up in. Did my instructors really expect me to desert the only teaching style I had ever considered (or known) after only six credit hours of exposure to the seemingly new and improved methods? Was this workshop stuff a fad? If not, why hadn't I ever heard of it before?

Although leery, I did have to admit to myself that the workshop method sounded like a wonderful way to teach. I thought back to when I was a student in high school and how much more motivated I would have been in English classes had I been given choices about what I read and wrote. Since there wasn't any room for choice, I was driven beyond the doors of school to write about the things I *really* cared about. I wrote at home—a place where there were no boundaries, red ink, or criticism. The writing I did at home was free. However, it was probably too safe. There wasn't anyone pushing me to take risks, develop drafts, or polish my writings.

So, after careful contemplation, I concluded that workshop classrooms probably were the best style of teaching. When the time came to write informed position papers, mine emphasized giving students the freedom to choose literature and to write about topics that intrigued them. I believed in tying together all aspects of English—literature, writing, and mechanics. I envisioned myself as a Linda Rief protégée, as I was enthralled by her *Seeking Diversity* (1992). By the end of the semester, I was content and couldn't wait to get back from winter break to dive into my practicum experience.

In the English 10 class at Northeast High School in Lincoln, my cooperating teacher didn't operate a Linda Rief reading and writing workshop *per se*, but she did incorporate aspects of a workshop into her classroom. For instance, students journaled three days a week, worked on weekly writings about topics of their choice, and read two books of their choice per semester.

Halfway through my practicum experience I found myself teaching a unit on *Of Mice and Men* ([1937]1965)—a novel I, along with my practicum partner, helped choose for the class. I felt the unit was going well. My practicum partner and I planned three weeks' worth of activities dealing with themes in the novel, along with an essay test and a final project. The students had a blast with the activities and seemed to be enjoying the book. Our unit wasn't disrupting the usual classroom routine, and I felt we had found a nice balance between pleasing our cooperating teacher (by giving essay tests) and experimenting with ideas we'd learned about in Methods (such as final projects).

Then, in one mere day, I was stripped of every ounce of confidence I'd gained as a teacher. My partner and I had turned in sets of lesson plans, objectives, and assessment procedures from our unit for response from Robert. I was looking forward to his comments; after all, our unit was going so well. We were having students reflect on friendships in their own lives compared with that of Lennie and George. We had them write poetry about friendships. We devised six freewrites where students reflected on the reading for ten minutes, and we responded to these journals extensively. The class also talked about the racial and other forms of discrimination in the novel. In the final project, students made abstract visual representations from quotes in the text. The essay test questions were passed out three days before the test was actually given, and they asked for the students' opinions, supported by evidence from the text. I expected to be commended for designing a creative unit that students were responding to in a positive manner.

When Robert handed back the materials from our unit, he also gave us copies of the IPPs we had written the prior semester. He underlined areas where I had praised the power of choice as a motivator in the classroom, and he asked why I had chosen the piece of literature for the class. He also pointed out that by designing our activities around the themes of friendship and discrimination, we were dictating what students would personally take from the literature.

My immediate reaction to his response was extremely defensive. The students loved our unit! Our cooperating teacher raved about it! But somewhere deep down I knew that the reason I was reacting so strongly was that Robert had pointed out inconsistencies between what I claimed to believe and what I actually practiced. My mind raced as I asked myself the dreaded question: Had I done the lowest of all evils? Had I gone traditional?

For the next week, I entered a minor depression and walked around worrying about my potential as an English teacher. I beat myself up about going against my IPP. But there was still a nagging voice in my head: Was the unit I had planned really so horrible? It was so similar to units planned by my cooperating teacher, as well as other teachers in the English department at Northeast.

I was caught in a workshop-versus-traditional conflict. Part of the reason for my conflict had to be that I was following the lead of my cooperating teacher. Yet I couldn't help but wonder: If the workshop methods were as effective as the research showed, why didn't more teachers use them? I felt an urgency to determine which method I truly believed in before I entered student teaching in the fall, but it was impossible. I felt my Methods courses were biased toward workshops, and eventually I just became angry. Why did I have to choose? Why are the two teaching styles so pitted against each other? Isn't there a time and place for both? Can't the styles ever complement each other?

I sorted through these issues during the summer before my student teaching. I had to admit that the traditional methods had some problems, especially when I reflected on my own education. But since I'd never seen an actual reading/writing workshop (besides the idealistic ones I'd read about), I couldn't wholeheartedly put my faith into that style of teaching, either. I needed to see a successful workshop in practice, not only in theory. I hoped to gain this experience during student teaching.

I was placed, however, with a cooperating teacher who did not advocate the workshop-style classrooms. In fact, any time I suggested using workshop teaching methods, she argued against the workshop. I began to think that maybe, in certain circumstances, she had a point.

I had been placed at Dawes Middle School, where I worked with four different sections of eighth-grade English classes. Dawes has a notorious reputation in town for being a difficult school. Many of my students were returning from detention centers or were on legal probation for behavior problems. These students made it clear on a daily basis that school was the last place they wanted to be.

It wasn't long before I realized that I was still far from the Atwellian classroom I had read about in my Methods sequence. Day after day, I would watch students struggle to follow the simplest of routines, such as freewriting. All students had freewrite notebooks and were supposed to write for the first five minutes of every class. We put topics on the board, but students were always free to write about whatever was on their minds. This procedure sounds simple, but it was like pulling teeth to get them to produce more than two sentences. I tried everything from modeling writing in my own notebook to giving extensive responses to their journals. The majority of students still struggled to stay focused for even half the writing time. And I expected to devise a unit incorporating fifty minutes of solid writing/responding time? I had to be dreaming.

I decided that maybe the workshop could initially focus on reading more than writing, but it wasn't long before I realized that this would be equally difficult. My cooperating teacher was teaching a unit on *A Raisin in the Sun* (1959), which we read aloud as a class. Some students were bored with how slowly the reading of the play was moving, while others were struggling to keep up. I suggested to my cooperating teacher that maybe if the classroom were more individualized (e.g., a reading/writing workshop), students would be free to move at a pace that was right for them. She argued that many students wouldn't comprehend the play if they read it on their own. I had to agree with that. Some of them were at fourth- or fifth-grade reading levels, so the play would have just overwhelmed them.

When the time came for me to take over the reins, I did not implement a reading/writing workshop. Because of the environment, my focus shifted to fine-tuning my classroom management skills. So, once again, I selected a novel for the classes. Once again, my cooperating teacher praised the unit, and my students thoroughly enjoyed it. But deep down, I knew I had made the same mistakes as I did during my practicum experience.

Looking back, I realize how essential it was for me to be placed in a student teaching environment where I would gain experience in a workshop-style classroom. Unfortunately, this was not the case. Without this experience, which could have reinforced what I'd learned in my Methods courses, it was just too easy to fall back on the only type of teaching I'd ever known.

Open Conflict with the School Institution

Richelle: "I think that your biggest problem with these students is that you are too nice. The best advice I can give you is to be more grumpy to the students." This advice was given to me by my cooperating teacher during my student-teaching experience in the spring of 1995. I will remember this advice for the rest of my life, not because I agree with it, but because during the few seconds in which it was spoken, I truly questioned myself as a teacher. The advice expressed a depressing interpretation of teaching: that the roles of teacher and student are so constrained in our country, and so much in conflict, that we have to be "grumpy" to maintain discipline. For me, the advice highlighted the conflict I experienced throughout student teaching, as I wrestled, perhaps unsuccessfully, to find a way to explore how I wanted to teach within a context that pressured me to teach in other ways.

Looking back, I realize that I had felt in conflict with school as an institution for most of my life. Like Staci (with whom I was paired at Northeast for Practicum), I grew up in a largely traditional school system and found I did my own meaningful reading and writing at home. The best atmosphere I could have been in at that time was an English class that incorporated life and feeling with reading and writing, but since that type of atmosphere was never offered, I can only assume that my educators thought it was silly.

When I came to the decision of adding a teacher certification to my college degree, I hoped that I could give to high-school students what I had never received in my secondary English classes: the freedom to come to terms by themselves with what literature was saying to them. Drawing on my reading of Nancie Atwell and Linda Rief in my Composition Theory and Practice and my English Methods courses, I determined how I wanted to teach: workshop style. I wanted my students to journal over their readings, form small groups to discuss ideas the literature had brought to them, and represent their feelings through anything but a book report. I felt confident in the way I wanted to teach. All I needed was the experience to put my theories to work.

To my surprise, the practicum and student-teaching experiences I was so looking forward to caused more stress in my life than comfort. What I found when I entered the secondary schools was that most of the teachers and students were not willing or ready to implement a workshop into their class curriculum. This new style of teaching, which the University of Nebraska Teachers College promised to be the wave of the future, was simply not wanted in these settings.

Staci and I worked in the same classroom for our practicum. As she explains, this class did contain some workshop features, and she and I tried to help our cooperating teacher incorporate even more workshop methods into her classroom by developing lessons that involved group work, class discussions, and student choice. My stress occurred over the issue of five-paragraph essays. Our cooperating teacher asked us to provide an essay exam in addition to the final project in our unit on *Of Mice and Men*. At first, we did not mind the addition. We felt it would be good for students to respond to the book as a whole as long as they didn't need to write the boring and treacherous five-paragraph essay. But we soon found out that that essay was what our cooperating teacher had planned, based on a curriculum requirement. We followed her wishes, taught an essay unit, and expected the students to write something that our Methods class had told us was outdated. I felt we went against our own beliefs about teaching in our IPPs in order to teach the way our cooperating teacher wanted.

My student-teaching experience the following semester at Lincoln High School again emphasized to me the enduring power of traditional curricula. For student-teaching, my primary interest was an American literature course, one in which I hoped to explore the connections between reading and life and feelings. My class consisted of juniors who were not at all interested in literature. But I felt I could take on this challenge by introducing them to a book I hoped all of them could relate to in some way. I used *Black Boy* ([1937] 1966) and encouraged the class to relate Wright's experiences to their own lives.

After we finished the unit, many students asked about other books by Wright. I felt this would be the perfect time to have them choose the texts they wanted to read for the next unit.

This was where my first conflict arose. Though my cooperating teacher had approved my lesson plans for the *Black Boy* unit and had seemed comfortable with my introduction of small group work, journaling, and class activities that made personal connections to the literature, she disagreed with the idea of students reading different books. She felt that if they read different books, there would be too much confusion and not enough structure in the classroom. She felt there would be no way to keep the students on task.

I honored my cooperating teacher's wish and didn't do a unit based on books of choice. I began teaching the next book on the syllabus, not knowing how the students would respond. As it turned out, they did not like Rudolfo Anaya's *Bless Me Ultima* (1972). In fact, they asked me if they could read books they chose. I had to swallow everything I wanted to say.

But it wasn't only in accommodating my cooperating teacher that I felt I was pushed into traditional teaching. In subtler ways, the students themselves had so internalized traditional classroom structures that they too pushed me toward those methods. Many students seemed not to understand what I was offering them with my workshop methods. For example, they had trouble discussing in both small and large groups. Several had nothing to write about in their journals, other than "I like the story." In response to these behaviors, my cooperating teacher encouraged me to focus on the maintenance of control in the classroom more than the content I was teaching. Therefore, I began giving assigned topics and page limits for the journals. I began giving points to those who came to class with questions. I began handing out worksheets and giving unit tests instead of having small group discussions. I began taking away any freedom of choice I had so much wanted to give them. I became more and more a traditional teacher.

What interests me in all this is that, even though I was retreating into traditional methods in an attempt to deal with the mechanics of the class, the class remained close to unruly. Students refused to quiet down when I began talking and made negative comments about other students and me during class. It was at this point that my cooperating teacher told me not to be so nice to the students. If I were grumpy, they would behave better. So I became grumpy. I no longer asked students what they did over the weekend. I didn't crack jokes or show interest in them. I only told them what to do. My cooperating teacher said, "Stay grumpy; it's working," clearly feeling my teaching strategies had improved.

I, on the other hand, began to question myself as a teacher. How could all of the positive soul-searching I'd done in my Methods course lead me to this? I was teaching like a traditional teacher and hating it.

After I spent some time talking with fellow student-teachers about my feeling totally useless, I understood, somewhat, why my experience turned out this way. The teacher I was working with had practiced her traditional methods for years. In the same way, the students in American literature had been taught by traditional teachers their whole school experience. In both cases, the parties did not know anything but the traditional method of teaching. I came into this setting thinking I could change the methods—and the expectations that go along with them—in the course of one semester. I think I underestimated the degree of change I was asking for, and the care with which I needed to institute such change.

Negotiation and Conflict

Robert: As Staci and Richelle's stories show, novice English teachers experienced ongoing tensions over their developing role as teacher, tensions that arose from their own past education, the schools they were teaching in, and the various competing models for pedagogy offered them through the Teachers College program. As their teacher, I wrestled with these same issues myself.

I came to the English/Language Arts Methods Sequence to learn how to teach them. For some years, in the privacy of my own teaching world in the English department, I've noticed where I have points of stress. It isn't in my writing classes (354 Advanced Composition; 150 Composition). I feel comfortable with the student-centered writing workshop approach I use there. It isn't in graduate seminars (971 Literary Theory: Texts and Selves; 920J Contextual Research in English). There, I also feel comfortable, aware of my role, in Donald Schon's phrase, "educating reflective practitioners" (1987, 1). The stress comes in one specific course: 457 Composition Theory and Practice. Something about that course, something about the weight of working with about-to-be teachers while also trying to provide experience with student-centered direction for learning, ends up creating stress. Predictable questions arise, all about the individual's future role as teacher, all about the coming relation of self-to-institution: "If this stuff works, how come I've never seen it before?" "This feels great, but feeling isn't learning, and where's the rigor?" "Hey, be consistent: First you ask me to write about what I most need to write about, and then you ask me to write about myself as a teacher? What do you want?" "If I get a job teaching, will 'they' really let me do any of this?"

I am self-reflective enough to realize that, as a teacher of Composition Theory and Practice, I have a lot at stake. I believe in workshop teaching, teaching that connects with the National Writing Project and the classrooms described by Lucy Calkins, Donald Graves, Nancie Atwell, Linda Rief. I want my course to make a strong argument for such pedagogical principles and methods. Frankly, I want converts. I grew up in an Anglo-Catholic minister's family, attended Jesuit school. I exhort with the best of them.

And, of course, such exhortation is in direct conflict with the principles I teach by: a focus on identifying the individual needs of students as growing writers; the encouragement of open dialogue between peers about writing; ownership of learning. My work in the course grounds itself on a double message: On the one hand, I argue that you need to turn the course to your own needs, discover your own writing practice; on the other, I argue that you need to teach in a way that makes the individual student learner the center of the learning experience.

I went to Teachers College because I felt I couldn't continue to have it both ways, to live the contradiction, especially since class after class of 457 students threw the contradiction back at me: "You're biased. You're just like every other educator—wanting us to believe what you do—you're just sneaky about it, pretending you're interested in our own ideas." I thought that if I had the opportunity to work with a group of future teachers through their Methods sequence and initial encounters with the schools, I might better understand the tensions I face in 457 and maybe better find my way through them.

Now, two years later, I must confess that I haven't resolved this tension. It still exists—I still feel the contradictory pulls of exhortation versus practice, between wanting to encourage future teachers to adopt student-centered methods and practicing those methods by working with the individual, contrary needs of this particular group. What's different, however, is how I see this tension. I now see it as the founding tension for the whole teacher development enterprise. It won't go away. It's the very structure of that enterprise.

For me, my year working with Shannon, Richelle, Staci, Melanie, and their peers was one that confirmed the ongoing presence and complexity of this tension. I started by assuming I would just use the syllabus and materials designed by Dave Wilson, the Teachers College professor who had switched assignments with me, and whose work on writing projects and teacher change has influenced my own. For most of the first semester, I did use his syllabus. But as the year went on, I found myself living the same stresses I had lived before: aware of the principles and practices I was advocating they adopt in teaching, and at the same time growing more and more aware of the life choices, directions, needs of these people as individuals. The one change I made in Dr. Wilson's syllabus during our first semester highlighted the stress: I added a series of conferences in which (as I do in writing courses) I negotiated a set of individual goals with each student. In these conferences, I discovered the huge range of ways these people positioned themselves in relation to the material. Shannon and Melanie and a few others, for example, were from the very early moments of the course already focused on developing the kind of teaching I admired. Shannon immersed herself in working out connections between language learning theory, her own children's growth, and the kind of classroom she wanted to have; Melanie took off after "enabling response" as the crucial teacher's moment in the classroom. But, for the group as a whole, Shannon and Melanie were oddities. Several others were, more than anything else, wrestling with fear of the classroom, fear of speaking in front of students, pondering what options they had for careers other than teaching. These folks expressly did not need, and frankly didn't care about, the nuances of what pedagogy to adopt, because the looming issue of career choice was so significantly stressful. And other students, like Staci and Richelle, who were taking 457 at the same time as the first Methods course, were living in a moment I can only describe as overwhelmed by the complexity of teaching: aware for perhaps the first time that teachers can choose their pedagogies from a range of possible methods, any of which are based on clear principles, and that in their future development they would need to make their own choices among them. These student-teachers wanted room to explore, to sample, to test options; they knew this, and quite sensibly resisted the demands of the course writing assignments, which asked them to take a position on principles and pedagogy *right now*.

In short, the needs of the growing teachers I worked with were so plural, the life issues so diverse, that I realized my own personal desire to advocate student-centered pedagogy was in many ways just plain irrelevant to the real learning that was taking place. The real learning was exploration and negotiation, trying to work out (given the personalities and tensions of the program) what they could discover for themselves about their future professional roles, inside or outside of teaching. And for this learning, my exhortations really didn't matter.

In the second semester of Methods, this range of individual needs grew wider and wider. As a consequence, I found myself, as teacher, relying more and more on dialogic structures that left behind all but entirely my own desire to emphasize a certain kind of pedagogy. Borrowing an idea from Ira Shor's *Empowering Education* (1972), I set up a cooperative planning group so that, as much as possible, class members' needs guided the seminar. I scheduled a regular Tuesday evening meeting at a local restaurant where all interested students could help me plan Thursday's meetings, and usually a quarter to a third of the Methods group came to these meetings. I extended the individual conferences, giving up entirely on Dr. Wilson's requirement of a unit plan complete with lessons for the course, instead having each student negotiate with me a project of equal effort that fit his or her own place in the program. Several students wrote career choice pieces, using the career placement office to explore alternatives to teaching; Staci and some of her peers took the opportunity to create a teaching portfolio for themselves; Shannon wrote an extended justification for her teaching ideas, using her ongoing reading in language development; others, like Richelle, completed the traditional unit, but on the basis of personal choice rather than requirement.

I left the second semester, thus, aware that on one level I had failed as a teacher converter. Looking at the class as a whole, I had to accept that very few of them had adopted the pedagogical principles I most believe in. Yet, on another level, I felt that I understood quite a bit more about what a teacher education program can and can't do, and what the place of an individual course within a program is. My ongoing dialogue with these people taught me that, for them, the crucial learning wasn't at all about specific pedagogy, but about the resolution of the individual tensions they faced as they tried to imagine themselves inside or outside the teacher role. To the degree that I merely exhorted for my own favorite pedagogy, I couldn't help them with these tensions. To that degree, I merely added my own voice to all those already urging them to become one kind of teacher or another. Far more crucial, I have come to believe, were the other sites for interaction our work together offered: the Tuesday planning group, the individualization of projects from goals conferences, the writing group that produced this article.

These other sites provided something that the Methods sequence and my department's Composition Theory and Practice course didn't: a chance to step outside or away from the dynamics of the teacher development courses in order to reflect and plan. In these sites, those individuals who took the opportunity could ask questions about their own development, about their needs, their confusions, their worries, and they could to some degree create ways to act out of these questions and concerns. They could design extended projects that they felt would help them address their issues. They could plan weekly activities that might spark the kind of thinking they saw as necessary *right now*. They could, in short, take active parts in their own teacher development.

Of course, providing experience with alternative pedagogy, student-centered pedagogy, is important. I continue to believe in such pedagogy and need to continue arguing for it through the structure of my courses. I see the need as well to locate the argument part of my courses within other structures that provide space for the kind of active, reflective engagement in the whole context of teacher development that these people clearly needed and wanted—the active, reflective engagement that some of them claimed.

Negotiated Practice:
Managing the Plural Politics of Schools

Negotiation in Practice

Shannon: As Staci and Richelle have shown, our experiences in our teacher development program were at times frustrating and stressful, and as Robert has suggested, it may even have been necessarily so. I too experienced these stresses. But my particular journey through my initial encounters with schools suggests that sometimes, if we remain aware of the negotiation and politics that occur, we can find ways to develop teaching methods we believe in. In this section, I'll share my experience to illustrate how this negotiation process operated for me.

I had come out of my teacher training at UNL wanting to find ways to foster literacy growth with a more student-centered approach to teaching English rather than the traditional behavioristic model of teaching that I had endured in my education. My first taste of this type of education came in Robert's Composition Theory course, where we were allowed to practice workshop principles: choice in writing, engagement in small group discussion with feedback, creating personal portfolios, and journaling. The biggest factor in my conversion to this more transformational teaching was my own confirming experiences of self-directed learning. As I reflect on my rather mediocre high-school education, I remember most vividly one class, a product of the let-it-go 1970s: the mini-course. For six weeks, I was permitted to choose my own selections to read during a fifty-minute class period. There was a teacher in charge who sat at the desk while we read, and all we had to do was inform him of our reading choices. I don't remember at all how we were evaluated, but I do remember the content and specific books I chose—books about biblical archaeological evidence—and the lasting impact my self-directed studies had on my life. Later in college, after reading books by Lucy Calkins, Nancie Atwell, and Peter Elbow, I discovered that the name for my independent reading experience was responsibility. I had exercised it as a reader in charge of the scope and direction of my studies.

During my final year of Method, I worked hard to articulate my beliefs about how I wanted to teach. I searched for matching methods in Peter Elbow's *Writing with Power* (1981), studied Ann Berthoff's ideas for engaging learners into higher levels of composing, and analyzed how language learning takes place. But it was still my own confirming experiences in student-centered environments that kept me from reverting to more traditional methods of teaching the language arts. With these few glimpses from my own school life and little actual practice in teaching a collaborative approach, I was ready to enter teaching with a desire to make learning more authentic for other students.

However strongly I believed in the pedagogy I had immersed myself in, brick walls did arise in my relationships with teachers and students when I began practice teaching. During my first extended English practicum at Lincoln Northeast, I faced resistance and discouragement when I suggested incorporating workshop principles in my cooperating teacher's tenth-grade classroom. She did not share my enthusiasm and faith in structuring a classroom like Atwell's model or Robert's workshop. When I brought up the words *workshop* or *Nancie Atwell*, she was pessimistic and warned me of the impracticality of many of Atwell's techniques, such as writing along with my students. She smiled at my inexperience and warned me that my beliefs might not work in the real classroom.

What was important to my cooperating teacher was maintaining control of the class by engaging only in activities that were restrictive and inflexible compared to the student-centered workshop I envisioned. Her approach to writing included step-by-step directions, worksheets, and identified stages in the writing process. She did, however, allow her students two days of in-class, free choice, silent reading every week. Her methods of teaching reminded me of Ritchie and Wilson's words, "a teacher may hold one set of beliefs about teaching writing and another about teaching literature" and that new or different ideas often aren't fully integrated into an existing curriculum because of the "power of this traditional orientation" (1993, 78). Given what I had studied and believed in, I didn't think it was effective to blend a traditional approach with a student-centered one.

My dilemma was how to match the practical experience of teaching in someone else's classroom with the beliefs I held about how best to teach English. Since I was being evaluated by a cooperating teacher who seemed to represent a lump of conflicting pedagogical principles, I was tempted to conform to the more curricula-guided teaching. The trap of slipping back into a traditional classroom frustrated me and made me feel that my walk was not my talk. One day during my practicum at Northeast, for example, discussion bombed, digressing to arguments, insults, and hurt feelings among the students, whom I had arranged in a large circle. My cooperating teacher had already voiced her disapproval of the large circle for these students. She felt they could handle expressing themselves only in smaller groups. Although these students had previously worked well in a large group, I worried. Since this particular day was a flop, did this mean that my pedagogy was all wrong and I should conform to the more structured recommendations of my cooperating teacher? Was I simply using a method—the circle—because I liked it (as my cooperating teacher suggested) and not assessing whether these students could learn better in this form? My temptation was to agree with my cooperating teacher and give up my new methods, but my beliefs and own experience were strong enough for me to know better. I realized that, while in a teacher training program, the limitations and temporariness of the setting make it difficult to draw firm conclusions about the validity of my beliefs.

Despite the conflicts I felt from the school and teacher I was hooked up with, I was given the freedom to attempt a simple writing workshop for six weeks. I believe I accomplished this by not trying to sell my cooperating teacher on the workshop format, but instead by focusing on how best to meet the needs of these particular tenth-grade students. When I presented my plans to my cooperating teacher, I did not use the words *workshop* or *Nancie Atwell*. I tried to present other examples, besides Atwell's, that allowed writers time with, ownership of, and choice over their writing. I conceded to my cooperating teacher that my ideas weren't foolproof, but pointed out to her that nothing else was working that well with this particular class either, so why not give it a try? I also pointed out that the students clearly enjoyed the choice and ownership in their reading days and that I felt we could extend choice successfully into their writing activities. She agreed that my practicum was a place where I could try out my beliefs about teaching and allowed me to implement my plans. As a result, these tenth graders participated in a six-week writing workshop and produced a class anthology of their writing. Although I was often disappointed in the limitations of my setting, it was clear in the end that much time and effort is required before one can successfully integrate transactional principles of learning into the existing structure. But it can be done.

I considered alternative ways of practicing my theories with a minimum of conflict when I student-taught again in the fall. Initially, I felt certain pressures because I would be student-teaching in my hometown, with a good friend as cooperating teacher who didn't necessarily share my teaching ideas. Also, this was probably the place I would land a job. To smooth the waters, before I even entered the door of the school, I had given my cooperating teacher my IPP, which I felt was an honest explanation of my beliefs. This would prepare her without bombarding her with my philosophies. I had learned not to assume that other teachers would welcome my approach, so I needed to be more politic when attempting to make changes. My plan for the semester was to wait, watch, and listen, and when the opportunity arose, I could incorporate my beliefs without causing too much friction.

My first opportunity arose when my cooperating teacher unexpectedly became disabled and her unit was turned over to me. Although I was still restrained by my teacher's heavy curriculum plans, I could choose how to implement them. I pulled the students into circles for discussion groups, introduced them to freewriting, asked them for feedback about what we were doing, and used their responses to alter lesson plans. What I was slowly inching toward was a way to escape from teaching American literature in the traditional manner of reading together, bit by bit, some excerpts of literature from the textbook. Although my cooperating teacher had been absent during most of my trial teaching time, what she observed of me during her periodic, checks of the classroom had made an impression on her. She was receptive to the alternative ways I was presenting American literature to these two sections of juniors.

After she returned full-time, she was ready for me to make my curriculum plans for the remainder of the semester. She liked to write a day-to-day agenda for the whole year, and hence pushed me to quit procrastinating and lay out my plans. In my mind, I wrestled with planning out the entire semester while also finding a way to create choice and ownership for my students.

How it happened as I look back on it seems somewhat miraculous. I started to discuss with my cooperating teacher ways we could create a classroom where the students could choose what they wanted to read from a list of selections, ways we could allow time for in-class reading and small discussion groups, and ways to use the computer lab for writing. We had a giant brainstorming session together. As I explained the basic structure of my plans, my cooperating teacher immediately started sketching out ways to put my ideas into practice. She was enthusiastic about the anticipated student response to using class time for reading, writing, and discussion. My cooperating teacher latched onto this idea and called it a learning lab. Whatever she called it, we had created a workshop setting allowing the students much more ownership over the choices in their reading and writing, as well as time to discuss literature with one another and their teachers. Obviously, the favorable impressions my cooperating teacher had of my performance during her absence contributed to her enthusiasm for my plans.

When I entered this student-teaching assignment, I was apprehensive about offending my cooperating teacher by introducing my ideas. Instead of trying to push my plans too soon, I waited for opportunities where I could slip them in while still accomplishing the existing curriculum goals. I learned I needed to be more subtle when entering into dialogue with other teachers about my philosophies and the techniques to implement my beliefs. I needed to avoid overwhelming a seasoned teacher with my different principles and to discover ways within the existing restrictions to practice my beliefs. Gradually, working within the existing curriculum, we collaborated, combining our knowledge, ideas, and strengths to create a better learning environment.

What Is a Workshop Anyway?

Melanie: When I think back over my years as a student and over the classes I've since taken part in as a substitute teacher, I realize that subtle ways to work on change always exist. In fact, I think of many classes now as a kind of developing hybrid of methods. I suggest that what's more important than the labels we attach to pedagogies is the ongoing spirit of innovation that leads good teachers to continue to find ways to guide their students.

Unlike many of my peers, I did not solely experience the traditional classroom or teacher as I grew up. I did not always sit in rows, always take tests, always do this or that. Especially in high school, I was fortunate to have what many would consider innovative teachers who were willing to experiment with their methods in class. The one class that I truly think made the greatest impact on me as a student—and now as a teacher—was my AP English class my senior year.

I honestly doubt I will ever forget the day that I got my first AP paper back from my teacher. I took *her* class because I knew her to be a bit out of the ordinary. I saw the way her classroom looked physically: the words from floor to ceiling, the colored cellophane on the windows, the desks arranged in a circle. I really wanted to be *in* that room. Once in her class, I quickly realized how different this English course was compared with others I had taken. As a class, we did freewriting on the first day and frequently thereafter; we had writing families to share our drafts of papers with and to receive feedback from. So far, I loved this class. It was what I needed: It was extremely creative, open, but still tough. She still *really* pushed us to work. Our first assignment was to read and analyze a section of Wordsworth's "Ode"—the likes of which I had never before encountered.

As the papers were handed back, it took me several minutes to get the nerve to turn my paper over to see the dreaded grade. Staring at the paper on my desk, I could see the red ink bleeding through. I thought right then that she had crucified me—me and my writing. To my complete amazement, when I turned my paper over, the blood I had seen through the paper was not error corrections, it was simply comments. My teacher had marked where words and ideas had struck her as strong or interesting. She made notes about how words, sentences, and ideas made her feel as she read. At the end of the piece she had left me a note saying *what* she thought, *how* she felt, and how she interpreted *my* thoughts.

In that class, the grade was not the deciding factor in whether or not I thought my papers were good. I knew I could write—I just never knew if other people knew! How could I know if I was really communicating with someone if no one ever responded to me? In essence, my teacher's feedback was one of her ways of individualizing instruction for all of us. She responded to each of us as people—not just with a grade.

In her class, we would work on themes or ideas as a class, but would choose individual authors and pieces we each wanted to read and write about. We often selected the specific writing skill we were working to improve in each piece (from integrating quotes to specifying pronouns) so that we could focus on what was important to each of *us*. I think it was this class that finally made me decide to teach. I would love to see kids as excited about their work as many of us in that class were. So, when I first heard about the workshop style classroom at UNL, I knew that this was what I would someday have.

In retrospect, I'm not quite so sure now that my high-school class fit the true definition of the Atwellian workshop, which I believed in college to be the one and only workshop. I have met many teachers in high schools and in colleges and have been fortunate to see what many of them consider workshops. Ironically, every single one of these classrooms is in some way different. AP and Contemporary Literature classes use feedback on writing from many sources, mini-lessons, student choice of books, guest readers, grade contracts, journals, projects, writing families, and discussion circles. Composition classes use "boxwrites" (creative writing prompts), journals, drafts for editing groups, tons of feedback. Eastern Philosophy class uses small groups, discussion circles, group book selections. Women's Literature and Culture class uses "coffee houses" (open informal discussions), small group work, lots of feedback, and journals. English Methods class uses journals, conferences, freewrites, reading tables, individual projects, and small groups.

In my substitute teaching, I see many teachers use a combination of methods. I see reading-response journals in almost every English classroom, but very different uses for them. Some journals are personal, some require students to write on specific questions, some cover literature, some are graded, some are not. I see many teachers set aside reading days or writing days in class. Some have this set every week; others use it as necessary. Some teachers comment very briefly on student writing, while others are truly in-depth. Teachers I have seen try to conference regularly with their students to keep track of *each* student. Other teachers use self-evaluation types of activities to communicate with students regarding attitude and growth in class. More and more classrooms have student projects on the wall—ownership of the room—but with so many traveling teachers now, this is pretty difficult to do.

There just doesn't seem to be one type of workshop for a classroom. Now, when people say to me that they have a workshop class or want to implement a workshop, I'm not quite sure what they mean. Although completely changing methods can be difficult for teachers, the fact is that they try—they add bits and pieces of the workshop method as they understand it. But is adding one or two methods that are aspects of a workshop really a true workshop?

It seems to me that the issue is and should be innovativeness, constant learning, and flexibility. I don't know that an all-or-none attitude is necessary or good, whether it's for the traditional or workshop method. If a teacher can keep the classroom alive and fresh, keep new ideas coming in, give students ownership, encourage organization and responsibility, expect and encourage learning beyond rote memorization, and develop relationships with each one of his or her students, then that would be a successful classroom.

Possibilities for Improved Teacher Development Programs

Shannon, Richelle, Staci, Melanie, and Robert: Our stories collectively show that growth into the teacher role is a process of negotiation among competing institutional forces: Shannon, Richelle, Staci, and Melanie each had to wrestle with the competing visions of what teaching is, offered to them by their Methods teacher, cooperating teachers in both practicum and student teaching, the institutions in which they taught, and their own past educational experiences. To form their own stance as teachers, they had to decide how they would place themselves in an institutional environment that demonstrated many ways of teaching. Dealing with such plurality requires active negotiation and decision on their parts.

Such active negotiation is a source both of stress and of possibility. As Staci, Richelle, and Robert describe, the stress exists because it's often difficult to decide what you believe when you find yourself acting out different belief systems, and often the pressures from institutional figures like cooperating teachers and university faculty just increase this stress. But, as Shannon shows and Melanie argues, if student-teachers can find ways to negotiate within their institutions, they can often make a space for their own practices.

Unfortunately, the institutional structures provided for developing teachers aren't currently set up to encourage such negotiation. At present, they operate on different principles: Isolated classes like Robert's Composition Theory or English Methods supposedly teach students how to teach. On paper, the courses supposedly are additive—students pick up composition here, language there, methods in yet another place—even though as they move from classroom to classroom students don't find additive so much as competitive views of teaching. The instructors of these classes recognize at some level the failure of the additive training, and hence are tempted, as Robert describes, to use their classes as opportunities for one-shot conversion. But the consequence of having each class be a single teacher's (or program's) attempt to make a strong argument for their kind of pedagogy is that it forces students, as learners, to go underground and be intellectual chameleons, rather than openly confront the conflict between pedagogies in their teacher-development program.

Since education as an institution is so clearly plural and conflicted at present, we want to argue that teacher-development programs desperately need two kinds of educational improvements. The first improvement calls for programs to provide *many opportunities to become engaged in different pedagogies*, so that developing teachers can do their own thinking from a wide base of experience. To a degree, the current system does provide such opportunities. As Melanie argues, many classrooms now use a variety of methods. Additionally, we were able to identify classes outside of Teachers College that provided us with models of alternative teaching, from Melanie's AP class to Shannon's mini-course.

Second, we recommend programs provide *more opportunities for reflective action on the process of becoming a teacher*, such as the opportunities Shannon, Richelle, Staci, and Melanie had doing individualized projects, setting individualized goals, and writing this article. Developing teachers need opportunities where they can reflect critically on the negotiating they are doing as they move from class to class, context to context, school to school. Other opportunities might include advising and mentoring, regular collaborative learning groups adjacent to required classes, and ongoing portfolio development. All such opportunities create structures for regular reflection on the processes of becoming a teacher.

If, as we suggest, teacher development is more about negotiating among approaches than it is about learning any specific set of information or content, then teacher-education programs like the one we worked in can improve by focusing explicitly on such negotiation. What we must do to develop as teachers is identify the possibilities and restrictions that exist in the complex, plural world of education and negotiate our own place among them. At present, most emerging teachers deal with this process in their own ways, because academic institutions don't fully recognize that it goes on. But we believe in imagining possibilities and can envision an educational world where negotiating one's role as learner and teacher is an explicit focus of teacher-development programs.

Eight

Out of Control

TA Training and Liberation Pedagogy

Mary Anne Browder Brock and Janet Ellerby

1

Mary Anne: I arrived at the M.A. program in English at the University of North Carolina at Wilmington after a seven-year hiatus from formal education, and I entered my first semester as a graduate student and teaching assistant (TA) feeling tremendous pressure to succeed. I remembered only two rules from my undergraduate years: (1) Students should always address a professor with "Dr." rather than "Mr." or "Ms.," as it is much better to err with a compliment than not to acknowledge someone's advanced degree, and (2) the first impression a student leaves with professors is indelible and therefore must be a good one.

During my first semester as a graduate student and TA, I followed the rules. I worked relentlessly in my three graduate classes, calling each professor Dr. Whatever—unless or until that professor invited me to do otherwise—and making sure I invested considerable extra effort on most assignments. That semester was a crucial one: In my eyes, everything was a test that I would ultimately either pass or fail, a test on which I desperately wanted to earn more than just a passing grade.

In that first semester, I achieved several successes that eased my fear of failure. My mentor in Freshman Composition I, Philip, encouraged and supported me while inviting me to go beyond the minimal requirements of merely attending and observing his class regularly and then meeting with him for an hour each week to discuss the class dynamics. In those conversations, I questioned him, challenged his comments, and offered my perceptions and interpretations of how the students were responding and developing their thinking and writing skills. Philip, a mentor who readily declared the class his—not ours, listened intently to my views, enthusiastically offered his own, and questioned me in return. Those conversations provided the necessary first moment of liberation in my TA career: I learned that a full-fledged tenure-track associate professor could respect what I had to say.

My confidence grew. And with my confidence so grew my willingness to take risks. I accepted each extra responsibility that Philip suggested. I developed a few class exercises and taught two class sessions, and I graded student essays, keeping Philip blind to my evaluations until after he had graded each one. The results of my test: Students responded well to my exercises and fairly well to my leading of the class sessions, and my evaluations of student papers corresponded almost exactly with Philip's. My confidence soared.

I knew, however, that I would have more responsibilities as a second-semester TA, continuing in Freshman Composition II with a new mentor who would give me an official evaluation as I taught at least one unit independently. With the new challenges came a renewed fear of failure.

When I learned that Janet would be my new mentor, I was thrilled. I wanted to work with a woman after having observed a male mentor already. I arrived in her office equipped with a pen, a notebook, and a two-pronged agenda: to receive the information she would deliver to me and to discuss what my role would be in her class. It would be months before I would understand that what Janet said to me that day had something to do with a concept called *team teaching*. I now know that she was inviting me into the realm of liberation pedagogy, but at the time, I felt anything but free.

2

Janet: Often overlooked in discussions of liberation pedagogy is the challenge of how teachers actually learn a pedagogy that liberates rather than restricts students. By *liberation* I mean the ability to ignore the prescribed, constraining pedagogical role of the teacher as the controlling authority—the ability to step out of that overdetermined role into a space of dispersed authority, ambiguity, and empowerment for all members of the classroom community. Though many new teaching assistants perform well in their own classrooms, their training is often so casual and truncated that it is not surprising that they frequently feel out of control. Rather than risk the uncertainty of experimentation, they gravitate toward prescriptive teaching, nervously marching their students through step-by-step assignments provided by their director of composition or a required rhetoric. Ira Shor admits that he started as a traditional teacher, lecturing on writing, teaching grammar, and concerning himself with correct usage (1987, 19). Shor's own transformation from a conventional lecturer to a participant in a learning community inspired me to develop new models of possibility for teachers-in-training so that they might create the kinds of productive activities that disperse authority and control in the classroom while building an atmosphere conducive to cooperative writing.

Liberation pedagogy requires courage even for experienced teachers, but it is asking a great deal of novice teachers to simultaneously celebrate multiplicity, affirm uncertainty, and strive for an active, democratic community of critical learners. If we encourage novice teachers to alter the prescriptive methodologies and traditional authority they are most comfortable with, we are in danger of abandoning them in poorly defined and vulnerable instructional territory. Rather than empowering them, a pedagogy that tries to resist the asymmetrical relationship between the knowing teacher and unknowing students can leave these teachers anxiety-ridden, silenced, and in danger of losing an already fragile control over the activities of their students. If our teachers-in-training are to help us in our attempts to transform disempowering institutional practices, we need to find better ways to redefine and reshape the ways students and teachers construct socially conscious discourse.

I am fortunate to teach in an English department that gives teaching assistants an entire year of training during which they work as mentees in actual writing courses. When I found out that Mary Anne was to be my mentee, I knew I wanted to use her expertise, enthusiasm, and energy in team teaching. I was not interested in the traditional expert/initiate relationship. Instead, I believed that together we could build a democratic partnership that might resist patriarchal models. I wanted to create pedagogical possibilities that would allow for collaborative teaching. I hoped Mary Anne and the students would be able to avoid the easy passivity and submission that usually comes with comfortably assumed, traditional student roles. Unfortunately, I was told Mary Anne would be my mentee only a few days before classes would begin, long after I had chosen my reader for the course and planned my syllabus. Such logistics took away the possibility of involving Mary Anne in designing the time frame of the syllabus, an arrangement I was not happy about but could not change at that late date. Nevertheless, I wanted to erase as much as possible the hierarchy of the mentor/mentee relationship.

My education as a teacher has been a process; it still is. Now Mary Anne was to become part of that process, and I knew that she was expecting to be taught the steps to become a conscientious teacher of composition. What would she think when she realized that what I wanted to demonstrate for her did not involve carefully crafted lesson plans with accompanying worksheets, but instead allowed students to be involved in setting the agenda of the class? It had taken me so many semesters to have the moxie to hand over my control. Could I really expect to illustrate for Mary Anne the benefits of reconfiguring authority in just sixteen weeks?

In effect, I was asking her to skip painful but useful steps I had had to take in my own teaching evolution. I decided the most constructive way to guide her through the challenges of liberation pedagogy was to ask her to be a participating member in the community that was about to emerge, hoping that without having to take my circuitous route, she would find that relinquishing dominion might be a positive first step for a beginning teacher.

At the semester's commencement, I indisputably knew more about liberation pedagogy than Mary Anne, and I had a plan in mind that would allow me to demonstrate for her that a decentered class is not only socially appropriate but also pragmatic. Because of my conviction, I knew I could not just tell Mary Anne about this different way of teaching. I would have to move forward self-reflectively, always conscious of the drawbacks of the novice/knower hierarchy. And so I began, trusting that we could both explore together ways in which our potency as teachers could be realized.

Mary Anne: I was not surprised that Janet, like Philip, had completed her syllabus before I arrived in her office: I was well aware of the recent date of our assignment to one another. Her syllabus included a complete reading and writing schedule up through the first essay due date, as well as due dates for the remaining three essays. The reading schedule for those final three essays was to be announced as we progressed through the semester, and I was excited with this open structure that would allow for my participation and would help me learn how to construct a syllabus and to coordinate readings and writing assignments.

Disappointment, however, soon overshadowed my joy. Unlike Philip, Janet had already decided—without talking with me ahead of time—specifically how she wanted me to contribute to this team. She had thought about it, she told me, and had decided that she wanted me to be totally in charge of the students' reading logs. She also had already determined that she wanted me to conduct individual conferences with all of the students as they were preparing each of their four essays for the semester.

Of the myriad other details we discussed that day, I remember only a few. Janet said that we should decide later which unit I would teach for her official observation; I felt grateful that we would decide this together. I recollect most vividly my final question to her.

"Do you mind if I call you Janet," I asked rather sheepishly, "or would you prefer that I call you Dr. Ellerby?"

"Oh!" Her near-giggle puzzled me. "Please! Call me Janet."

I did not understand Janet's amusement, nor did I understand the great trust she demonstrated in me by the participation she asked of me. What echoed in my ears were the words, "I have decided that I would like for you to. . . ." I perceived not an invitation, but rather a list of mandates. Consequently, I felt not respected, but rather overwhelmed, fearful, out of control, and angry. I do not recall whether or not Janet asked me how I felt about her plan. Knowing my feelings on that day, I suspect that if she asked, I did not answer honestly.

Instead, I carried my worries to my fellow TAs—*my* colleagues—crying and whining about all that Dr. Ellerby had planned to make me do. They commiserated with me, wailing their sympathy: "Mary Anne! What are you going to do?" I did not know what I was going to do, but I knew that I surely felt more oppressed than liberated.

I worried the most about time. The student conferences alone—*if* I could pare them down to twenty minutes each and *if* I could get the writing lab to adjust my schedule so that I could see only Janet's students when on duty there—would require five and one-half extra hours per week during four different weeks of my busy semester, dates that had been predetermined by Janet without consulting with me or my schedule. How could I carry nine graduate hours, work three hours per week in the writing lab, and add an additional twenty-two hours worth of conferences—thirty-four additional hours if the writing lab could not accommodate me? Could I fulfill these extra responsibilities and keep up my graduate work?

I also felt uneasy about grading the reading logs. Philip had graded papers *with* me. How, I wondered, did Janet know I would do a good job with the reading logs? What if I messed up? Was this fair to her students? I, all by myself, would be determining twenty percent of their grades, a percentage Janet had already put on the syllabus. I was only a TA. She was the professor. This arrangement just did not seem right.

I quieted my anxieties and prepared myself to meet this unexpected set of challenges, experiencing what many students—especially first-year undergraduates—experience when they find themselves in a classroom operating under the principles of liberation pedagogy. Janet was asking me to contribute something to this class, and my contribution would be far more than a token one. My contribution would make an important difference in how successful this class would be, and my effort in the class would be costly in time and energy.

Janet: One of the features of liberation pedagogy that is immediately apparent to my students is my resistance to the discourse of the omniscient professor. In my classes my language and concerns clearly count, but so do students' and so would Mary Anne's. From day one, I try to create an atmosphere that will be as conducive as possible to students' authentic, explicit responses while at the same time asking for agreement on a policy of considerate language. Because Mary Anne and I—as it turned out—openly disagreed in class about interpretations of the course's assigned readings, it was easier to set the example of mutual respect for different opinions and to set the tone for a democracy of expression. Students could witness firsthand how conflict could expedite our drive to understand and make for much more interesting classes. Often when I tell students that I expect them to take that '60s bumper sticker seriously and question authority, it takes them a while to believe me and to act on that invitation. But with Mary Anne and me at odds with one another over a variety of subjects, the example was set and "teaching the conflicts" became a reality much more readily (see Graff 1992).

In addition, because in class I talked frankly about my life, my own forthrightness helped Mary Anne and the students to speak out more readily with less fear of being embarrassed by the revelatory nature of their participation. For example, I have found that students begin to trust their own experiences as valid evidence if I use my experience to demonstrate why I have taken a particular position. As a member of the discourse community I try to establish in the classroom, I speak openly about such normally taboo revelations such as my childhood, my adolescence, my extended family, and my struggles as a single parent. Mary Anne and my students were all surprised when I expressed my fears that my nineteen-year-old son was psychologically dependent on marijuana, and they listened thoughtfully and responded ardently because this subject was relevant to all of us. Since I see this personal side of my life as germane to my convictions and opinions, I ask the other members of the community also to draw connections between their personal contexts and the opinions they hold. Mary Anne was no exception since she too was a part of our community, and she joined in readily, talking about her experiences growing up in a working-class family and about the pains and frustrations of being a first-generation college student. Although some students seemed self-conscious and diffident, the directness and attentiveness that both Mary Anne and I demonstrated encouraged them to take responsibility for communicating their experiences and ideas during discussions and in their writing that followed. But the important thing here is that I did not just tell Mary Anne about the importance of the personal in critiquing dominant values, nor was she able to sit back safely and observe while the rest of us took the risk of self-exposure; instead, she experienced firsthand not only the initial discomfort in providing the personal as legitimate knowledge, but how valuable and valid it is for building a sense of trust and community.

Our students were motivated when they themselves were taken seriously as the integral, necessary focus of the course. By being participating members of this evolving community—not observers—TAs see how exciting a discussion can become when we create the space for the diverse idioms reflected in student discourse. When discussing gender roles, for example, we all sat back in delight while an African-American woman made her sassiness serious as she spoke in dialect about her boyfriend. We listened carefully to the quiet, shy, and brave first-generation Asian-American woman as she told us of her ongoing battle with her tradition-bound, authoritarian father. Students listened sympathetically and closely as I told about the heartbreaking experience of watching my commanding grandfather fall into the labyrinth of senility and with empathy as I told of my brother's dependency on a nightly alcoholic haze.

In a classroom that encourages a range of competing discourses that may even clash, students make riveting observations about issues that are close to their experiences, including racial and gender discrimination, substance abuse, sexuality, and conflict with authority. Together Mary Anne and I, along with our students, revealed the narratives of our lives, allowing these stories to become the social texts with clear, enunciated connections to the written texts we were reading and producing in class.

Mary Anne: Initially, I saw Janet as a stern and insensitive mentor: My participation on the team felt like a mandate from the hierarchy. Today, my perspective more balanced, I am grateful to her for the opportunity she provided me. My initial discomfiture with Janet, however, serves as a warning to others who would marry liberation pedagogy to TA training programs: Students—even graduate student TAs—traditionally residing at the lower levels of the educational hierarchy bring that hierarchy with them to classrooms and instructors' offices (see Freire [1970] 1990, 32). The hierarchy cannot be erased. In our initial meeting, I could not see past Janet as a person who was over me. I did not know that I had the freedom or right or power to protest her decision about my role in her class that semester.

I had internalized the institutional hierarchy all too well. And Janet, perhaps, had ignored it too readily. She was more knowledgeable than I—I had not yet even heard the term *liberation pedagogy* when we first met—yet she treated me as an equal, perhaps *too* much so. She spoke to me as if to a colleague; she did not acknowledge explicitly our positions in the hierarchy; she did not say how she hoped our work together would break the institutional hierarchy; she did not tell me *why* she wanted me to do the tasks she asked of me. Her silence about the hierarchy only embedded me more deeply into it: I passively received information. I accepted the assignment dutifully, if resentfully, wondering all the while, with the dramatic wonder that graduate students muster so easily, whether or not I would survive the ordeal of this second-semester TA training program.

Despite my emotional and mental turmoil, I accepted a shared responsibility for this class, and I was well on the way to perhaps the most important lesson of my TA career: Feeling out of control does not necessarily mean that chaos will reign; instead, it may well indicate the abandonment of unexamined, unspoken assumptions. The crucial activity, the one that lay before me, was to identify explicitly and then to question the many unexamined assumptions I had been carrying with me.

Janet's lead on the first day of class did not help me to examine or challenge my assumptions, but rather reinforced for me—and, I feared, for the students—my as-yet-unspoken assumptions that she was in charge and I had to obey her instructions for my role in this class: She stood at the front of the room (I had taken a seat in the front row), called the roll, introduced herself to the class as Dr. Ellerby, and then introduced me as Mary Anne Brock, a graduate teaching assistant. The hierarchy was clearly fixed. This was her class. I was but a lowly TA, and now all the students knew the hierarchy as well. How, I wondered, could I ever gain their respect?

I stewed over that first class for only a few moments before deciding that I must say something to Janet. I needed to break my silence and tell her of my discomfort. I did not yet hold a jot of concern for the students' own lowly place in the power structure; I simply wanted to make sure I gained enough power and respect that I could control them and teach a good session for my formal evaluation. After that first class, I went with Janet to her office intending to confront her. I did tell her that I did not want to sit in a desk as a student, that I felt it very important that I be up front with her. I wanted to tell her why—that I was insecure, that I needed to earn the students' respect—but I feared that she would not approve of these feelings and expectations, and I still believed that she had full authority over me in that classroom. I told her instead a reason I believed she would find acceptable, a partial truth: I wanted to be up front so that I could desensitize myself and be better prepared when the time came for my solo teaching and evaluation.

I thought I risked reprisal in this confronting, but none came. Janet responded with such warmth and understanding, pleased, it seemed, that I wanted to stand up front, delighted that I had contributed something to our structure, that I felt soothed and hopeful. She received what I had said as if we were equals. What I wanted seemed to be important to her. My preferences counted. In that brief conversation, some of my anxieties melted, and I sensed a new beginning.

My move to the front of the room helped me feel like Janet's teammate, and I soon learned that I need not have worried about the lowly position of the students or how to emancipate them. If the first class session highlighted our hierarchy, the second and subsequent classes forged community.

Janet led the class, not by delivering information to the students, but by inviting them into a conversation about the day's readings. As we all wrote and spoke on the topic of the day, Janet and I became two voices among many. And as she spoke honestly and with conviction about her life and her beliefs, I saw hesitant students blossom. I saw students respond willingly and enthusiastically. They agreed with her, disagreed with her, and learned to risk sharing their own stories. Janet gave her students—our students—permission to risk by respecting views different from her own, showing the students that she was there to learn with them, valuing their contributions, and modeling for them how to communicate with those who hold differing opinions.

I took courage from Janet and soon felt that my discourse in the classroom was as important as hers. Some students rallied to her position on various issues; others responded to my comments with equal fervor; still others had opinions all their own. When Janet and I disagreed on an issue, students joined in the debate with enthusiasm rather than hostility. I had joined Janet as a teammate, eager to understand the dynamics of this liberatory classroom, eager to imitate this mentor who led us to such meaningful discourse.

3

Janet: As I have continued in my attempts to relinquish authority and renegotiate power, I have learned that—no matter my best intentions—the established hierarchies of the institution continue to reinsert themselves into the democratic contexts I work to create. I do have power over my students, my mentees, and now, as an associate professor, over assistant and adjunct professors when I am called upon to evaluate them. Antithetical to what had become a collaborative arrangement, part of my task as Mary Anne's mentor was to observe her as she took full responsibility for the class—choosing the readings, planning the class, and teaching the material she had chosen. Meanwhile, I was obliged to take copious notes, telling her exactly what worked and what didn't. It appeared we were still very much under the dominion of the institution and not yet daring enough to question its valuative authority.

Our willingness to go along with the program, break stride in our collaborative effort, and become the evaluator/evaluated is common and continues to be a stumbling block for all kinds of innovation. Whenever I talk with colleagues or teachers-in-training, they bring up evaluation as proof that no matter what my intentions, relinquishing authority ultimately fails as soon as my evaluation is required. Mary Anne and I obediently went through the steps of the formal observation, and she performed quite well, taking full advantage of the discourse community we had become. The power in a liberatory classroom is always shifting, and her test was a dramatic and ironic shift. It gave her the power to meet with our discourse community on her own terms (though I am sure my presence in the room had some effect), but it also disempowered her because it reinstituted the mentor/mentee, knower/learner hierarchies we had been trying to disassemble. Nevertheless, the requirement to evaluate should not subvert the intentions of the teacher committed to liberation pedagogy. Institutional policies will often conflict with our pedagogical intentions, but in spite of these frictions and disparities, we must persist in our commitment to share authority for learning.

Because I was self-conscious about assuming the subject position of evaluator (which implicated me as the only one with the knowledge and expertise), I was to some degree freed from this role's limitations and able to shift to the position of fellow scholar. Not as evaluator but as part of our community of learners, I watched and learned from Mary Anne's conversations with the students. I found her approach to interacting with them quite different from my own and one that I wanted to try. I took from our relationship a most important lesson—I learned I had further to go in being "out of control." As I observed her, I noticed Mary Anne had a way of listening intently to each individual student that was quite different from my appreciative but short-lived attention. My tendency was to focus on the direction of the discussion rather than on the specifics of a particular student's comments. Mary Anne focused more on the student and less on the relevance of the idea. I could also see that the students appreciated her keener interest and her eagerness to probe deeper into their experiences. Mary Anne was doing her master's in creative writing, and she had a much greater appreciation for the students' stories than I did. I had declaimed about the importance of the personal, but what I learned by participating with Mary Anne was that I was using the personal only as a step toward larger issues, which I highlighted. I always got nervous when discussions seemed to get too anecdotal and not linked closely to the "more important," more general social issue at hand. Mary Anne taught me something priceless—that the telling of the story is just as important as the conclusions to be drawn. By listening and participating, Mary Anne showed me how to slow down and sometimes abandon the pace I had been imposing on discussions, to take more time to hear individual student narratives rather than focusing so exclusively on the final destination of the discussion—in other words, to relinquish control!

Mary Anne: When the day finally arrived for Janet to observe my teaching, the disparity between our positions sharpened. She was the professor. I was the TA about whom she would submit an official report to the director of graduate studies. This was my test, the one that I would either pass or fail. Janet's judgment would be significant; here she clearly had power over me.

Ironically, though, the process was not totally enervating. One pleasant surprise was that as Janet and I held forthright discussions about how our collaborative model collided with the approaching evaluation and the institution's vertical structure, the institutional hierarchy seemed to shrink. The existing power structures and the conflicts we feel from them lessen somewhat as soon as we talk openly about them. The evaluation process empowered me by highlighting the parallels between myself as an instructor and Janet as my mentor. After my performance as solo instructor, I understood better several paradoxes of the role of teacher. My job was to be both facilitator and learner, one who would lead the class and encourage students to speak, to reflect, and to think, to move beyond received opinions and formulaic responses. My job was to share the power given me.

I also faced the conflict common to one who has more acquired knowledge than her students: I wanted the classroom to be liberatory, but I also wanted to *lead* the students to new heights of critical thinking and to a deeper appreciation and understanding of language. I wanted to give them what I thought they needed to know rather than to allow them the freedom to discover what they were ready to learn, knowing all the while that I must relinquish my need for control and give the students room to contribute to the discussion. The focus for the day was AIDS, and I winced as one outspoken student denounced need for common concern for this disease that affected "just a bunch of queers." Rather than telling him that this view was narrow, I let the class struggle in dialogue with one another, and while most participants did not move significantly from their original positions, all of us seemed better able at the end of the discussion to articulate our views and the reasons behind those views.

After class, Janet shared her observations about the classroom conversation, and I heard for the first time that Janet was learning from me. I realized in this moment that I was still clinging to the vision of Janet as a superior teammate and that this paradigm could no longer work. Janet seemed to respect me as much as I respected her, and herein I discovered another vital ingredient for success in the collaborative model: understood mutual respect. Although my relationship with Philip was always securely grounded in the hierarchy and never hinted at a partnership, we maintained a sense of mutual respect throughout our time working together. With Janet, the road toward mutual respect had been rockier.

I had managed to accomplish all the tasks Janet had set before me in our initial meeting, and my resentments had gradually subsided. I was managing the reading logs with little trouble; the writing lab staff had adjusted my schedule so that I saw only Janet's students in the weeks preceding their paper due dates; I had managed to squeeze the remaining five and one-half hours of conferences into my schedule during those weeks while keeping up with my graduate classes.

I had taken courage from Janet's presence in the classroom, and I had begun to share more honestly with her after class as well, contributing as an equal to our plans for the course despite my not yet feeling like her equal. I had modified the assignments for the reading logs, selected some of the readings for the remaining units, and developed exercises designed to help the students recognize assumptions and question them. I had followed Janet's model in the classroom, speaking boldly while respecting comments from her and the students. Although I still felt forced into a prescribed role, I had abandoned the drama of the persecuted graduate student and wallowed in the joys of collaboration in the classroom.

I also, however, had continued to think of myself as a lesser partner. Janet and I tried to flatten the hierarchy, but I could not participate as an equal partner without knowing she respected me. The formal evaluation process forced a conversation in which I learned for the first time what she thought of me in the classroom. Having heard her evaluation of me, I felt rewarded by her respect.

4

Mary Anne: My elation was short-lived, however, as I soon slammed again into the wall of hierarchy and power, this time as it materialized in personal relationships. One day, when sharing with the class some of the struggles of being a single parent, Janet talked of how she handled a situation between the man she was dating and one of her children. I stood beside her as she shared, wishing that she had not. Janet had indeed urged the class forward into risky dialogue about various personal and social issues. This particular moment of sharing, however, only reminded me of a painful internal struggle. The person she was dating was one of my professors that semester, and he was a professor from whom I felt little nurturing support.

This professor and I—or at least our ideas—clashed regularly, and I saw little room in his class for my views. Very much an intellectual, this professor, like Janet, seemed to privilege the ultimate point of the discussion more than the story being told. Because he disagreed with my ideas and perhaps because I heard no explicit affirmation for my contributions, for the story I told, I believed (rightly or wrongly) that he considered me his problem student.

What wonderful fodder this would have been for Janet's and my ongoing talks about liberation pedagogy. I could have told her my firsthand experience of being the disagreeable student. I disagreed openly and regularly with the views of this professor, and because I routinely left his classroom having *not* received what I as a student needed from him—some explicit indication that he valued me as a contributor to the discussion—I believed that he did not value me as a participant. And I refused to risk discussing with Janet my discomfort in his classroom.

Janet and I had become friends and shared some personal stories, but I decided that my equal relationship with her was not nearly so equal as was her relationship with this professor or, for that matter, with any of her other colleagues. I compartmentalized my struggles in my graduate classes into a world I labeled "private," and I held fast the door against Janet's entry. My relationship with Janet skewed further along the vertical plane because I also stopped speaking as boldly on issues concerning our class. I sought her ideas on upcoming readings and class discussions before sharing my thoughts, and if I disagreed, I did so as tactfully and softly as I could. I feared that if I angered Janet, my graduate professor might also become angry with me and I might not do well in his class.

Only now, nearly four years later, can I acknowledge my lack of trust. I initially felt ashamed that I consciously chose this path of nonresistance, that Janet learned of these feelings only as we prepared a near-final draft of this paper. I also know that I made the right choice for myself at the time. My standing in graduate school was too important to me. This was one risk I could not take. And while I completed graduate school unscathed, the price for my silence was high, my relationship with Janet having suffered due to my belated honesty, our dialogue with one another having now ended.

The painful reality with which the practitioners of liberation pedagogy must contend is that no instructor can completely eliminate hierarchy in the classroom, and no mentor can eliminate it with a TA in the office. And even though power may fluctuate in the classroom or between a mentor and TA, those in the lower positions feel the weight of the vertical structure more heavily than do those granted power by the institution.

We, whether TA, associate professor, full professor, or community college instructor, stand amidst the structured policies and practices of our institutions at least as much as do our students. For mentors who would offer a liberatory model to TAs, a keen sensitivity to the power structure seems essential for any degree of success. It is certainly easier for the TA if the mentor extends the invitation to talk about the structure. The TA, however, must be willing to accept the invitation to the dialogue. Honesty is needed from both partners. The unfortunate reality for me was that I feared being completely honest.

Janet: Liberation pedagogy should come about in very concrete ways. It is important for us to read Shor and Freire, as well as other commentators on liberatory education such as Stanley Aronowitz, Henry Giroux, Gerald Graff, and Jane Tompkins, but as Freire remarks in *Pedagogy of the Oppressed*, "The teacher is no longer merely the one-who-teaches, but one who is himself [/herself] taught in dialogue with the students, who in turn while being taught also teach" ([1970] 1990, 67). Teachers-in-training can witness that students and teachers are jointly responsible for the process in which all grow, that authority as an absolute vertical pattern will no longer serve in the construction of knowledge. When professors passively deliver prepackaged information to students, they are taking the path laid out for them by institutions uninterested in dynamic inquiry into the status of power. By not risking passionate involvement, they are squandering rich possibilities for personal and intellectual growth.

Nevertheless, there are precautions that must be taken when we choose liberation pedagogy. Giroux lauds an emancipatory critical pedagogy that builds on solidarity, community, and compassion; however, he wisely warns us that getting students to merely express their own experiences can collapse teaching "into a banal notion of facilitation, and student experience becomes an unproblematic vehicle for self-affirmation and self-consciousness" (Aronowitz and Giroux 1991, 117). As teachers and learners we need to remember that our purpose is not only to create dialogues and celebrate student voices, but to help our students recognize the limits of their historically and socially constructed positions and to extend their concern to those beyond their particular experience.

The collaborative community of our liberated classroom was created so the students, Mary Anne, and I could work on developing and honing the critical consciousness that would help us recognize and resist positions of domination. Together, we dealt with the tension of the power I had by virtue of my position as the experienced teacher, the power the institution held over both of us, and even the coercive power of aggressive or resistant students who wanted to claim authority from us. Although that semester has long passed, it is only right that Mary Anne and I as fellow teachers continue the conversation—the process of continuously reflecting on the authority that our institutions grant us as teachers and the possibilities for collaboration. Hence we write this narrative to demonstrate how the dialogue proceeds.

It came as a great surprise to learn in the final stages of our revising this essay that Mary Anne had felt too vulnerable to tell me about her reservations about her work load in our class and about what she perceived as her ambiguous status in her graduate class. In hindsight, I feel quite certain I would have responded with genuine concern had she revealed her anxieties. I believe I would have readily readjusted her responsibilities and reassured her that her distrust was unfounded.

In her graduate course, Mary Anne was apparently experiencing, perhaps more self-consciously than her own composition students, a quite natural but, nevertheless, destabilizing sense that disagreements with authority will get one in trouble. Perhaps it is too much to have hoped that Mary Anne would have come to me with her insecurities, but if she had, I would have tried to assure her that the last thing her professor wanted was any kind of silence or passivity. There is a crucial lesson here: The personal is as relevant a dynamic in the graduate seminar and the undergraduate writing class as it is in the collaborative mentoring model. Even mature graduate students feel insecure about forthrightness—about the complexity of the personal within the politics of a discourse community. Since that seems to be the case, we must be especially reassuring, open, and honest with our more uninformed and vulnerable undergraduates. Unless professors and teaching assistants can confront the complexities of the personal, we probably will not be able to allow all of our vibrant psychological tapestries to weave their way into the life of our undergraduate classrooms and our collaborative endeavors.

Finally, it is important for the teacher-in-training (and the liberatory associate professor) to experience the democratically exciting conflicts that necessarily occur when we begin to examine contradictory versions of truth. Clearly, Mary Anne and I had and have very different conceptions of all that a liberated pedagogy might exact and how it might best be implemented. Yet, consensus is not a goal of liberation pedagogy; instead we hope to create a place where we can hear "the dissonance, contradiction, or oppositional impulse that goads us to interrogate and problematize the givens of traditional reading and writing" (Clifford 1990, 260).

When we open our classrooms and our writings about classrooms to the lively exchange of oppositional discourse, it is not just our students who move from passivity to animation or from unexamined acceptance to critical awareness—we as teachers are also caught up in the intellectual and psychological adjustments that liberation pedagogy ignites.

5

Mary Anne: After three years of postgraduate teaching experience in two different institutions, I see that Janet's and my class can serve only as a representative anecdote and not as a blueprint. Because each class is different, the thinking, assumptions, discussions, and learning will be uniquely organic to that class. I began my independent teaching, for instance, trying to force the AIDS script onto my new students, trying to be prepared for the same comments Janet's and my students made in the spring of 1992. (The need for control dies hard.) Some of those subsequent students expressed virtually no interest in AIDS but exploded with ideas about other issues: abortion, sexism, affirmative action. The element of uncertainty, I learned again, is central to liberatory teaching methods.

I now try to be explicitly honest with my students about where we sit in the power structure. In the community college where I teach, some of my students are recent high-school graduates and others are my age or older. I invite them to call me "Mary Anne" or "Ms. Brock," whichever will make them more comfortable. I say out loud that I will be assigning grades to their work. I also say that their words and ideas matter and that I want them to speak as boldly as they can. I also remind them that I am human and that I may not be able to maintain objectivity if, in their bold speech, they insult me personally. In doing all this, I acknowledge the hierarchy, admit where it poses problems, and ask my students to risk with me.

My experience working as Janet's mentee was a most rewarding one, and it was so largely due to the fact that we moved our working relationship toward a collaborative model rather than grounding ourselves in the existing hierarchy. The experience was successful also largely because of the built-in paradoxes of what we attempted. These two models collided throughout our semester together, resulting in several vital lessons: I learned the need and earned the courage to risk a collaborative approach with my students. I learned that I must earn my students' trust, must be ever willing to challenge, encourage, and support them, and must let each class develop organically. I learned that I must risk sharing the power, and I must remember that my students believe their risk is greater than mine.

TAs need the support and guidance of nurturing professors who are willing to be out of control—in other words, to share authority with their TAs. The best training challenges TAs not only to see risks in action, but also to take risks of their own so that they can enter classrooms knowing for themselves and holding before their students the assurance that being out of control does not mean chaos.

Nine

Telling Secrets, Telling Lies, Telling Lives

A Dialogic and Performative Approach to Teaching Autobiography

Bob Myhal, Lynn Z. Bloom, Valerie Smith Matteson, and
Elizabeth Bidinger

Writing Autobiography/Writing Criticism

Bob: When you've studied English in fairly traditional undergraduate and graduate programs (and most programs are still traditional) and you've become accustomed to the critical and the creative occupying separate floors in the ivory tower, if not separate towers altogether, then a course such as Professor Bloom's autobiography seminar, in which both are so strongly present, sort of throws you a curve. I've taken what seems like dozens of literature courses in fiction, poetry, and drama, and not once was I asked to actually write in any of these genres.

Lynn: This course was a three-credit graduate seminar of a dozen students at the University of Connecticut called Autobiography: Telling Secrets, Telling Lies, Telling Lives. I described it this way in the course bulletin:

> This course will focus on autobiography as a literary genre: its history, artistry, and changing theory as understood by critics, readers, and autobiographers themselves. We'll explore the major modes of autobiography, including diaries, letters, writer's notebooks, confessions, oral history; and we'll study artistic and intellectual constructs, such as models of an exemplary life, childhood, social and political protest, historical interpretation, and mixtures of fact and fiction. We'll read ten major representative autobi-

ographies (ranging from St. Augustine to Eudora Welty, Benjamin Franklin to Virginia Woolf, Frederick Douglass to Gertrude Stein, Black Elk to Maxine Hong Kingston), a multicultural anthology, and current criticism. In addition, students will write two short papers, one autobiographical, one critical, and will prepare a critical or autobiographical oral class presentation as the basis for a term paper.

None of us, neither teacher nor students, could have predicted the dialectic, dialogic nature of this course. Our dialogue here is an attempt to explore and explain a course that surprised us all.

Elizabeth: I thought the whole class had an air of adventure from the beginning. It always felt like there was going to be something surprising around the corner. We didn't, any of us, know how it was going to go, and there was an awful lot of vitality in that.

Bob: With the uncertainty comes anxiety, however. The tendency as a student is to want to know exactly what to expect. It's perfectly natural—the known is easier to approach than the unknown. I give open assignments in the undergraduate courses I teach, assignments that involve a great deal of choice on the part of individual students. Inevitably, students ask what *exactly* it is that I'm looking for. Instruction manuals and blueprints can be reassuring; they can also be extremely confining. Likewise, it's easy to tell students what to do, but it's more difficult but ultimately more empowering to allow them to struggle with their own rhetorical decisions.

Valerie: Anxiety can be either productive or deadly. It can force you to new heights or it can block all possibility. I know that most of my efforts in writing critical papers are successful; knowing this, my level of anxiety is automatically reduced. In this seminar, on the other hand, I saw people begin writing their autobiographical essays with tremendous anxiety. In fact, our inability to get started was the main topic of conversation for some days in the grad student lounge. No one knew *what* to write about. A number of us were afraid of being either terribly trite and obvious or melodramatic and silly, considerations we don't usually have when producing academic work.

Elizabeth: I think my anxiety came from realizing that while I may not be able to write the great American novel, I certainly better be able to write about my own life with some art and skill. That seemed the least I could do to justify my identity as a writer. Thus, a great deal of personal pride was at stake for me. I realize that writing a publishable memoir is not the kind of achievement that traditionally makes you marketable in academia, but in Lynn's class I discovered I was deeply ambitious to do it anyway. I certainly don't see writing autobiography as compromising my academic aspirations. The myth that a person cannot be at the same time both a good critic and a creative writer is crippling and sad for the profession. Asking graduate English students to make a serious attempt at writing about their lives is an appropriate assignment, and for students to feel anxious to do it well is also appropriate.

Lynn: Autobiographers have to learn to do what creative writers already know how to do. You have to relearn how to tell a good story. The process itself, it seems to me, is ultimately aesthetically as rigorous as the process of writing a good critical essay. While you may be making an argument in an autobiographical piece, you're embedding it in character and action and activity, or reflecting on it in many ways that are not analytic—and that's different from the usual academic writing. Writing autobiography is counterintuitive to what we as critical writers know, because the important point is to tell the story in a way that makes it credible and engaging.

Bob: Donald Murray calls this "unlearning to write" (1989, 103). The more formal education you have, the more difficult it is to just tell the story. The discourses of academia just keep getting in the way.

Dialogic and Performative Approach

Lynn: Annie Dillard in *Pilgrim at Tinker Creek* says that the natural world is full of "unwrapped gifts and free surprises" (1974, 16), and I do like my class to be that way. It seems to me that also keeps you alive as a teacher. You have to be willing to be surprised. And of course if you're willing to take the risk that the surprise will be a happy one, you're also running the risk that it will not.

Bob: One of the things that surprised me most was the way the class was in a sense charting and revising its own course week by week. When it became apparent that many of the students were interested in writing extensive autobiographical pieces—which in itself was something of a surprise—the course moved in unforeseen directions. Interestingly, rather than diminish our involvement in the autobiographical and critical readings, workshopping on our autobiographical pieces actually seemed to enhance our experience of those texts. Being writers in the process of creative composition made us better readers in the process of self-discovery.

Elizabeth: Writing autobiography is different from every other writing task, and experiencing it from the inside out helps to illuminate important issues for approaching published works critically. That our class was a rigorous literature course implied that we should strive to write about our lives according to discipline, grace, restraint, artfulness, and emotional honesty.

Bob: An important point of demarcation in the development of the class's personality occurred when Lynn read from one of her own autobiographical pieces in progress.

Lynn: I dove in first, with a draft of my "Growing Up with Doctor Spock." During the week before I was to read it, I kept slipping into the students' mailboxes ever more condensed revisions of the most difficult material: my parents' anti-Semitic rejection of myself, my husband, our marriage, and ultimately of my biography of Doctor Spock. Three rewrites on the very day of our seminar. What outsiders might interpret as an act of academic arrogance ("How dare the teacher take up valuable class time by imposing her life on her students!"), the students accurately perceived as an act of humility and vulnerability. I was literally laying my life on the line.

Bob: Lynn did this during the period when we were first working on our own autobiographical pieces. There were times during her reading when it was apparent that Lynn had difficulty continuing. But continue she did, and by doing so, by taking such a risk, she enabled many of us to also take some chances in our own writing. In the following weeks everyone in the class would read from his or her own autobiographical essays. Although the essays in themselves were clearly different—some evoking tears of laughter, others tears of grief—in sharing them with each other, the class members became a community. During the class I began to think of myself more and more as a writer or, more precisely, as a writer among writers.

Valerie: That was my experience, too. At first I was extremely uncomfortable with the idea of opening my life up to people in a classroom situation; I've inherited a large dose of my mother's British reserve. But Lynn's generosity with her own life stories broke the ice, helped me more fully realize that autobiography is not some kind of static truth that is told in only one way. The arrangement and rearrangement of words, information, tone, could be played with. There wasn't one right way to produce an autobiography. Suddenly, before us, was an autobiographer, accessible and vulnerable, and full of questions of her own.

Elizabeth: Lynn was concerned about the ending of her essay. She would ask us whether the tone seemed too angry or clipped, too restrained, too vague, too personal, and so on, with each revision. She was trying to achieve that difficult balance between offering the reader some honesty and letting the writer's own feelings about her subject control the prose. She was open about the fact that even an experienced, professional writer such as herself can at times not know how parts of her writing are coming off.

Bob: For me the key part about Lynn's work with the class was not only that she was sharing her autobiographical essays, but that she was sharing the writing process itself. It seems to me that it's in the revising process that the links among teaching, writing, and studenting are most significant. It's one thing for an instructor to bring a published, and thus polished, piece into a class (this in itself, especially with personal or autobiographical work, requires a great deal of courage), but it is something altogether different— something more honest, more difficult, more risky—for the instructor to share a work in progress. This not only makes it easier for students to share their own works in progress, it also gives them insight into the revision process of a professional writer. Thus, it's doubly effective. The entire *process* of the class becomes dialogic.

Lynn: As Tobias Wolff says, "The writing of autobiography is the opportunity to catch oneself in the act of being human" (1991, xiii). Autobiographers don't need to have all the answers to life's problems in order to write about them; the writing can in fact become part of an exploration, if not a resolution.

Valerie: And the exploration inherent in writing autobiography is very risky. It means self-exposure, both intentional and unintentional. You may think you're covering your tracks, concealing that which needs to be concealed, but autobiography has a sneaky way of revealing through concealment. Exclusions automatically imply inclusions, and sometimes you want them to and sometimes you would rather they didn't.

The writing of my own autobiographical essay drastically changed the way I read and critiqued other autobiographies. I was suddenly intimately aware of how many choices and decisions must be made in the production of an autobiography: how many scenes left out, how many positions negotiated, how much compromise is inherent in any autobiography, and how much those choices and decisions influence both the autobiographer's interpretation of her life and readers' interpretations of the life story to which they are responding. I stopped looking for the truth factor and started listening and responding to how writers were *telling* their lives.

Lynn: Sure, once you learn that there's not just one right way to read a text or one right way to write a text or one right way to write your life or to read your life or live your life, you have to be open. This is the essence of being dialogic, for you have to be open to multiple perspectives. You don't abdicate authority, as a teacher, as a reader, or as a writer, but you do abdicate absolutist judgment.

Bob: Yes, and by abdicating such judgments the classroom becomes a more democratic place, a place of possibility rather than a place that reinforces the teacher's authority. Of course, the realm of possibility can sometimes be a bit messy, but I enjoyed how the class was not always predictable. The blurring of the lines of authority did not result in a sense of chaos as much as it resulted in a sense of freedom, the freedom to spend more time discussing our own works than was originally planned, for instance.

Lynn: I think the best courses are a bit messy. It can be messy, yet it can't really be out of bounds or out of control.

Bob: Any class environment is a structured environment just by its nature. You meet at a certain time, there are certain requirements, etc., but it's important to have some freedom within that structure to move in different directions. We had that in the autobiography class. In particular it seemed to me, and correct me if I'm wrong, Lynn, that even you didn't expect there to be that much class time devoted to workshop-type activities.

Lynn: No, I didn't. Each class meeting (fifteen two-and-one-half-hour sessions) was originally planned to focus on a published autobiography or pair of autobiographies that illustrated a particular type, such as the autobiographies of Benjamin Franklin and Frederick Douglass as exemplary American lives, and related criticism. Into this format I eventually inserted three hour-long workshop sessions: one on my paper and two student papers, the other two on the rest of the students' short autobiographical papers. So on the three workshop days, we had to compress our discussion of the literature by about an hour. The literature still dominated—the course *was* a literature course—but it *felt* different. The final session of the course was scheduled from the start as the time for students to read their major papers; that so many were autobiographical evolved over the semester.

That did surprise me, but I think as a teacher you have to trust your students a lot. This may mean you have to trust that the class won't become anarchistic, that it will stay within the implicit boundaries, whatever they may be, such as trying to concentrate on the text at hand rather than providing group therapy, a *major* taboo. You trust your students, which may mean you have to have a lot of confidence in yourself as a teacher just to keep your mouth shut and let the students take over.

Bob: Of course it would be much easier to go into every class session with a set agenda and go through the list, one item after another, but that's not the way a dialogic class works. You have to continually fight against the tendency to want to make everything nice and neat. The course became increasingly dialogic in the sense that roles were frequently changed and exchanged. In working on our own autobiographical essays, it was clear that we became something other than students, critics, or even scholars: We became, first and foremost, writers. Of course, as graduate students in English we had all done our share of writing, but autobiographical writing seemed unquestionably and perceptibly different. Where in the past we had always been asked to write, at least in our course work, from a distance (as it were) about authors long dead or works already analyzed in minute detail, now we were being asked to write about ourselves. The rules of the game had changed.

Lynn: I felt that this course was dramatically different from much of my other teaching. I was in a genuinely collegial relationship with the other people in the class. We became colleagues—peers in sharing the risks, in assuming authority over our own texts, in earning the right to offer critiques of each others' writing and the published works we were reading. Did you feel that we were breaking down the conventional hierarchical structure of the classroom?

Bob: Well, it's always still there, but I think we were working against it in numerous ways. The nature of a graduate seminar is that there are going to be grades and, like it or not, usually there is one person in control of those grades. So you're usually working to impress that person.

Lynn: Is that what you were doing in this class?

Bob: The most honest way to answer that question is to say that in this course, rather than trying to impress someone for a grade, I felt more like I was trying to reach out to an audience as a writer. Writing well, rather than getting a grade, was always the major concern. Perhaps this was because our own essays were being given the kind of attention usually reserved for published reading materials only. That was terribly important. Classmates brought in revisions, works in progress, exchanged them with others and with you, Lynn. You made several significant changes in your own piece based on ideas generated in discussions both in and out of the classroom. You kept us up to date on your revision process. The reality that such an experienced writer was struggling with her own art—a reality too often hidden from students—eased some of my own anxieties and uncertainties.

Elizabeth: I thought that it really did influence the climate of the class to have the teacher engage us in her own writing process; it made me less self-conscious about doing so, made me see it as another businesslike activity that an English professional undertakes.

However, Lynn's sharing of her revising did not suddenly make the class more democratic for me, in the sense of diminishing Lynn's authority as a critic, writer, teacher, and student. I was a neophyte in this territory and well aware of that fact.

Valerie: That's true for most of us, I think. One other point I'd like to make is that we were given the opportunity to read through Lynn's work outside of class, so we actually had more time to spend with it. I think the same strategy, having the opportunity to review essays outside of class, would have worked well for student papers too. That way, students could have received a bit more criticism on their work, which, given the time constraints during the class sessions (twelve students reading their papers in three one-hour sessions), was impossible.

Lynn: The next time I teach the course I'll supply copies of the autobiographical essays in progress for students to read in advance and to follow while the author reads in class. That should address some of these problems.

Telling Secrets, Telling Lies, Telling Lives

Valerie: If you remember, during the second reading of student essays, one of the students in the course expressed his desire for more critical commentary. He wanted to know what we thought of the writing of his essay; we wanted to know (and who could blame us, his was the tale of the death of his child) when the genetic disease had been diagnosed and how his other children were handling the baby's death. The often lengthy and complex essays we heard our fellow students read for the first time were difficult to comprehend on first exposure. We could grasp ideas, events, emotions, but the subtleties of authorship are easily lost under such conditions. It's easy to be appreciative; it's difficult to maintain critical distance, to provide in-depth commentary.

Elizabeth: I did not have a problem maintaining critical distance when listening to other students share their essays. I was prepared to offer criticism on the written presentation of an experience, and felt confident in my ability to distinguish between the life and the work. It so happened that the student essays that depicted the most dramatic events or circumstances were quite well written, and so what may have seemed like a hushed, respectful response on my part to the events described, such as the death of the writer's baby, was also a genuine feeling that the writing itself was quite finished.

Bob: In this type of class—really, in any class—it's okay if critical distance momentarily suffers at the hands of compassion. As long as the focus returns to the work of art itself, there's nothing wrong with being human, even in a graduate seminar.

Elizabeth: If you have people learning how to write about themselves, it's very important that they have a qualified and skillful person giving feedback. Don't misunderstand me. I would never say that a writing teacher should be in the role of a therapist, but in a course like this the emotional stakes are very high. Because of the nature of autobiography, a teacher can greatly influence the way students see the facts of their own lives; an insensitive teacher can be quite destructive.

Doing the personal writing for the autobiography class, for example, helped me to see that my family history is rich and valuable, rather than something to be ashamed of and to disguise. My essays centered around my parents' penchant for turning their marital battles into gothic, often public, spectacles; about my own involvement in their physical fights; and about the legacy of humiliation all of this left me to wonder at into my own adulthood. Writing about it helped me to distinguish their pain from my own.

At first I found myself overwhelmed by the task of distilling huge, deep feelings about an entire childhood into meaningful details and a manageable narrative scope. The resulting essay was uneven, unfocused, and fragmented. I knew what was wrong with the piece, that it lacked cohesion, but I didn't know how to fix it. I concluded I simply was not capable of personal writing. Lynn's comments were businesslike, kind, and to the point: She suggested that I was trying to explain everybody, and that I was making the common mistake of trying to provide the reader with the whole pie all at once rather than with a single, sharp, concrete slice. Her advice was liberating; when I wrote the next essay I described only one illuminating incident. I had so much more control as a writer.

Valerie: In her assessment of our autobiographical essays, Lynn wasn't grading our lives. I trusted her enough to know she would never do that. Her comments on my essay were mostly questions for clarification's sake, such as, "Why were volunteers [for kibbutz work during my year in Israel] paid at all?" and advice on ways to condense certain sections—important reader-to-writer commentary. The comments I received after reading my essay aloud in class were much less satisfactory. My classmates wanted to know what had happened to the people I'd described in my essay. I was glad they'd responded to my descriptions, but at the same time I wanted advice about presentation. I wanted a focus on my use of craft and language, the fashioning of sentences and the narrative persona: Is it too controlled in some places? Too flippant in others? Does it work as a whole? How can I improve it? What I wanted was feedback on the art of the essay rather than the event described.

Bob: During some of the workshop sessions it was initially difficult to separate the lives from the texts, but my recollection is that in every case we were able to do so. I remember a piece in which the author described how she as a mother was coming to grips with her adolescent son's homosexuality. She was struggling with the notion that she had contributed to her son's sexual orientation. After she read what was a long and emotional piece, there may have been a moment of awkwardness, or rather thoughtfulness, on the part of the class, but numerous comments were offered about the piece as a written composition. Several people mentioned published pieces that dealt with similar issues, and eventually rhetorical suggestions were made about tightening the paper, eliminating some quoted material and unnecessary exposition. The class was sophisticated enough to treat the piece as a work of art in progress, while still remaining sensitive, caring individuals.

Elizabeth: Given the often high emotional stakes that such writing carries, do you think such a course could successfully be taught by a less experienced teacher and writer? And taken by less experienced students?

Valerie: That's a good question. I'd been teaching composition for only a year when I assigned an autobiographical essay to the students in one of my first-year composition classes as their final paper. This was after we'd read and discussed a number of autobiographical pieces over the course of the semester. We'd discussed the rhetorical strategies various writers had used, their craft. Some of the students' papers were highly successful, some less so, although there was not one I would have deemed a complete failure. And at that point I wouldn't have considered myself very experienced as a writer of autobiography. As a writer and reader of critical essays, yes, I had some experience. As a reader of autobiographies, yes, I had some experience, and as a writer of short fiction, yes. The students felt comfortable writing essays that were much more personal than I had initially anticipated when I'd given the assignment, and for the most part, they did a good job in creating interesting, well-written essays.

Lynn: Although undergraduates aren't as likely to write in critical academic prose as graduate students are, their generally simpler style doesn't automatically make them good storytellers. For autobiography expresses the logic of the heart, the truth of the story; it doesn't make points through rational argument and analysis, buttressed by the balanced opinions of others. Autobiography doesn't frame a coherent thesis that embeds the argument's key words; it doesn't have a clear, logical, predictable plan of organization or lead inexorably to a foregone conclusion. It makes no pretense of objectivity. And it's messy, for it doesn't tie up all the loose ends. Maybe that's why it worked well for your less experienced students—they're not worried about all those loose ends yet.

Valerie: The potential unraveling of loose ends was definitely inhibiting for me, and I wasn't alone with my discomfort during our class workshops when we focused on event rather than form. Many of us were somewhat uncomfortable with the telling of our highly personal stories in the first place, and even more so with answering questions from well-meaning classmates about events we had chosen to leave out of our tales. I didn't want to answer questions concerning the end of a ten-year relationship I'd chosen to discuss the beginnings of in my autobiography—a relationship I almost left out of the essay completely because I was afraid the gaps I'd left surrounding it might evoke just the type of questions they, in fact, did. Readers do not get the chance to ask such questions of a published autobiography. I wanted to talk about youth and hope and innocence, to capture that perfect moment of self when one is young and has both limited vision and unlimited faith. Suicide, incest, and addiction all belonged in a very different essay—they were, though perhaps implied, deliberately left out of what I read aloud.

As the second reading of autobiographical essays came around, a couple of classmates approached me and asked me to read their stories outside of class. One had specific questions as to what did or did not work as far as her transitions went—they were valid, technical questions. I suggested she ask them to the class as a way to facilitate the discussion's direction, since she was extremely anxious about the personal questions the class might ask on their own concerning issues that were implied, but deliberately not elaborated on in the essay. She did this, and thereby guided the class to address her technical concerns.

Elizabeth: I very much looked forward to the second readings. I think when we talk about students' discomfort with reading their personal stories aloud, we have to try to tease apart the different reasons for the discomfort. Before either of our readings, the least of my own worries, for example, was that anybody would ask me questions about the people or events I chose to write about. This was mostly because by the time of our first readings, even, I had developed a great deal of trust in the sophistication and spirit of my teacher and classmates. But it was also because I felt that by writing about these particular people and these events, I was inviting my audience to contemplate them, to be curious about details beyond the scope of the essay. In fact that's what we strive to do in our writing, isn't it, to arouse the reader's curiosity? The story had been about one particular fight between my parents that occurred when I was a teenager. After my second reading, I was delighted that my classmates wanted to know more about the situation I had described. They asked questions and made comments about my parents' relationship and about my family members as people. They did not strictly comment on the writing, but this was fine with me, because the kinds of remarks they made suggested to me that they had gotten from the essay much of what I'd hoped to convey. Also, their questions indicated to me the points of the story where I could be more precise and clear.

It's ironic, I suppose, that though I was not apprehensive in the least about my second reading, the reading, as those who were there know, turned out to be quite an emotional experience for me. I had not anticipated—not even a little—just how wrenching it would be to read that essay aloud, and I was completely surprised when I started to cry—and more surprised and terribly embarrassed when I felt I might never stop! I was not prepared to feel how deep the wound was that I had uncovered in the acts of writing and reading that story to other people. But though I was embarrassed by that sudden rush of emotion, I felt very confident that the people in the room were not going to let the essential tautness and professionalism of the meeting fall apart. They were patient, giving me a moment to get back to reading, and one or two even made some funny comments to keep the atmosphere light and to make me feel less conspicuous. One thing I learned from that experience is how unexpectedly vulnerable you can feel when you read your personal writing aloud in the presence of others; an intensely listening audience gives the room, the writing, the reading, an energy. I felt as if I were hearing the story for the first time, through the ears of my listeners, and somehow that really broke me up.

Lynn: Having myself become teary-eyed during students' readings and my own, as well, is simultaneously a reminder of one's vulnerability to an audience and solidity with them. But make no mistake, these readings are not group cry-ins, as in Gunter Grass's "Onion Cellar" chapter of *The Tin Drum* ([1962] 1964), where patrons gather to peel onions for public, therapeutic cleansing of their collective guilt as perpetrators of World War II. I have never felt that the occasional tear compromised my authority as either a writer or a teacher, nor did it transform the class into a sodden mass of Kleenex-carriers.

The Final Project

Elizabeth: Part of the problem I experienced in writing about my life before this literature course was my own erroneous superstition that I would somehow diminish the complexity and fullness of my past if I tried to articulate it in writing. Anything I wrote never seemed to capture the entirety of the experience, I felt, and so I never finished writing about any event—I was perpetually overwhelmed with the hugeness of life. At the beginning of the course, we discussed Janet Malcolm's *New Yorker* piece ([1994] 1995) about writing biographies. I found Malcolm's comparison of the writing of a life to the cleaning of a house a useful insight at the time, but I didn't fully appreciate its truthfulness until I was pushed to clean my own house. Then I experienced what a daunting task it is to choose which details of a life, or even an incident, to tell and which to leave out. Where to begin? What will be meaningful and revealing to the reader? Hearing the pieces written by classmates, then hearing how they made such choices about craft, and how they dealt with such issues as memory, subjective meaning, ethics, loyalty and so on, gave me a sharper appreciation for all the choices involved in fashioning an autobiographical text.

Valerie: My concept of what constitutes autobiography changed drastically during the course of the semester. Autobiography was no longer limited by externally imposed criteria, but only by the power of the autobiographer, by her choices, by her negotiation of language—of past with present, truth with memory, memory with interpretation, and interpretation with self-consciousness and the unconscious—and by the reader.

Bob: After having experienced this course and having done some autobiographical writing, I do think differently about autobiography as a genre. In all honesty, before I took this course I thought autobiography was just fiction in disguise. I thought that the autobiographic text was just that—a text among others, no more or no less authentic. I still feel that the line separating autobiography from other genres is not solid, but over the semester I came to recognize that there is something unique about the autobiographical act. The text produced by that act may still be a text, but the act itself is recognizably different from other acts of composition. Maybe there is a closer link between the process and the product in autobiographical writing than in other types of composing. For there is in autobiography a unique relationship between the author and text in terms of power: The subject of the autobiography is rhetorically in control of the autobiography. And that rhetorical control does count.

Valerie: I wrote a critical paper for my final project, but I did so with about a page and a half of autobiographical introduction. That's something I had never attempted before. So I was taking a real writing risk, yet I felt comfortable doing it given the class environment. Ironically, in light of my initial resistance, I now write autobiographical essays all the time. I find I have lots of stories to tell, as well as lots of stories not to tell.

Bob: For me the course reinforced the power and the importance of good writing. It showed me how writing—and yes, even my own sometimes awkward writing—can be much more than just an academic activity, more than something only a few professionals and students do. The real value of this course is that it brought before my eyes for probably the first time the connection between writing and living. In the past I've heard friends and colleagues say that they enjoy writing so much that they *live to write*; this course has shown me that many of us who take writing seriously may actually *write to live*. We write to discover who we are, to make sense of our worlds and our lives, to connect ourselves with others.

Lynn: I'm a restless teacher. Just as I'm always pushing my own writing to make it better, and my students' work—graduate and undergraduate, too—to make it publishable, I am always tinkering with my teaching. Even if something works well in the classroom, I want to make it better. This course validated Robert Scholes' claim in *Textual Power* (1985) that it makes theoretical, critical, and pedagogical sense to write literature in response to and as a way of understanding the literature that the students are reading. That it created a community of readers, writers, scholars, critics, and friends is clear from our dialogue—and not at all serendipitous.

Our initial community has expanded in scope. Several students have presented conference papers written in this course, half the class led a conference workshop embodying the course philosophy, two autobiographical papers won graduate creative nonfiction prizes, four of us have worked—and worked—on this paper. This is not to mention my own publications that took shape in this course. I really expected the students to do as well as they've done, though I didn't want to frighten them at the outset by identifying such Great Expectations.

What surprised me the most about the course was its impact on my own writing. In the process of writing a critical/pedagogical book over the last few years, *Coming to Life: Reading, Writing, Teaching Autobiography,* I've begun to write autobiography. The validation I got from these students enabled me to treat my own autobiographical writing seriously. So recently I've been publishing autobiographical essays and incorporating autobiographical segments into much of my other writing. I also continue to foist drafts on my former students, friends and colleagues all, and I take their commentary as seriously as they took mine.

Elizabeth: The class as a whole, meaning the design of the course and the way it was conducted, as well as the students as a group, was permeated with a spirit of intelligence, warmth, generosity, and respect for both literature and the process of creating it. There was in the class, in the books we read, and the essays we wrote, a palpable respect for human experience, which is what most of us come to literature to be enriched by. Because of this class, I was inspired to continue the journey of personal writing. The experience has already changed my teaching, my reading, my thinking, my writing, and even some of my life choices for the better.

Ten

When Pedagogy Gets Personal

Manners, Migraines, and "Pedagogy of the Distressed"

Katharine M. Wilson

Spring, 1988. Two-thirds of the way through my second year of graduate school. Today's class, Professor Jane Tompkins' graduate seminar Emotion in the Humanities, has just started. I am watching another graduate student sob and wipe her cheeks, one finger at a time. Through her tears she is saying, "I define sin as fracture, and this class has sinned against me." She is sitting in front of the blackboard, facing us all. Her breakdown, apparently, is her presentation.

I sit in the second row. If I get up to leave, everyone will see me. More to the point, I'll pass right in front of the sobbing student. What kind of confrontation will I be embroiled in if I try to walk out on her? So I stay, and a claw-hammer headache digs in behind my eyes. My vision darkens steadily. When the presentation is over, Professor Tompkins calls a break, leads me into the ladies' room, murmurs something about how she knows how bad migraines can be, and strokes my temples. Several years later I turn up as a bit player in her *College English* article, "Pedagogy of the Distressed": "The course was in some respects a nightmare. There were days when people went at each other so destructively that students cried after class or got migraine headaches" (1990, 658–659).

My fifteen minutes of academic fame have stretched to eight years, because from the day Professor Tompkins's article appeared, people have responded voluminously: Articles and letters about it have been printed not only in *College English*, but also in many other journals; it has been extensively cited in later articles; and even as recently as 1993, I attended a discussion group on teaching methods that charted its course largely by "Pedagogy of the Distressed." Oddly, though the responses I have seen and heard come from people who were not there in 1988, they match what I remember about the class: not its fascinating overview of social and literary constructions of emotion, intellect, and the so-called mind/body split, but the way Professor Tompkins taught it. And while I still consult her Course-Pak and reading lists once or twice a semester to teach my own classes (I especially rely on Genevieve Lloyd's provocative *The Man of Reason* [1984]), I refer to her pedagogy every day. Migraines and all, Professor Tompkins and that class taught me how I can play on the hierarchy of the standard teacher-directed classroom like a kid on the monkey bars, to dramatic and useful effect—and, even more importantly, how I cannot. In matters as broad as manners and free speech, and as personal as emotional vulnerability and Professor Tompkins' inventively-named "good sex directive" for classroom chemistry, what I saw her do in the Spring of 1988 has informed my teaching ever since.

First of all, I must announce my bias, which I'm sure will annoy many of my colleagues who are better than I am at the decentered classroom. I *like* teacher-centered hierarchy, and anyone who tells me I can't have any in my classrooms will have to find a new teacher.

What do I mean by *teacher-centered hierarchy*? Simply, I mean that it's the teacher who calls the shots. The teacher sets the standards, gives or withholds approval, enforces the rules. It's the teacher, not the student, who says, "Yes, that's good enough," or "No, do it again." It's the teacher, not the student, who says, "Keep going," or "Sit down." The teacher is the authority, and whether I'm the teacher or student, I like it that way—partly because I attended Professor Tompkins's class. Having class directed by the most excited students didn't always produce a more exciting discussion; it sometimes produced a classroom version of *Lord of the Flies*. No authoritarian teacher ever bullied me, emotionally or intellectually, as badly as my fellow graduate students did in that class. Based strictly on my own good and bad experiences in school, I'm in favor of the teacher-centered hierarchy, and I doubt I'll ever change my mind. The twitch of horror I get even now as I recall that student's sobs, or consider the possibility of ever in my life enduring another scene like her breakdown, is enough to convince me that changing my views on hierarchy would require my complete psychological overhaul.

But what I learned from Professor Tompkins is not a reflexive "ugh" at certain classroom behaviors. From watching her teach, I learned what I might be able to do as a teacher myself, and from being in her class I experienced the cold-water shock a student gets when a teacher does challenge the prevailing hierarchized "Sit down and shut up" model of teaching.

Playing on the teacher-centered hierarchy like a kid on the monkey bars means I can (to mix a metaphor) jump out of it whenever I want to administer that cold-water shock. I maintain my right to set standards, to grade, and to eject students if they get out of hand. But being the boss doesn't mean I lecture to students as they sit docilely in rows, or more than a few times a semester, anyway. I question students until they take over the discussion and argue among themselves. I ask them honestly interested questions about what they see in the reading. I admit freely when someone's interpretation makes my own look paltry. That's what I mean by invoking classroom hierarchy sometimes, but stepping out of it sometimes: Students tend to think that if I'm a boss in the beginning, I will always be a boss, so their shock when I say, "Did everyone hear that? That is so much better than the way I explained it! You're right! I never thought of that! Shout it so everyone can hear," invigorates the class. The cold-water splash of an authority figure acknowledging another as an equal or a superior—that's when hierarchy becomes a powerful tool both in its presence and in its absence.

I did say that I'm all for teacher-centered hierarchy, in that I prefer to be in classrooms where the teacher is the ultimate authority. But I think this is possible while the students are leading the discussion, arguing with each other, even standing up and facing off with each other over the heads of their classmates. As long as I retain the power of saying, "You are making it difficult for others to get a word in edgewise, and you must let them speak," I have the power both to start the intellectual train rolling and to get out of the way as it picks up speed.

So is the dichotomy between teacher-centered and student-centered hierarchy necessarily an either/or proposition? Not on the surface. Certainly, when I quiet down while students question each other, or when I urge a student to put on the board an idea that reduces my lecture to rubble, I'm not using the traditional "I talk, you listen" teacher-centered hierarchy. But still, and always, if I say, "That's enough," my students know I expect them to stop what they are doing. They may be irreverent or even temporarily disruptive in my classroom, as we were in Professor Tompkins', but there is one crucial difference: My students never will have a chance to treat me the way we treated Professor Tompkins. I'm not brave enough to relinquish control completely.

Maybe a better word for "teacher-centered hierarchy" is *manners*. Perhaps if I could be sure everyone would adhere to academic etiquette (restrain abusiveness; be passionate but not murderous), I'd be more ready to hand over all control.

But I don't think I could ever become vulnerable enough to give up control both of a classroom's direction and of its personality. That's precisely what Professor Tompkins did. This vulnerability began, simply enough, with her lesson plan, which was basically to turn the intellectual shape of the class over to us. "Pedagogy of the Distressed" outlines it accurately, though not (as a description of the class experience itself) completely:

[T]he students are responsible for presenting the material to the class for the most of the semester. I make up the syllabus in advance, explain it in detail at the beginning of the course, and try to give most of my major ideas away. The students sign up for two topics that interest them, and they work with whoever else has signed up for their topic; anywhere from two to four people will be in charge on any given day. (1990, 656–657)

Not only will "two to four people be in charge on any given day," but also she herself stubbornly insists on giving away her power, asserting her authority mightily to get rid of it. Yet for all the tenacity of that classroom hierarchy, the changes Professor Tompkins made in it were profound. She didn't just put us in control nominally; she stepped as far as she could out of the traditional teacher role. She told us to call her "Jane." She sat in the back of the room with the students. She bowed out of moderating or directing many of the discussions at all, commendably refusing to give us the "right" answer even though we demanded one. So in almost every respect, the hierarchy in her classroom was greatly changed, but existed still.

Professor Tompkins' obstinate abdication, however, was not how the class's tantrums and migraines actually began. I think now that the fuse was lit when she brought up the idea of not just talking about emotions, but talking *emotionally*, asking us where discussion of a subject ended and the subject itself began. In other words, along with handing over the responsibility for knowing and discussing the material, she removed the barriers that traditional academic expression puts around transmitting that material. Perhaps examining emotion meant bringing it into the classroom, living it out in front of others, like conducting a lab experiment? So we started to test what we could do.

Professor Tompkins' class was already challenging some of our most basic assumptions about what went on in school: From scratch, we had to figure out how to communicate controversial knowledge to others, and how to disagree, without killing each other. We had to decide how to treat a teacher who deliberately sat among us and refused to act authoritarian. And then here was this new idea as well about how we participated in emotion as we talked about it. Given the way I timidly tried to do what I thought Professor Tompkins wanted me to do, I think it's likely that at first many of us thought that we were *supposed* to bring lots of emotion into the classroom and act it out as part of our work. So dutifully, we did, and then we started to revel in it, and because we were running the class, we didn't stop. At first, we did what we thought the hierarchy had told us to, and eventually, the results were poisonous.

That feeding frenzy in the class, the academic and social misbehavior, the turf wars and sobs and physical pain, occurred because we not only unleashed our emotions, but also (and this is important) started misusing our power. There wasn't one acknowledged head of the class who assumed enough authority to say, "This classroom is taking on a mean personality, and I am going to redirect things until everyone stops abusing everyone else." Because different people were in charge every day, we had little sense of continuity in the structure of the class, so we tried to provide that continuity for ourselves socially. We huddled into loosely organized warring fiefdoms: the religion students versus the literature students, Hatfields and McCoys physically dividing the room between them with rows of empty desks. Of course, divisions and loyalties materialize in classrooms all the time. There's the class clown, the teacher's pet who gets away with things others don't, the bullies: But imagine the clown, the pet, and the bullies all fighting to run the show.

The day the student wept marked the turning point in the personality of the class because for the first time since the beginning of the semester, Professor Tompkins went (briefly) to the front of the room. She did it, not because of the student's breakdown, but because after the midclass break, several other students used class time to dissect Professor Tompkins' role and classroom performance with respect to the "sin" and "fracture" we had experienced. They decided—in class, out loud—that she was sadly lacking. Perhaps the heady feeling of actually teaching a class, and of having power over a teacher, went to some students' heads. The fact that students could dissect a professor's performance lengthily and publicly, *in a way that no responsible professor would do to a student*, tells me that power went awry in that classroom. I don't understand how Professor Tompkins ever got the courage to go to the front of a room full of people who had attacked her. I do understand that when she stood in front of the class and said she felt under siege, I got my first splash of cold water in the face: "You mean teachers are affected by what happens in class?"

So what did I learn in school that day? First, I learned about free-speech issues that I still wrestle with every semester. Paradoxically, giving people the freedom to speak their thoughts sometimes means setting up boundaries: Not only may you not shout "fire" in my movie theater, you may not shout "nigger" in my classroom. You may say it to discuss it, but you may not use it as a club. Why? Because it wrecks what the classroom is for: experimentation. Condoning verbal terrorism discourages free inquiry.

The second thing I learned from Professor Tompkins' class is really just a different version of the first: that sometimes students, like any other human beings, have to be restrained from being mean. As students trying to follow a teacher who had insisted, firmly but kindly, that we direct things ourselves, we had to work out what was acceptable. But we didn't do a firm or kind job—or even a sensible or economical one. Of course, we had never taken a class like that before—how were we supposed to know how to run it? But experienced or not, timid or not, afraid of the students at the top of the hierarchy or not, I am still ashamed that during the post-breakdown discussion I did not stand up and say, "We are dissecting the woman who has given us the freedom to do it, and it is personally and intellectually unfair." God help me,

I even volunteered a comment myself, because I didn't have enough information then to realize that (1) Professor Tompkins' class was pedagogical gold,
teaching me twenty-four-karat ideas, and (2) teachers can have their feelings
hurt too. But when Professor Tompkins reacted to our discussion, I learned a
lot all at once about pedagogy, classroom dynamics, and what can happen
when there is no single leader.

What happens is that things might go fine. Or they might become perfectly ghastly. There's always one student in every class whom one shudders to
imagine in charge of a vehicle, much less a group of people. Whether I'm a
student or teacher, I certainly don't want to be controlled by that student, no
matter how instructive it might be for future teachers who are witnessing the
carnage (as it was for me).

At this point, I hear my colleagues shouting that perhaps the whole problem with the traditional hierarchized classroom is that no student ever has a
chance to learn how to wield power kindly and effectively. After all, we students in Professor Tompkins' class didn't. We were dazzled by the authority
we had over someone who normally would have controlled us; perhaps that
was why we did not use that authority well. And perhaps if more classrooms
had less of a standard "Shut up and sit down" hierarchy, students would learn
more about how to use power wisely, and more about the academic subject
while they're at it. And I say, "Amen."

Yes, I do. Of course, I say it with reservations. I don't dislike hierarchy
enough to offer myself up unreservedly to the class, as Professor Tompkins
did. And I maintain that, no matter how authority-free the classroom, there
exist some lines that should not be crossed: A student can disagree profoundly with me, but may not call me a bitch. I can loathe a student's politics, but I
may not flunk him or her because of them. But *lessening* the imbalance of
power? Well, yeah. It's scary, but if the learning process can be helped by de-
hierarchizing, then I will give up large amounts of control. Peeling my own
fingers hesitantly off the reins, maybe. And ready to grab them again, certainly. But, at least for a while, we'll travel without my direct guidance.

I try to dehierarchize very much the way Professor Tompkins did: Besides taking students seriously as living, thinking beings, I put myself out
there as one too. I do reserve the right to toughen up and eject troublemakers,
but I still try to relax enough to be personally vulnerable as well.

You see, what happened in Professor Tompkins' class, both good and
bad, happened because she made herself personally vulnerable. (I have no
idea if she set out to do that, or if she believes that this is the main facet of
what went on in class. I'm writing about not *what she taught* but *what I
learned*—a difference that anyone reading this article is probably achingly
familiar with.) Yes, it's contradictory to talk about controlling vulnerability,
measuring defenselessness in driblets, calculating and titering my own free
fall. Yet in life and in teaching, one always balances control and vulnerabili-

ty: "This far I will go, but no farther," whether one is talking about how much money one is willing to trade for a vacation, how many health problems caused by medication one should accept, or how long one can bear the ride when one's students are in the driver's seat. I may not allow myself to be completely vulnerable in class, even though I'm espousing vulnerability, but so what? Perfect vulnerability means that the class might become vital, alive, and interesting; given the right students, we could leave the room each day wrapped in a haze of excitement and brainwork. But, given many of the real-world students in my courses, I don't think it will happen. Some of my students are bored, tired, hostile, or seeking a diploma rather than an education, so they merely go through the motions to humor me and the interested ones. With that deadweight, the class probably will be ordinary. Or stultifying. And given human meanness, the class might become flamboyantly toxic. So I don't take the ultimate risk of releasing all control to the students. I feel like a professor of anatomy who won't dissect his own body in class. Yes, the students would learn a lot about what organs are actually inside a human body, and they'd never forget the lesson. But the costs for everyone involved, including the professor, are just too high.

But vulnerability is still possible even if it's diluted. The part of Professor Tompkins' vulnerability that I try to imitate is both uncomplicated and profound: She simply allowed us to see her reacting to the text and to what was happening in the classroom. She stood up in front of us and said haltingly that she felt attacked. She got excited about *The Wide Wide World*, she got angry about *Uncle Tom's Cabin,* she reminisced about her own graduate school days and how awful she would feel on the way home when she'd made a fool of herself in front of her own professors. Sounds like a formula, right? "Let them see you being human. Teach with emotion." But there was one huge difference between Professor Tompkins and any number of mechanical, glad-handing teachers I've had who say with affected heartiness, "I love this book! It's my favorite!" Professor Tompkins not only let us see her emotions about books: *She told us when she was unsure of things.*

That sounds so insignificant, yet at the time I saw it as the most naked, revealing, vulnerable thing any teacher could do in front of me. Now that I do it myself in class, I realize I was right. And every semester, the first time I do it in my own classes, I notice that my students' attention suddenly sharpens: *"What now? She just said she didn't know!"*

From Professor Tompkins I found that admitting unsureness or insecurity can teach. There's a big difference between "Nobody really knows where this line in *The Boke of the Duchesse* came from. The best guess is that . . ." and "I don't know what Chaucer's line about the dog means for sure. I looked in five books and asked eight other teachers without getting the same answer twice. So I came up with an explanation myself. I don't know if it's right, but it's the closest I can get. Here's what I think . . . . Anyone have a better idea of why a person would describe a dog that way?" Both versions admit unsureness. But the second version instructs students in three vital areas: facts, research methods, and the sometimes flimsy underpinnings of authority. The second version gives evidence, shows the pile I have made of that evidence, shows the glue that holds the flimsy pile together, and shows what a fragile thing it is to have "the right answer." If an "authority" can admit unsureness or confusion, an education that looked insurmountable to the student might suddenly shrink by half: "If she doesn't have to be perfect, but she still knows all that stuff, then maybe I can learn it too." I think that's the light bulb that goes off in my students' heads because I know it went off in mine in Professor Tompkins' class.

Professor Tompkins didn't just show us she was human and explain why she was confused. She also demonstrated another priceless technique; she implemented the "good sex directive." That simply means to talk to the students about what is happening in the class as it is happening:

> Talk to the class about the class. For mnemonic purposes, we might call this the "good sex directive." Do this at the beginning of the course to get yourself and the student used to it. Make it no big deal, just a normal part of day-to-day business, and keep it up, so that anything that's making you or other people unhappy can be addressed before it gets too big or too late to deal with. (1990, 659)

Perhaps one of the few things that kept me from walking out of Professor Tompkins's class so pissed off with the world of academics that I never wanted to set foot in school again was that she let me peek, that day and every day, into the processes that occur in the classroom. She taught me to look at not only the literature about human interaction, but also the human interaction that occurred as we discussed the literature.

In class, she'd say something as simple as, "Notice we're sitting on two sides of the room as we discuss rivalry," and turn the spotlight from the text we were talking about to ourselves, and to the way we were living the text. Or she'd say, "Some of the quieter students seem to be almost disappearing, and I don't like the idea of people locked out of the discussion. Is something else happening that I'm not seeing? Do you even want to talk?" Because Professor Tompkins believed that class dynamics were important enough to question, she taught me that class itself is important; that students are not simply empty vessels that allow themselves to be filled with knowledge; that human nature, whatever it is, is such a strong force that it must be taken into account, implicitly or explicitly, in any discussion.

And thank God I learned that; one of the biggest explosions that *never* happened in my own classroom had to do with the human interaction of a class that was discussing human interaction. As preparation for Shirley Jackson's "The Lottery," I was giving my undergraduate literature survey class some ways to think about why people invent scapegoats, commit sacrifices, and participate in religions that involve ritualistic or real bloodshed. I sketched an abbreviated version of René Girard's *Violence and the Sacred*, emphasizing the "I got you back" model of reciprocal violence. To illustrate the model, I used myself and the students. I said, "If I scream at you because you gave me a wrong answer, what can you do? You need this grade. But it was humiliating, how loud I yelled. So maybe you wait till later, and up the ante to prevent me from embarrassing you again. You slash my tires. So I up the ante to keep you away from me. I shoot your dog."

One student interrupted: "And I come to your house and blow *your* dog away and shoot out your windows. That'll stop *that*." He was obviously agitated, bobbing his head for emphasis.

I answered swiftly, reacting to what sounded like unreasonable sass. "But Girard says I have to pay you back for that. So I come shoot your brother."

The student's face got red. "I shoot your whole *family!*" he snapped, just over the edge of too loudly.

The room got real quiet real fast. His classmates stared, waiting to see how far over the edge he'd go, and what I'd do. I waited to see what I'd do too, and whether the result would be irreparable.

I took a step back. I scanned the class. "See?" I demanded of the room. "Girard was right! We're civilized. We sit in straight rows in chairs in a building. We wear clothes and drink liquid out of cans. And here he and I are, upping the ante—in a schoolroom!—to more and more violence, just like the book said."

My students were simultaneously reassured and startled; they looked around at each other, studying each other's faces, chairs, Coke cans. The angry student subsided back into his chair, half-belligerent still, half-sheepish. I took a deep breath, "Let's see whether Girard is right about this next part too."

Professor Tompkins' model of talking *about* the class *to* the class saved that day for me. A battle of wills would have been useless and extraordinarily disruptive; instead, I somehow had the wit to defuse the situation and teach at the same time. I turned the spotlight and the inquiry from anonymous vendetta-riddled "primitive" civilizations to our classroom, showing how we all ran true to anthropological form, and I pointed out how a student and a teacher were interacting. All from following the "good sex directive." Thank goodness it worked that time.

But it's not every day I have to calm down a student who is shouting he'll shoot my family. Usually I face the opposite problem: student apathy. That's another reason I don't hand over complete control—if I did, the apathetic students might cancel class and go home for the day. But Professor Tompkins has taught me well. Admitting vulnerability and unsureness, and offering up the students to themselves as examples of what we are studying, piques their curiosity. They stare covertly at each other. They listen. They begin to question. Talking about the class to the class seems to invigorate uninvolved groups as much as it soothes the fiery ones.

I also believe a teacher-centered hierarchy should exist for the reason that, simply, I know more than the students. At least, I know more questions to ask that will get them thinking. I want to retain power in my classroom because my questions are often annoying or require a lot of work to answer. I might ask, "Have you ever judged someone by what they looked like? How about if you saw someone scary-looking coming toward you on the street? So what's the difference between common sense and prejudice? Okay, open up your Twain book. What's Aunt Polly's definition of common sense?" I want power enough so that students will feel compelled to answer me. Only a few undergraduates in any school I'm familiar with can achieve rigor on their own—most of them need a match lit under them, and that match, for me, is my power to demand that they indeed catch fire.

Besides, I know from both watching students and being one that many, perhaps most, don't step into a dehierarchized arena easily; and if they do, they don't believe it. You can sit in a circle and call your teacher "Jane" all you want, but she's still the one who gives the grades. No matter which side of the desk we're on, none of us can forget that. Unless the underlying system changes—for example, unless students and teachers alike are colleagues with the same pay—classroom hierarchy will continue in some form. So use it as long as it speeds up the process of inquiry and argument. When it gets in the way, push it aside—or at least disregard it as long as you can.

And, frankly, when there are facts that must be learned, or equations that must be remembered, the banking model of teaching does come into play. If I'm the only one in the room who knows the dates, facts, and equations that my students need in order to begin to question a particular issue, well then, they'd better listen to me, not each other. At the same time, to teach a process of thinking I must give my students space to practice it, and I must listen to the results and take them seriously—hence, a classroom where students don't, and in fact shouldn't, shut up and sit down. That you-listen-to-me, I-listen-to-you alternation is my definition of dialogic pedagogy.

One should not forget, however, that "dialogic" by itself can metamorphose into the talk-show syndrome—the apparently limitless ability of the American public to accept personal, supposedly true revelations from complete strangers and regard them as spectacle—and without the appropriate interventions, you can find yourself at the end of the semester wondering how to evaluate sixteen weeks of drinking-buddy banter that have had no apparent relevance to any of the literature or issues discussed. For unusual, personal, free-form discussion to be a learning experience, even if it's not the experience the teacher originally envisioned, someone in the room must have a pedagogic vision concerning its purpose. Or, at least, someone must know the procedures of inquiry and disagreement one generally uses to reach some undefined goal. I suppose my ideal classroom hierarchy is one in which both student and teacher are under the control of good manners, but are free to turn their telescopes and microscopes on anything they want, including the areas that good manners (or traditional academic areas of inquiry) would declare off-limits.

I remember Professor Tompkins' class in a gingerly way, as if thinking about it too hard will bring the migraine back, but for teaching uncurious or underprepared undergraduates I have had no better foundation. I try to be like Professor Tompkins, pushing the class off center so that unexpected things are brought to light; but I also try to remain in control of how far off center we get. That way my students cannot forget that it was the literature that started us on this strange discussion, and it's the literature we're heading toward. Eventually, I hope they reread the books for themselves. My fretting about manners and hierarchy exists to get students to own their reading, and to decide for themselves how they will think. I hope they can claim that power for themselves. Not a bad end for a teacher-centered hierarchy, really. Not bad at all.

Eleven

Dinner in the Classroom Restaurant

Sharing a Graduate Seminar

C. Ann Ott, Elizabeth Boquet, and C. Mark Hurlbert

> A great variety of things, some thriving and others declining, some joyful and others grievous, are set side by side and move onward together; this is precisely the way of this world.
> —Nijo Yoshimoto, quoted by Leslie Davis and Hoa Nguyen (65)[1]

We learned—are still learning—to share a pedagogy. In a graduate seminar, The Politics of Composition, at Indiana University of Pennsylvania (IUP), we analyzed the place writing occupies in English studies and the academy.[2] We examined the failure of institutional support for composition at many colleges and universities. We considered hiring and tenuring processes for composition faculty. We investigated the role of gender and non–tenure track teaching in composition. We examined professional activities such as publishing. And we did all this over food. We experienced, in other words, the confluence of the personal and professional, and in this article we try to learn new ways of documenting that convergence. In doing so, we seek to reclaim the right to represent ourselves as people different from those figured in university tenure packages and candidacy applications; as people different from those in theoretical writings about the classroom where teacher and students are abstract representatives: "the teacher" and "the students"; as people of more depth than those in classroom success stories where a teacher sees an educational problem and fixes it, recording the inevitable successful conclusion. This article is an attempt at making a documentary of a semester in which we shared a class and became friends. In it, we propose:

the creation of collectively produced documentaries,

the exploration of the shared emotional truths we find in our work as teachers and students,

and the elaboration of the serial nature of our work as teachers and students.

documentary: *"a new aesthetic space which complicates notions of 'actual' experience"* (Pamela Lu 141).

documentary: *"an arrangement or conformity of parts in a structure which transcends and explains its elements. Such an arrangement initiates the absorption of the activity of assembling objects/words/images into the method, as well as the subject matter of the work"* (Andrew Levy 130–131).

"Documentaries can exist in a conversation between friends, with imaginary others, in words, in drawings, music, and dance, assemblages of all kinds, and is rarely if ever centered in any singular mode or medium but is most powerful when made plural" (Andrew Levy 131).

emotional truth: *"I strive for emotional truth which I feel comes from an accumulation of images rather than from attempting to replicate the physical world exactly"* (Maggie Dubris 91).

documentary: *"both an effect of a social reality as well as its negotiator. . . . And by Social Reality I mean the entire set of social relations in a given period, regardless of whether we know the full extent of their consequences"* (Rodrigo Toscano 227).

"Well, I'm insistently uncomfortable even being in the same room as the word 'legislator,' but George Oppen's revision of that grandiose statement gets a little closer to my point: 'legislators/ of the acknowledged/ world.' If this is so, and if, as I say, the poem is a place, a structure, and if a place is a form of knowledge, then the poet is capable of enacting an epistemological shift. Perhaps the poem is a door out. Someone better be watching" (Liz Fodaski 98).

serial: *"But if we can avoid the corny and sentimental previewing, gainsaying, and self-promotional historicizing that marks the documentary as a vehicle for publicity, then we might look to it instead for its provisional, anecdotal, and performative character—as a model for some kind of 'serial theory' that can exceed its own limits and recognize the suspense (suspension) which seems to characterize the 'meanings' of our time, the intermediary span"* (Lyn Hejinian 113).

Mark: When I wrote the syllabus for The Politics of Composition, I included two objectives. I quote them here, not with pride so much as to develop the context of the course (objectives are expected by university evaluators at my school): "(1) to better understand the ways in which cultural institutions such as schools, government, and corporations intervene in the composing processes of students and teachers alike, and (2) to learn ways of composing and teaching that promote more democratic classrooms and a more democratic society." Readings for the course included Richard Bullock and John Trimbur's *The Politics of Writing Instruction: Postsecondary* (1991), Susan Miller's *Textual Carnivals: The Politics of Composition* (1992); *Composition and Resistance* (1991); which I edited with Michael Blitz; and various articles and manuscripts. Later the class added (this is explained below) Elspeth Stuckey's *The Violence of Literacy* (1991).

For this semester, I handed out a syllabus that was half blank and invited the students to design the second half of a course for us to follow, including the readings and writings we would do. I suggested that here was a chance for us to do interesting and inventive collaborative projects. My aim was to take with my students at least a small step toward constructing a more democratic classroom, one that would respond to student goals and interests. Second, in the completed part of the syllabus I included manuscripts of my own and book prospectuses by others. I did so to create a seminar in which students could investigate with me some specific ways—not to mention the sometimes arcane protocols—in which the profession worked. Lastly, following a procedure I started several years earlier and used in every nighttime graduate class, I invited the students to take turns, with me, bringing in food for each class period, so that we could eat together as we discussed the week's reading or writing in a circle.

Many semesters before The Politics of Composition, I was teaching a graduate seminar in postmodern literature at IUP. One night, the class and I decided to bring in food for our breaks. During these breaks, the students stood around the teacher's desk, which had been turned into a buffet table, to talk over the issues of the class. Week by week the food became more elaborate, progressing from chips and pretzels to fruit and vegetables and homemade dips and desserts. I also noticed, as the semester developed, that the students began to share more and more personal and meaningful responses to the literature we were reading, responses imbued with the authority of lived experiences and personal and cultural histories (two students were from the People's Republic of China). These ten students became close. Several of them even did a panel on postmodern literature at a Pennsylvania statewide university conference after the semester was over. Several of them have also stayed in touch with me and have sent photographs of the class, huddled around our table of food. These photographs hang on my office wall.

Because of the success of this class, I decided to suggest the sharing of food in all of my night classes.

Many of the students in The Politics of Composition had taken another graduate class, Rhetorical Traditions, with me the previous semester. The students in the English Department's graduate programs come from various parts of the country and the world. They are of various racial, ethnic, and professional backgrounds. On nights when these students brought foods such as spiced rice or hundred-year-old eggs for Rhetorical Traditions, it was a recipe from their homeland, and sometimes, in the case of a tea, a spice or some apricot candies, the food was actually carried by the student from his or her homeland. The sharing of food helped to make the study of rhetoric deeply personal. It concretized the ways in which our rhetorics were matters of individual as well as social and political investment. The sharing of food also suggested novel ways for voicing appreciation for rhetorical/cultural difference.

Eating in class, a way of supporting a collaborative environment. That practice, while hardly original with me, is successful because it draws upon some significant anthropological, feminist, and poetic principles: community-making, hospitality, caring, cooperation, need and ritual. As students feed each other and eat together, they learn meaningful, rich ways of being together, of connecting the theoretical to the personal, the political to the social, the study to the story. Recently, in *Teacher Research and Urban Literacy Education: Lessons and Conversation in a Feminist Key* (1994), Sandra Hollingsworth shows how while eating together a group of urban teachers came to share personal narratives of their lives and teaching. Hollingsworth eloquently relates the ways in which real teacher talk—the kind of deep questioning that teachers in their best moments do—is facilitated by sharing practices and settings that are traditionally thought of as outside institutionalized, disciplined work. And while the sharing of food was surely not the sole reason for the level of success that Hollingsworth achieved as a teacher, any more than it was for me, it was still a significant factor. The sharing of food, as anthropologist Bernard Guerin points out, is not only a consequence of social relations, it is a creator of them. Creating what in our classrooms?

> grief, mercy, language,
> tangerine, weather, to
> breathe them, bite,
> savor, chew, swallow, transform
> —(Denise Levertov "O Taste and See"
> A desire to share—to go on sharing?

Ann and Beth: It would be easy to say that our class didn't do much with Mark's half-empty syllabus. We allotted more time for reading the books Mark had already assigned, adding only one more selection, J. Elspeth Stuckey's *The Violence of Literacy* (1991), which Mark also suggested.

Looking back, we cannot escape the doubt that the class read Mark's syllabus as a nonnegotiable document. As students we feared failing to meet a course's requirements so much that we did not realize the opportunity we had to create the requirements with a teacher we knew and trusted. Perhaps this was because we were worn out from graduate courses with exhaustive reading loads that left little time for sorting out ideas and their connections to our personal and professional goals. Perhaps we all wanted to *appear* to want to read and write different things—reflexively responding to the enormous pressure in our society to compete. Hardly anyone wanted the position of seconding, of saying, "Me, too! I'd like to work on that, too!" as if the most important act of invention was coming up with an original topic and not identifying critical issues of mutual importance. That meant that each of us went through the possessive process of claiming a little area of the field of composition as our territory. This was discouraging because working alone is sometimes a serious deprivation. Company, talk, dialogue, choice, sustenance: We didn't quite grasp the possibilities that lay in what Mark was offering.

In any class, even in the best classes, some aspects of the course may fall short of the teacher's expectations. In this class, strong personal interests were surely at work—the students' individual plans for completing the course and graduate program (plans that graduate programs often demand, whether in writing or not), for giving conference papers and publishing articles, and for entering the profession (getting a job)—these undermined the collective we tried to develop and foregrounded our differences at precisely the times we needed to recognize our similarities.

In Mark's classes, the syllabus is like a menu. Students discuss which readings to keep, which to postpone, and which to discard altogether. Mark worries about the justness of the process, explaining the choices he made and all the reasons for dropping his selections from the syllabus in favor of others. So, in many respects, Mark's syllabi are always open to negotiation and change. Perhaps the half-blank syllabus wasn't really necessary.

The class's reaction to Mark's half-blank syllabus was similar to what people might do if they entered a restaurant only to have the waiter inform them that they can make up half the menu.

"Could you make eggplant parmesan?"

"Yes, we could."

"I've heard I should really try swordfish."

"Swordfish is good."

"Well, what do you recommend?"

"Any of the things you've already mentioned."

"Oh, I think I'll just go with one of the dishes you have listed here. . . . "

Mark: On the one hand, I was disappointed that the students didn't do more with the empty half of the syllabus. At first, I wondered why it was that, especially late in their degree programs, the students didn't seem able or willing to name books they wanted to read and work with as a group. On the other hand, I supposed that if the half-blank syllabus didn't inspire what I immediately perceived to be meaningful work, then I probably didn't immediately understand what constituted meaningful work in that classroom in that semester. I also realized that if students as good as the ones in this class didn't see fit to add more reading to the course load, then there were sound reasons for not doing so. It made perfect sense, after all, to spend more time reading fewer books well than it would have to race through several books poorly.

Beth: There's a wonderful restaurant in New Orleans called Tujacques, where the chef makes only two entrees per day and writes them on a chalkboard that leans up against the door. Take it or leave it. That's what we wanted; that's what we were used to; that's what we expected. We weren't prepared to make more choices.

Ann and Beth: Looking back, we see the value of the choices we did make. In selecting to review the required readings and to add only one more text for the second half of the semester, we allowed ourselves time to struggle over the texts that were important to us, connecting them, as we ate and talked, to our lives, teaching and writing. We gave ourselves, in other words, time to think and discuss deeply.

Ann: So, although we entered the class with our own interests as doctoral students (and admittedly emerged with them intact), we also began to cooperate on issues raised in class. The projects we undertook extended beyond the walls of the classroom—to local, regional, and national forums where many of us worked together. In fact, I would say that because of our early decisions the collective continued to exist as an operating idea in the class, continually suggesting alternate ways for doing professional work even when we saw the need to work alone. I would even go so far as to say that the collective idea won out. This essay stands as just one example.

Mark: Still, one of the things I learned from the half-empty syllabus is just how difficult it is to break the institutional and professional forces that divide students and teachers. Offering the possibility for negotiating an institutional document as sacrosanct as a syllabus is not the same as creating a classroom in which students claim that right. Suggesting collaborative projects to students is not the same as changing, in one fell swoop, a profession that does not universally value them.

Snacks Instead of Supper

While none of us can recall exactly what food appeared during the second class meeting or who supplied it, we suspect it was something safe: chips, perhaps, and probably brownies, the perennial favorite. We were, after all, only beginning to get to know each other. We were sampling each other, negotiating distances, testing the waters. And, during those first meetings, Ann remembers feeling homesick for the Rhetorical Traditions class Mark taught during the previous semester. In this graduate seminar, she realized, like previous graduate classes, everyone would have to start all over again, learning how to be together, how to negotiate ways into the talk and through the silences—how to carry on a dialogue—education as forever reinventing the wheel. Hand-in-hand with this discussion of what food to bring, we talked, typical of Mark's classes, about term projects, and how, if students chose, they could turn them into papers, articles, curricula, dissertations, or book projects.

> *Ann:* Unconsciously, I had expected that the dialogue we had developed in Rhetorical Traditions would simply continue, but I could see that we would have to start all over again, even though I had shared classes with almost every person in that room. Listening to the other students discussing *Composition and Resistance* (1991) during the second class meeting, I was disappointed with the level of the dialogue. Everyone seemed too eager to please Mark. I lost my appetite and remained silent.

Ann and Beth: Figuratively speaking, we snacked our way through these projects, talking about possible topics from early in the semester right through until the end. We opened the class with talk about our projects on some nights and closed class with talk about them on other nights. We all stood in awe of the array before us—so many possibilities that we could not decide on just one. We dutifully grabbed chips and brownies before class, stood near the table munching during the break, and tossed our remains in the trash on the way out. But we hadn't yet thought about bringing the food back to our seats with us, much less eating it during class.

Appetizers

As a class, we deepened our discussion of term projects during the third week, coming up with a list of nine possible ventures. These included learning what, if any, effect the doctoral program in composition had on the freshman writing program at IUP, developing a collaborative project with students taking a literary theory class, and a collaborative project in which women would tell stories about their lives as educators. This last one eventually evolved into Ann's project.

We were also facing the anxiety of deciding what we would do when we came to the blank place in the syllabus. What books did we want to read? How did we want to spend class time? We all felt the pressure to find a way to fill this space. With a mixture of curiosity, faith in his students, and teacherly concern, Mark wondered just what, if anything, would happen. In an attempt to offer us some direction, Ann made a list of books she wanted to read for comprehensive exams, thinking others facing the same task might add more and we could come up with a short list to discuss for the seminar. No one followed her lead.

The seminar's topic heightened our anxiety about issues as well, such as about finding jobs, how those jobs might be constructed, and how we might be composed by the institutions in which we would be working. We were hungry to learn about jobs, but that hunger was tempered by well-founded fears after reading Bullock and Trimbur's *The Politics of Writing Instruction: Post-secondary* (1991). The competition for good jobs would be stiff, and if we wanted to do research and teach in two- and four-year schools, we could expect a struggle. We began to fear that not many of us sitting in that room would reach that goal. The criticisms of the profession in that book were thorough, and many of them left us wondering how we could make any change if we couldn't even find employment.

The term "resistance" wove itself through our discussions from the beginning of the semester, with Mark observing, "We have bought into a system we may need to resist."

A student responded, "We have to resist things in ourselves, but often we resist things in ourselves we shouldn't."

With this comment, we acknowledged what we all knew to be the reality: that we might suppress important pedagogical ideas in order to meet immediate institutional literacy demands[3] or because colleagues wouldn't understand our theoretical orientation.

These talks heightened our growing misgivings. As the semester progressed through these difficult topics, food became a source of comfort, a safe place to begin as well as to retreat to when the going got tough. When discussions became intense, as a discussion about how to deal with physical intimidation against women did, we could always reach for and strategically place an oatmeal cookie. And we began to know each other as much by our preferences for food as by our political ideologies. By mid-

February, we had learned that chocolate chip cookies and brownies should be ever-present (Mark's and Beth's preference), countered by some healthy selections (pretzels or fruit) for Ann to munch on. Thus, we had begun the all-important but often neglected practice of accommodating each other, of making concessions for the other. Though this may sound as if we silenced opinions, as though we stuffed a potato chip into the mouth of someone desperately trying to articulate a thought, that was not the case. Instead, what we learned was that, like baking a cake, measuring and timing were everything.

Main Course

One of the most productive class discussions of the semester occurred when one woman, Karen, brought food prepared by her grandmother. Until that time, food had served primarily as fillers in class discussion, with students entering the room asking, "Oh, who brought the brownies?" or "What are these?" On this night, however, Karen's tins of pastries from her grandmother initiated our most substantive discussion about the connections between our home cultures and academic life.

As we sat in a circle passing the tins from one person to the next, Mark asked, "Where do your politics come from?"

His question stunned us into silence. Of course our politics had to be the product of our experience. Some of us had fought our ways through school. Some had endured harassments of various kinds. Some had had difficult home lives, yet others came from close, loving families. We launched into heartfelt explanations of our backgrounds and how they had shaped our political beliefs. In those responses, we heard what Victor Villanueva means when he describes Antonio Gramsci's idea of the organic intellectual—people whose efforts to solve problems had little chance of success, but who nevertheless found ways to improve the situations they found themselves in and to help others in that process. We hoped we were helping each other.

> *Ann and Beth:* In this seminar Mark invited the class, by deed if not by word, to get "close to the other of the other" with a few simple acts. He invited us to critique his work and the manuscripts of other scholars in the field; he shared his own experiences as we wrestled with difficult questions concerning our own; he solicited our opinions on the doctoral candidacy procedures at IUP and then returned to the graduate program's Candidacy Committee with our input; and he shared his tenure materials with us.[4] Simple gestures that told us so much.

Milestones are important individual markers in any graduate program: the completion of comprehensive exams, the acceptance of the dissertation proposal, or (as was the case with several members of our seminar that semester) admission to candidacy for the doctorate. This marker affected our relationship to each other in important ways, as we will discuss later in this essay. At this point, we would like to restrict the discussion to the ways that our in-class discussions demystified the process for us.

Ann and Beth: In class, Mark made the candidacy committee procedure the topic for discussion. "How do you read the program's official request for a letter of intent?" he asked us. "What do you think it is all about?"

We saw the candidacy procedure as a gatekeeping device, even though Mark outlined its intentions—to provide reminders to students if they missed a requirement for graduation or to help students who might want to do dissertation topics for which they weren't adequately preparing themselves. Mark explained that the idea was to provide feedback early in the program, to assist students by offering guidance at an important juncture in a student's progress through the program so that they might take necessary steps to acquire the knowledge or skills they needed to complete the comprehensive exams and dissertation. Some of us still felt that because the procedure was, in essence, a review process, it could become a means for eliminating students from the program. We never seriously questioned whether or not programmatic history justified this misgiving, nor did we discuss whether or not cases might arise in the future where removal from the program might be seen as a valuable thing. Some of us began to fear, however groundless our concerns were, for our own safety.

"We've lost some really talented people at the dissertation stage," Mark said. "Despite all efforts, they've just disappeared after course work."

During the next class, Mark made copies of the form the candidacy committee was designing to obtain feedback from the program's professors about students being reviewed for candidacy. We revised the document with Mark, replacing words we thought could be used, however unintentionally, to hurt students. For instance, we were concerned that in one section of this survey professors were being asked to assess individual students rather than to appraise their current work or estimate their ability to write a dissertation. One sentence, "Please comment on the student's ability to think critically," particularly troubled us, so we re-

> *Ann and Beth:* Mark's actions made us feel like we could contribute to the process, even though we still didn't really know much about how our program developed and how it was changing, a fact which is still true.

wrote it so that professors would evaluate student writing rather than the students themselves: "Please comment on the student's work. Does it demonstrate critical thinking?" Mark took this revision, along with other less substantive ones, to the committee, which included all of the class's suggestions in the final document.

Ann and Beth: In a gesture meant both to reassure us as well as to remind us of the realities of the academic institution, Mark brought his tenure box to class during the break one evening. He used it to remind us that this battle to be here was one we would fight for much of our entire professional careers, one we'd better get used to, learn to survive—or, at the very least, begin to see differently. As we all gazed wide-eyed at the box, he demeaned his accomplishments, hating the letters he had to write to the dean to prove he was worthy to be here. The file was so extensive—so much material. A box of blood. How could we possibly do all this work? And whoever pays any attention to it? What keeps Mark working?

As if by magic he answered, "I do this so I can be here with you."

Ann: It was the way Mark moved that made this moment memorable—like an elf carrying that box, skating in, setting it in the middle of the floor inside our circle of chairs, and sitting down with a half-smile on his face, silently reassuring us that he understood our concerns, that professors as well as graduate students are vulnerable, are kept in check.

Looking back, we see what he really meant to tell us: that we should not be deceived about what it means to become an academic, or what we think we'll enjoy about it: Losing sleep; having to relate to colleagues who might look at our work with derision and even hatred, fear; being sick a lot; working seventy hours a week; not having time for family. Feeling alone. All of this so we can do things with students, listen and talk, spring a little change in the world.

The professional work that Mark brought into class offered us yet another peek into the field. In one instance, he provided two book prospectuses—one for a cultural studies/composition textbook, the other for a scholarly collection of articles on composition studies and politics—and asked us to act as the editorial board.[5] We each read the prospectuses on our own and then came to class to discuss their merits. As we engaged in a spirited debate, we were able to get a glimpse of the world of academic publishing. Ultimately, we turned both proposals down because they offered little that was new or different about either cultural studies or the politics of the academy. (Both have since, ironically, been published.)

Ann and Beth: By far the most telling pieces that Mark shared with us, however, were his own. We read quite a bit of Mark's work that semester, and, while that practice is sometimes frowned upon and often might not work, it was invaluable to our seminar. With the published collections, Mark was able to talk about the genesis and de-

Beth: I remember reading the published version of one of those pieces, "Cults of Culture," several months later: I wasn't even going to reread it when I saw it in Berlin and Vivion's collection. After all, I figured, how much could it have changed? From what I could tell, it had already gone through some pretty extensive revisions before

Ann: During our next-to-last class in April, we workshopped re-visions of our projects. Mark brought in a draft of "Collective Pain: Literature, War and Small Change," an article he wrote with one of his undergraduate students, Ann Bodnar. He held onto it for some long minutes while people chose partners, then lay it on my desk. I think I knew he was going to do that.

"Is that too much to read?" he asked. "Will you have time?"

I just nodded.

I left the room. After trying, with little success, to find a quiet place to read, I finally settled, in the dark, in an empty classroom in Leonard Hall, where I was sure I wouldn't be disturbed. An hour later, with only five pages left to go, in came Mark.

"Ann! You'll go blind! You can't work in the dark here," he said, flipping the lights back on. "Will you have time to finish?"

velopment of each piece as well as the coming together of the works as wholes. His drafts were a window to the world. He presented them to us full of notes in the margins—his own, Michael Blitz's, and his editors'—with entire segments crossed out, reordered, rewritten, reconceived.

we ever saw it in class. When I began skimming through the published version, however, I realized that I barely recognized it. And I remember thinking to myself, "So this is what it means to revise."

I just laughed, and he smiled and sat down, peeking over at where I was in the essay and telling me the editors had asked that he cut nine pages from it. I remember asking him if he needed the long introduction that described IUP and postindustrial conditions in western Pennsylvania, and then I gave him a conference. I asked him why he didn't include the names of the novels and short stories he had used in the course so readers could find them if they wanted to, particularly since the content was related to the cultural and political issues involved in the war-making he and Ann were trying to make sense of. I felt honored to be included in Mark's writing process and have remembered the importance of that moment by sharing drafts of my writing with my students.

Dessert

We decided in class that our culminating activity for the seminar would be a dinner at Mark's house in Pittsburgh and that we would all contribute a dish. Toward the end of the semester, before-class discussions were filled with culinary possibilities: What would we cook? What does everyone like to eat? Because Beth and Mark shared a love of New Orleans in general and of Cajun cooking in particular, it was decided that Mark would make shrimp Creole and Beth would contribute her mother's sausage jambalaya. Ann jumped in with her mother's apricot pies. Other members of the class agreed to supply the salad, appetizers, and vegetables. Mark had decided that it would be no fun to cook alone, so Ann and Beth agreed to drive to Pittsburgh early so the three of us could cook together.

Looking back, that dinner seems to symbolize the development of our friendship over the course of that semester. When we entered the class, and even during the entire semester, we were all working on different writing projects. By the end of that class, however, we had begun the process of wanting to create together, a process that first became recognizable as we prepared that meal and has continued through conference presentations, dissertation drafts (Mark has directed both Ann's and Beth's dissertations), and this article. In fact, as we worked on this article, passing drafts back and forth, exchanging e-mail messages and telephone calls (which we do frequently whether or not we are writing together), we realized how much our disparate geographic locations (Ann in Maine, Beth in Connecticut, and Mark in western Pennsylvania) and personal circumstances all keep us apart. Writing together: Ann so methodically progressing forward, undaunted and focused; Mark obsessing over all the potential interpretations of what we write; Beth blundering through, able to make sense of events only as she looks back on them.

Thursday Night Supper Club

The afternoon of the second week of the seminar, Beth called Ann about the evening's class meeting, "You feel like getting some dinner before class?"

"Sure," Ann replied, "that sounds good. Let's see if Mark wants to join us."

When we approached Mark he said, "Great idea. I'd love to, but I can't tonight. Let's do it next week. I'll get my work out of the way earlier."

So our supper club began. Beth, Ann, Mark, and sometimes Shelly, another member of the class, met for dinner every week for the rest of the semester. While the invitation was extended to the class as a whole, and was repeated throughout the course of the semester, we were the only ones clear of prior commitments.

During our first meal at the Classroom Restaurant, which was near campus, we talked about a lot of things, but we remember specifically focusing on conflicts in our families. Mark mentioned tough times growing up and how much he missed his son when he taught night classes and couldn't be with him when he went to bed. Beth talked about the different ways her father and mother handled her misbehavior when she was a teenager. And Ann talked about how she and her husband had dealt with the conflicts they had had with their daughter when she was a teenager.

> *Beth:* Our Thursday night dinners gave me a little piece of home. Growing up in Louisiana, I remember faking illness in order to stay home and share lunch with my family, all of whom—parents, grandparents, aunts, uncles, and friends—arrived on their noon break to exchange gossip, talk politics, discuss the fate of the nation or even the world. I used to think that if school were as interesting as our lunches, then it might be a place I wanted to be. Though, admittedly, our seminar was interesting, it was no substitute, for me, for the exchanges that took place as we sat down to our weekly meals together.

This was unusual. We suddenly found ourselves, teacher and students, with time to be with each other as we are outside of the classroom: Mark asked Ann parenting questions and Beth mused about how hard she'd been on her mother in between such comments as, "That looks good," or "I could have ordered shrimp." And that's the way it stayed throughout the semester. Dinners provided us a chance to get to know each other in a more personal way. They were also the sites of some highly emotional events that profoundly influenced class discourse.

Not all of the dinner conversation was removed from academia. We were still near campus, eating before class, and in the Classroom Restaurant. In fact, some of our dinner hours contained painful reminders of just how much distress the academy could cause us.

One evening, a night when Shelly did not come along, Mark told Beth that her candidacy had been approved at the meeting of the Candidacy Committee earlier that day. They joked about it. But Ann began to have a horrible feeling that her own application may have posed a problem because Mark hadn't mentioned it. When she asked Mark about it, he had trouble remembering it. Then he recalled that he had seen her name on a list of several students whose applications were as yet incomplete, but which would be taken up at the next candidacy meeting. Together, they were able to determine that her application cover letter had been misplaced.

Ann: Thursday night dinners became, for me, like visits to my Aunt Mimi. Anything could happen: She might tell me another teaching story about my grandmother, share the food friends regularly bring her, or ask me to articulate something that was bothering me.

"Would she feel comfortable in this class?" Mark asked the night I brought in a tin of cream candies Mimi sent from Kentucky.

"She'd love it," I said, immediately picturing her in her gold lamé loafers, asking everyone questions and making sensible, comforting comments.

Ann: I was trying to be inconspicuous, but Mark had already learned to read my face. I remember with excruciating embarrassment the moment he asked me, "Ann, what's wrong?" I couldn't talk because of the lump in my throat. The first feeling I had was pain, loss of face. In order to answer Mark's question, words would have to be forced around that lump and that would mean I was sure to cry in front of both him and Beth. I muttered something about having sweat blood over that letter and lashed out a little about why it took five months for the committee to meet. My advisor had discussed the candidacy application with me, and she had told me mine was fine, so I was confused.

Beth discreetly got up and went to the bathroom while this was going on. Then I discovered I was short on cash and went out to use the ATM machine, hoping I could cool out during that little walk. But my eyes kept filling up with tears, even while we fished for change for the tip and paid the cashier. Just a hopeless well of anxiety and shame.

In that tense little walk back to campus, how important that awkward little half-hug from Mark was—I said, "I feel like a complete idiot." We laughed a little. Beth's face in profile, maybe wondering just what had gone on here. I was experimenting with being honest about my feelings with people I could trust in the face of academic processes that force professionals to turn out documents that continually monitor—from an administrative distance—the fitness of those who want to work in the academy. Later, Mark described spending three hours staring at a computer screen, trying to compose a letter for a friend's tenure file. "Why is this so hard?" he asked. What is most threatening about such tasks is the possibility of rejection after investing so much time, expense, and commitment.

Mark: I was really at a loss to figure out what was bothering Ann. When she finally told me that it was her candidacy application, I was amazed. The only power the committee had was to advise advisors about what requirements students might need to meet for admission to candidacy or to offer suggestions to advisors about how to help students through the dissertation process. I had no idea that Ann or any student in the program worried so about candidacy. No student could ever be summarily dismissed by the committee. In fact, so few students seemed to get their applications submitted in a timely manner, I figured that the committee wasn't taken too seriously.

Still, I determined that if Ann was worried about candidacy, then I should make it an issue for the night's class—and remember to take it more seriously myself.

I was also reminded, in this moment, and in very stark terms, that even when teacher and students become friends, the gulf between their perceptions of institutional practice could be enormous.

In class, Mark made the candidacy committee procedure the topic for part of the night's discussion. What did we think the process was about? Some people stayed quiet; others expressed fear. That was also the night that Mark dragged his tenure box into class. The hours spent in class discussing the candidacy and tenure process made Ann feel better—not quite so inadequate. But she left class uncharacteristically early that evening.

Beth later asked, "Where the hell did you go?"

Ann responded, "I had a lot of thinking to do."

The dinner at the Classroom Restaurant before our ninth class meeting was difficult; every one of us was upset in some way that night and we were in a rut: We couldn't make up our minds about what to eat or what could become a social conundrum. Our imaginations were so preoccupied with work that even small decisions such as choosing what to eat could become a social conundrum.

On the walk downtown, Shelly could hardly keep from crying. She had a student in the composition class she was teaching who was bright, yet upset, engaging erratically in the work of the class. The student would not come to class, or come late and not participate. Finally, she had chosen to share her enormous personal difficulties in a piece of writing with Shelly. Shelly had responded by trying to find her a counselor and a job. The student was a presence as we entered the restaurant and chose a booth.

There was silence while we studied the menu; Mark and Beth finally decided on pasta, Ann ordered a fish sandwich, Shelly had a club sandwich. Shelly's eyes kept filling with tears; she couldn't stop thinking about her student. Beth, Ann, and Mark offered advice and consolation. Later in the meal, Beth got into an argument with Mark about student representation on the Rhetoric and Linguistics program committee. Beth argued that student representation was essential to the running of a democratic program, and while Mark agreed, he also felt that, for issues of student and teacher privacy, students could not be privy to the kind of information that was sometimes necessary to making an informed vote on the program committee. Beth counterargued that it might be good for the program if all decisions were made publicly. Neither would give an inch. And Shelly kept trying to wash down the lump in her throat with lemon tea.

Near the end of the meal, Mark told a story about a student who told him her father had died and that she was going home for the funeral. Mark had given her special consideration but wondered whether the student had lied when he later saw her walking and laughing with a group of students on campus.

Ann replied that it would be difficult to find out if she had lied, but that the loss would be hers. Ann also thought that this student might not fully appreciate the consequences of a father's death at that point in her life, and might not want to appear different to her friends. Then Ann told the story of her student, Jane, whose mother died two weeks before the end of the course. Jane refused to take more than a day off and turned all her work in on time, but the image of her face as she broke the news has remained unforgettable, along with her courage in writing about that death.

Quietly, Mark told us his mother died of a heart attack while he was finishing his last semester of course work in his doctoral program and that, yes, he would give his student every benefit of every doubt. A dense space of grief and commiseration settled over the table—no clean plates that night. Fleetingly, we gazed at the homemade cookies in the glass case under the register as we figured out who owed how much, and what to put on the table for a tip.

One More Cup of Coffee / One More Cup of Tea

"Truth as a sort of tone."
—Dodie Bellamy (25)

Professors write syllabi; students follow them. Professors make assignments; students write them; professors grade them. Professors have tenure-track positions, and sometimes they also have tenure and advanced ranks—some of the marks of status that students enter graduate programs to earn. Most times, in other words, graduate school is a reminder of the professional and personal distances between professors and students.

This, the ending of our article, is the perfect place to say that all is well, but writing "Dinner in the Classroom Restaurant" has also deepened our awareness of the institutional forces in operation here. Candidacy separates us; employment separates us; tenure separates us. These are realizations of the fact that democracy, transformation, liberation, and affiliation are problematic, even in the best of circumstances.

What has it meant to write an article about the development of our friendship? What—after years of talking, laughing, and arguing—could we possibly still have to learn? For one thing, that we've only begun to hear our differences.

At the same time, we've only begun to learn our connections: how deeply they go, how they connect us to each other despite the distances.

Beth stood with her back to Mark as he draped her doctoral hood over her head. Then, he turned her around to hug her before facing her forward again. All the while, Ann elbowed her way through the crowd, snapping pictures of Beth and Mark and standing in Beth's parents' stead when President Pettit suggested that the families rise so the graduates could honor them.

In "The Institution('s) Lives!," Hurlbert and Blitz argue that "documents and their literacy demands teach us our place(s) within the institution, institutionalize us, (con)figure us into the autobiography of the institution, incorporate us, make us part of the institution's scene. They tell us what to do and where to do it as they describe, for us, what *we are doing*" (1992, 63). Institutional documents seem to capture our minds, our subjectivities, molding them into acceptable forms, into stasis—containing no sense of the collective, the emotional truths, or the serial nature of our work. Institutional documents are artless snapshots taken of us in what are often our most stressful and awkward moments. They seem never to reflect the fact that our work in any given semester continues into the next and the one after that. The institution's endless search for immediate results is decidedly anti-aesthetic and anti-serial.

How do we get elsewhere?

The title of this book is *Sharing Pedagogies*. But what does it mean to share a pedagogy in the clumsy situations in which students and teachers find themselves? In our experience, sharing a pedagogy means accepting others' stories, hosting others' thoughts and questions, sorrows and joys (and all while resisting being taken for hosts by institutional objectivity). It's Ann crying in a restaurant; Mark talking about his mother's death; Beth laughing too loudly and talking too much. A wise host has emotional intelligence and senses when to listen closely, how to respond. Eating together. Learning to work together differently. It's sharing beyond the time and space allotted for a course. It is a way of learning that is intimate as well as academically legitimate.

Candidacy documents and tenure packages are documentaries of who we are supposed to be—an oversight, many times, of who we are. This article is, in other words, a documentary of who we are despite the institution's other documentaries. Or as Trinh Minh-ha argues, "Writing is above all releasing oneself from external censorship" (1991, 130). At the beginning of this article we quoted Andrew Levy's take on the documentary's multimodal form: *"Documentaries can exist in a conversation between friends, with imaginary others, in words, in drawings, music, and dance, assemblages of all kinds, and is rarely if ever centered in any singular mode or medium but is most powerful when made plural"* (131). The idea of documentary offers, then, fresh ways for *performing* classroom realities: sculpture, dance, song, poetry, theater, painting, video art, cartoon, puppets, and performance art. *Performance*: recitals, readings, interpretations. Performance is not, Jeff McMahon tells us, "analytic or linear, and leaves us with much that cannot be explained; a causality that does not always follow the plot. It represents more than it explains, or it makes the explaining itself the content. It *is something*, not about something" (1995, 129). This sense of the aesthetic and social possibilities of performance has traditionally had little place in graduate composition studies—except performance as food for assessment.[6] There must then be something else we can commit to:

the creation of collectively produced documentaries,	the exploration of the shared emotional truths we find in our work as teachers and students,	and the elaboration of the serial nature of our work as teachers and students.
document: Institutional documents provide "one of the most perceptible sites at which the institution's 'autobiography' is composed" ("To: You, From: Michael Blitz and C. Mark Hurlbert" 1989, 8). An autobiography that is and is not our own. Who might we be if we could make a new aesthetic space in which to subvert the power of documentation? The candidacy and tenure documents served as powerful warnings about the dangers we	**documentary:** What emotional truths are teachers missing every day? The ones we experience but do not document? What change can come from the missing? **documentary:** One of our goals in this article is to try to demystify the student-teacher relations in a graduate class we shared. During the class we learned about our friendship. We learned about	**serial:** Multiple, open-ended, and connected in aesthetic/political/social performance. **serial:** A postmodern stance in the face of totaling fictions about the classroom. It introduces the multiple, different, and disruptive into the representations we make (Downing and Bazargan 3–44) about the classroom.

may be in or are in to members of our class, rather than as performances one might make toward more meaningful social experiences.

documentary: To tell a narrative as both true to the experience and a meaningful reworking of it. To tell it as an aesthetic construct—human beyond objectivity or subjectivity.

And always as fair to the characters (protection of anonymity, fair usage, careful—ethical—representation, etc.). Academics are good at using representation and interpretation to hurt others.

documentary: A work has form. When the form works, it performs meaning; it shapes and reshapes living for the participants and readers.

When the form works, we hear multiple voices speaking at once—a sound closer to the "tone of truth."

our shared concerns about the tenure process, which we all loathed but hoped to face successfully. At the same time, we also learned about some of the distances between us. Ann viewed candidacy differently from Mark and Beth. And Mark and Beth never reached a reasonable consensus about student representation on the graduate program committee. This last fact strikes us as particularly odd given the powerful perspective on faculty committees that Ann's candidacy concerns made available. What do teachers and students see? Share? Who is recording it?

Someone is watching—and documenting what we are doing. Now! while they're looking for something in our files—let's do something else.

serial: Not the merely repetitive, but the open-ended performance. Marian Yee's improvisation about "something written for the moment. Having a limited impact, and then moving on. I think there's something necessary about things having short-lived lives and then ideas transforming, taking another shape and going on" (92).

serial: Similar to Sandra Hollingsworth's commitment to "staying in the question" (230). Being willing to keep things open. Being committed to resisting the totalizing myths and foreclosures of disciplinary conclusions. A commitment · to sharing what we are not sure of. Performing the work from within an ensemble.

serial: Storytelling invites other stories, invites us to then move on while staying in the questions we have raised.

Notes

1. All italicized text in this first section of our article is taken from the second edition of the literary magazine *Chain* (Ohman and Spahr). The writers and artists in *Chain 2* follow their poems and pieces of fiction and visual art with various statements about the genre, "documentary." It is from these critical afterwords that we quote in this first section.

2. Throughout this narrative, we do not designate the semester in which this course took place or name many of the students in the class. We do not do so because we and our colleagues explored the borders between the political and the deeply personal natures of academic experience in our class.

3. The concept of "literacy demands," or "complex sets of explicit and implicit institutional instructions for certain forms of literate behavior," was developed by Michael Blitz and Mark in their articles, "To: You, From: Michael Blitz and C. Mark Hurlbert, Re: Literacy Demands and Institutional Autobiography" and "The Institution('s) Lives!" (1991). Since we read these texts in class, it became a useful concept for members of the class interested in critiquing institutional ideology—equatable, in the scope of this article, with the ill health offered in much institutional food. For an example of how the concept is used, see Derek Owens' *Resisting Writings* (1994).

4. Because the Candidacy Committee is so important in another part of this article, it is necessary to say a few words about candidacy. Near the end of course work, each student is asked to turn in an application for candidacy. This application includes a letter of intent, a plan for finishing course study and meeting requirements, such as the program's research requirement. Assessment forms from faculty, transcripts, and a Graduate School Candidacy Form are then added to the application folder by the Graduate Program in Rhetoric and Linguistics and it goes to the Candidacy Committee. The three faculty members of this committee read the folders and make recommendations for future work to students and advisors. Most currently, a committee has been formed to review and revise the candidacy process. The work of this committee is ongoing at the time we write this article, but it seems that the committee will become more of a review mechanism while retaining its advising capacity.

5. We do not name these texts because we were reading them in manuscript.

6. We realize here that we are shortchanging the possibilities for social activism inherent in cultural studies as community action programs or in the best examples of performance ethnography or in other places we have yet to look. The problem is that it is hard to say how widespread these movements will become at this juncture in the history of composition studies.

Bibliography

Anayo, R. 1972. *Bless Me Ultima*. Berkeley: Quinto Sol.

Aronowitz, S. and H.A. Giroux. 1991. *Postmodern Education: Politics, Culture, and Social Criticism*. Minneapolis: U of Minnesota P.

Atwell, N. 1987. *In the Middle: Writing, Reading, and Learning with Adolescents*. Portsmouth, NH: Boynton/Cook-Heinemann.

Axelrod, R.B. and C.R. Cooper. 1993. *The Concise Guide to Writing*. New York: St. Martin's.

Bartholomae, D. 1988. "Inventing the University." In *Perspectives on Literacy*, ed. E.R. Kingten, B.M. Kroll, and M. Rose, 273–285. Carbondale: Southern Illinois UP.

———— and A. Petrosky. 1990. *Ways of Reading: An Anthology for Writers*. 2nd Edition. Boston: Bedford.

Bateman, C. 1991. "Map." In *The Bicycle Slow Race*, 24. Hanover, NH: UP of New England.

Bellamy, Dodie. 1995. The Eternal Repository. Interview with Lyn Hejinian. *Chain/2: Documentary*. (Spring): 19–25.

Bernstein, R. 1994. *Dictatorship of Virtue: Multiculturalism and the Battle for America's Future*. New York: Knopf.

Berthoff, A. 1981. *The Making of Meaning: Metaphors, Models, and Maxims for Writing Teachers*. Montclair, NJ: Boynton/Cook.

Bishop, W. 1993. "Students' Stories and the Variable Gaze of Composition Research." In *Writing Ourselves into the Story*, ed. S.I. Fontaine and S. Hunter, 197–212. Carbondale: Southern Illinois UP.

————, ed. 1993. *The Subject Is Writing: Essays by Teachers and Students*. Portsmouth, NH: Boynton/Cook-Heinemann.

———— and S.G. Teichmann. 1993. "A Tale of Two Writing Teachers." *English Leadership Quarterly* 15(3): 2–7.

Blitz, M. and C.M. Hurlbert. 1989. "To: You, From: Michael Blitz and C. Mark Hurlbert, Re: Literacy Demands and Institutional Autobiography." *Works and Days 13: Essays in the Socio-Historical Dimensions of Literature and the Arts* 7(1): 7–33.

———— and C.M. Hurlbert. 1992. "Cults of Culture." In *Cultural Studies in the English Classroom: Theory/Practice*, ed. J.A. Berlin and M.J. Vivion, 5–23. Portsmouth, NH: Boynton/Cook-Heinemann.

Bloom, L.Z. 1993. "Growing Up with Dr. Spock." *a/b: Auto/Biography Studies* 8 (1993): 271–285.

——. (Forthcoming). *Coming to Life: Reading, Writing, Teaching Autobiography.* Englewood Cliffs, NJ: Prentice-Hall.

Bontemps, A. 1969. Introduction to *Cane,* by J. Toomer. New York: Harper and Row.

Brooke, R., R. Mirtz, and R. Evans. 1994. *Small Groups in Writing Workshops.* Urbana: NCTE.

Bruffee, K.A. 1993. *Collaborative Learning: Higher Education, Interdependence, and the Authority of Knowledge.* Baltimore: Johns Hopkins.

Bruner, J. 1959. "Learning and Thinking." *Harvard Educational Review* 29 (Summer): 184–192.

Bullock, R. and J. Trimbur, ed. 1991. *The Politics of Writing Instruction: Postsecondary.* Portsmouth, NH: Boynton/Cook-Heinemann.

Calkins, L. 1986. *The Art of Teaching Writing.* Portsmouth, NH: Heinemann.

Cather, W. [1932] 1974. *Obscure Destinies.* New York: Vintage.

Cisneros, S. [1984] 1989. *The House on Mango Street.* New York: Vintage.

Clifford, J. 1990. "Enacting Critical Literacy." In *The Right to Literacy,* ed. A.A. Lunsford, J. Moglen, and J. Slevin, 255–261. New York: MLA.

Dewey, J. [1900] 1971. *The School and Society.* Chicago: U of Chicago P.

——. [1938] 1963. *Experience and Education.* New York: Collier.

Dillard, A. 1974. *Pilgrim at Tinker Creek.* New York: Harper.

Downing, D.B. and S. Bazargan. 1991. "Image and Ideology: Some Preliminary Histories and Polemics." In *Image and Ideology in Modern/PostModern Discourse,* ed. D.B. Downing and S. Bazargan, 3–44. Albany: State U of New York P.

——, P. Harkin and J.J. Sosnoski. 1994. "Configurations of Lore: The Changing Relations of Theory, Research, and Pedagogy." In *Changing Classroom Practices: Resources for Literary and Cultural Studies,* ed. D.B. Downing, 3–34. Urbana: NCTE.

Elbow, P. 1981. *Writing with Power: Techniques for Mastering the Writing Process.* New York: Oxford UP.

——. 1993. "Ranking, Evaluating, and Liking: Sorting Out Three Forms of Judgment." *College English* 55(2): 187–206.

Eliot, T.S. 1943. *Four Quartets.* New York: Harcourt Brace.

Fontaine, S.I. and S. Hunter, ed. 1993. *Writing Ourselves into the Story: Unheard Voices from Composition Studies.* Carbondale: Southern Illinois UP.

Freire, P. [1970] 1990. *Pedagogy of the Oppressed.* Trans. M.B. Ramos. New York: Continuum.

—— and D. Macedo. 1987. *Literacy: Reading the Word and the World.* South Hadley, MA: Bergin & Garvey.

Geertz, C. 1973. *The Interpretation of Cultures: Selected Essays.* New York: Basic Books.

Girard, R. 1979. *Violence and the Sacred.* Trans. P. Gregory. Baltimore: Johns Hopkins UP.

Giroux, H.A. 1983. *Theory and Resistance in Education: A Pedagogy for the Opposition*. South Hadley, MA: Bergin & Garvey.

———, ed. 1991. *Postmodernism, Feminism, and Cultural Politics: Redrawing Educational Boundaries*. Albany: State U of New York P.

———. 1992. *Border Crossings: Cultural Workers and the Politics of Education*. New York: Routledge.

Goleman, D. 1995. *Emotional Intelligance*. New York: Bantam.

Goodlad, J. 1984. *A Place Called School: Prospects for the Future*. New York: McGraw-Hill.

Graff, G. 1992. *Beyond the Culture Wars: How Teaching the Conflicts Can Revitalize American Education*. New York: Norton.

Grass, G. [1962] 1964. *The Tin Drum*. Trans. R. Manheim. New York: Vintage.

Graves, D. 1983. *Writing: Teachers and Children at Work*. Exeter, NH: Heinemann.

Guerin, B. 1992. "Social Behavior as Discriminative Stimulus and Consequences in Social Anthropology." *The Behavior Analyst* 15(1): 31–41.

Hansberry, L. 1959. *A Raisin in the Sun*. New York: Random House.

Harkin, P. 1991. "The Postdisciplinary Politics of Lore." In *Contending with Words: Composition and Rhetoric in a Postmodern Age*, ed. P. Harkin and J. Schilb, 124–138. New York: MLA.

Harris, J. 1993. "The Course as Text/The Teacher as Critic." *College English* 55(7): 785–793.

Helmers, M. 1994. *Writing Students: Composition Testimonials and Representations of Students*. Albany: State U of New York P.

Hollingsworth, S. 1994. *Teacher Research and Urban Literacy Education: Lessons and Conversations in a Feminist Key*. New York: Teachers College P.

Hull, G. and M. Rose. 1990."'This Wooden Shack Place': The Logic of an Unconventional Reading." *College Composition and Communication* 41(3): 287–298.

Hurlbert, C.M. and M. Blitz, ed. 1991. *Composition and Resistance*. Portsmouth, NH: Boynton/Cook-Heinemann.

——— and M. Blitz. 1992. "The Institution('s) Lives!" *Marxism and Rhetoric*. Spec. Issue of *PRE/TEXT: A Journal of Rhetorical Theory*, ed. J.A. Berlin and J. Trimbur. 13(1/2): 59–78.

———and A.M. Bodnar. 1994. "Collective Pain: Literature, War, and Small Change." In *Changing Classroom Practices: Resources for Literary and Cultural Studies*, ed. D.B. Downing, 202–232. Urbana: NCTE.

Hutchins, R.M. 1952. *The Great Conversation: The Substance of a Liberal Learning*. Chicago: Encyclopaedia Britannia, Inc.

Knoblauch, C.H. and L. Brannon. 1984. *Rhetorical Traditions and the Teaching of Writing*. Upper Montclair, NJ: Boynton/Cook.

———. 1993. *Critical Teaching and the Idea of Literacy*. Portsmouth, NH: Boynton/Cook.

Koontz, D. 1987. *Twilight Eyes*. New York: Berkley.

Levertov, D. 1962. "O Taste and See." In *O Taste and See*, 53. New York: New Directions.

Lionnet, F. 1989. *Autobiographical Voices: Race, Gender, Self-Portraiture*. Ithaca: Cornell UP.

Lloyd, G. 1984. *The Man of Reason*. Minneapolis: U of Minnesota P.

Malcolm, J. [1994] 1995. *The Silent Woman: Sylvia Plath and Ted Hughes*. New York: Vintage.

McMahon, J. 1995. "Performance Art in Education." *Performing Arts Journal* 50–51 (27.2/3): 126–132.

Miller, S. 1990. *Textual Carnivals: The Politics of Composition*. Carbondale, IL: Southern Illinois UP.

Miller, S.M. 1992. "Creating Change: Towards a Dialogic Pedagogy." *National Research Center on Literature Teaching and Learning*. Report Series 2.18.

Minh-ha, T.T. 1991. *"L'Innécriture*: Un-Writing/Inmost Writing." In *When the Moon Waxes Red: Representation, Gender and Cultural Politics*, 119–145. New York: Routledge.

Morrison, T. 1993. *Playing in the Dark: Whiteness and the Literary Imagination*. New York: Vintage.

Murray, D.M. 1989. "Unlearning to Write." In *Creative Writing in America: Theory and Pedagogy,* ed. J.M. Moxley, 103–113. Urbana: NCTE.

Ohman, J. and J. Spahr, ed. 1995. *Chain/2: Documentary*. (Spring).

Owens, D. 1994. *Resisting Writings (and the Boundaries of Composition)*. Dallas: Southern Methodist UP.

Pratt, M.L. 1991. "Arts of the Contact Zone." *Profession 1991*: 33–40.

Rice, S. 1992. "Emotions." In *Singing Yet*, 219–221. New York: Knopf.

Rich, A. 1993. "Claiming an Education." In *The Dolphin Reader*, ed. D. Hunt, 657–661. Boston: Houghton Mifflin.

Rief, L. 1992. *Seeking Diversity: Language Arts with Adolescents*. Portsmouth, NH: Heinemann.

Ritchie, J.S. and D.E. Wilson. 1993. "Dual Apprenticeships: Subverting and Supporting Critical Teaching. *English Education* 25(2): 67–83.

Rose, M. 1989. *Lives on the Boundary: A Moving Account of the Struggles and Achievements of America's Educationally Underprepared*. New York: Penguin.

Roth, H. [1932] 1991. *Call It Sleep*. New York: Noonday.

Schlib, J., E. Flynn, and J. Clifford, ed. 1992. *Constellations: A Contextual Reader*. New York: HarperCollins.

Scholes, Robert. 1985. *Textual Power: Literary Theory and the Teaching of English*. New Haven: Yale UP.

Schon, D. 1987. *Educating the Reflective Practitioner*. San Francisco: Jossey-Bass.

Shaugnessy, M. P. 1977. *Errors and Expectations: A Guide for the Teacher of Basic Writing*. New York: Oxford UP.

Shor, I. 1992. *Empowering Education*. Chicago: Chicago UP.

———— and P. Freire. 1987. *A Pedagogy for Liberation: Dialogues on Transforming Education*. South Hadley, MA: Bergin & Garvey.

Smart-Grosvenor, V. 1992. *Vibration Cooking or the Travel Notes of a Geechee Girl*. New York: Ballantine.

Sommers, N. and D. McQuade. 1989. *Student Writers at Work: The Bedford Prizes*. 2nd Edition. New York: Bedford.

Sowell, T. 1993. *Inside American Education: The Decline, the Deception, the Dogmas*. New York: Free Press.

Steinbeck, J. [1937] 1965. *Of Mice and Men*. New York: Modern Library.

Stuckey, J.E. 1991. *The Violence of Literacy*. Portsmouth, NH: Boynton/Cook-Heinemann.

Tompkins, J. 1990. "Pedagogy of the Distressed." *College English* 52(6): 653–660.

Toomer, J. [1923] 1993. *Cane*. New York: Livewright.

Villaneuva, V. 1993. *Bootstraps: From an American Academic of Color*. Urbana: NCTE.

Welch, N. 1993. "Resisting the Faith: Conversion, Resistance, and the Training of Teachers." *College English* 55(4): 387–401.

Wilson, D.E. 1994. *Attempting Change: Teachers Moving from Writing Project to Classroom Practice*. Portsmouth, NH: Boynton/Cook-Heinemann.

Wolff, T. 1991. Introduction to *Broken Vessels*, by Andre Dubus. Boston: Godine.

Wright, R. [1937] 1966. *Black Boy: A Record of Childhood and Youth*. New York: Harper and Row.

Wynne, J. 1994. *The Other World: Stories*. San Francisco: City Lights.

Yaeger, P. 1991. Afterword from *Feminism, Bakhtin, and the Dialogic,* ed. D.M. Bauer and S.J. McKinstry, 239-245. Albany: State U of New York P.

Yee, M. 1991. Transcript. In *Composition and Resistance*, ed. C.M. Hurlbert and M. Blitz, 92. Portsmouth, NH: Boynton Cook-Heinemann.

Young, I.M. [1986] 1990. "The Idea of Community and the Politics of Difference." *Social Theory and Practice* 12(1): 1–26. Rpt. in *Feminism/Postmodernism*, ed. Linda J. Nicholson, 300–323. New York: Routledge.

Young, R.A. and J.D. Young, ed. 1993. *African-American Folktales for Young Readers*. Little Rock: August House.

Contributors

Brian Arbogast de Hubert-Miller is a semiretired sculptor and a student at Rollins College in Winter Park, Florida, majoring in Interdisciplinary Studies. His undergraduate degree is focused on social commentary in humanities, philosophy and religion, and communications. His graduate studies will focus on rhetoric and ethics and prepare him for a career as a professor and essayist.

Jennifer Muret Bate graduated from Southwestern College in Winfield, Kansas, in May of 1996. She has recently returned from student teaching in Athens, where she enjoyed being surrounded by the culinary culture of Greece.

Elizabeth Bidinger is an English doctoral student at the University of Connecticut. She has done editing for Beacon Press and *Yale Review*, and has taught a variety of creative writing courses, including a writing workshop in autobiography for older students.

Melanie Bills is a first-year teacher in Liberty, Missouri. She currently teaches advanced eighth-grade language arts and eighth- and ninth-grade critical thinking at Liberty Junior High. She plans to return to school to complete her gifted certification and to begin work on her master's degree.

Lynn Z. Bloom is professor of English and Aetna Chair of Writing at the University of Connecticut, Storrs. Her teaching and writing focus on autobiography, women writers, and composition, and her work in these areas appears in books such as *Coming to Life: Reading Writing, Teaching Autobiography* (forthcoming); *Forbidden Diary*; and *Composition in the 21st Century: Crisis and Change*.

Elizabeth Boquet is an assistant professor of English and director of the Writing Center at Fairfield University in Fairfield, Connecticut. Her work has appeared in *Composition Studies*, *The Writing Center Journal*, *The Writing Lab Newsletter*, and *Landmark Essays in Writing Centers*. She also has essays in the forthcoming edited collections *Stories from the Center* and *The Ethics of Writing Instruction: Postsecondary*.

Mary Anne Browder Brock is a full-time English instructor at Fayetteville Technical Community College, where she teaches developmental and college-level writing classes and literature. She presented papers at the

1993 Conference on College Composition and Communication and at the 1993 Associated Writing Programs Conference. She plans to continue teaching, writing, asking questions, and searching for paradoxes in life.

Robert Brooke is professor of English at the University of Nebraska–Lincoln, where he teaches writing classes at all levels and works with the Nebraska Writing Project. Some of his publications include "Underlife and Writing Instruction" (1987), which won the Richard Braddock Award, *Writing and Sense of Self* (NCTE, 1991), and *Small Groups in Writing Workshops* (NCTE, 1994), which he coauthored with Ruth Mirtz and Rick Evans.

Roland Cooper has published poetry in *The Sheath* and is currently working on a book of poems. He has recently been accepted into the Fine Arts Program at Union County College in New Jersey.

Carman Costello is currently a junior at Southwestern College. She is majoring in both English Literature and Theatre. Carman plans to attend graduate school to study English literature after she graduates from Southwestern in May of 1997.

Lezlie Laws Couch is associate professor of English at Rollins College in Winter Park, Florida. She teaches literature and writing courses in nonfiction genres, primarily autobiography and the personal essay. She is currently working on a collection of personal essays exploring the theme of reunion.

Richelle Dowding graduated in 1995 from the University of Nebraska–Lincoln's College of Arts and Sciences with a B.A. in psychology and secondary certification in English and Psychology. She has worked as a reader/grader for the Southeast Community College Composition course for penitentiary inmates across the country. Currently, she is teaching English at Central High School in Omaha, Nebraska, and completing a second Arts and Sciences major in English.

Janet Ellerby teaches and theorizes about gender, pedagogy, and twentieth-century fiction. Her work has been published in *Signs*, *MELUS* (in press), and *Reader*. She is associate professor of English at the University of North Carolina, Wilmington.

Sandy Feinstein has developed her teaching methods at a number of different institutions, including the University of the South—Sewanee, UCLA, The American University in Bulgaria, Southwestern College, where she currently teaches, and at teacher training institutions and gymnasia in Denmark while on a Fulbright there. Her writing in different genres has also contributed to her teaching: She has published fiction, poetry, and scholarly articles on literature of the Middle Ages and Renaissance.

Amanda Folck is a junior at Southwestern College, where she majors in Mass Communications and Film and English. She spent the past summer as a marketing intern at KAKE TV Channel 10 in Wichita, Kansas. Amanda hopes to work in the broadcast journalism field upon her graduation in May 1997.

Michael Gilland is a musician of twenty-five years currently working as an engineering technician and attending school part-time. At the University of Cincinnati he is completing studies on a B.F.A. in electronic media and working toward a B.A. in English and a B.S. in Secondary Education.

C. Mark Hurlbert teaches English at Indiana University of Pennsylvania. He is coeditor, with Samuel Totten, of *Social Issues in the English Classroom* (NCTE) and *Composition and Resistance* (Boynton/Cook Heinemann), with Michael Blitz.

Rosemarie Lewandowski is an instructor of developmental English at Union County College in New Jersey. Her paper, "Visualization in Natural Language: Four Case Studies in Discourse Analysis," has been accepted for publication by The Educational Resources Information Center (ERIC). She is currently pursuing a Ph.D. in English Education at New York University.

Valerie Smith Matteson is an English doctoral student at the University of Connecticut. She specializes in twentieth-century literature.

Bob Mayberry is a playwright whose one-act *The Catechism of Patty Reed* was recently included in a collection from the University of Nevada Press, *Lucky 13*. His academic work includes a book of dramatic criticism, *Theatre of Discord*, and five years as editor of *Freshman English News*. His academic career has been an excuse to tour the country, teaching at UNR, URI, OU, UU, TCU, UCI, UI, UNLV, UAS, and now Grand Valley State University.

Bob Myhal is an English doctoral student at the University of Connecticut, where he has been the winner of two Aetna graduate essay prizes.

C. Ann Ott is a doctoral candidate at Indiana University of Pennsylvania and an adjunct instructor at Northern Essex Community College. She is a published novelist and has presented papers on narrative and literacy and collective research at state, regional, and national conferences. Her article "Collective Research at an Urban Community College" is forthcoming in *Teaching English in the Two-Year College*.

Michelle N. Pierce is a poet who has been published in *Conceptions Southwest* and *Blue Mesa Review*. After graduating from the University of New Mexico she moved to her birthplace, Japan, where she has been teaching English and studying her mother's language and culture. She recently organized and presented a workshop on effective team-teaching.

Staci Quigley is currently teaching eighth-grade language arts and literature at Marrs Middle School in Omaha, Nebraska. She started on her master's degree in June of 1996.

Lucille M. Schultz is an associate professor in the Department of English at the University of Cincinnati and former director of Freshman English. In journals including *College Composition and Communication*, *Rhetoric Review*, and *Written Communication*, and in edited collections, she has essays on the history of writing instruction in the nineteenth century, on the history of school/college collaboration, on portfolio assessment, and on literacy acquisition. Her work in progress is a book call *Muted Voices: Writing (Instruction) in Nineteenth-Century Schools.*

Ira Shor is developing a new composition and rhetoric Ph.D. at the City University of New York Graduate School. His books include *Critical Teaching and Everyday Life, Empowering Education, A Pedagogy for Liberation* (with Paulo Freire), and *Culture Wars: School and Society in the Conservative Restoration, 1969–1991.* His new book on negotiating the curriculum and merging critical pedagogy with democratic learning is *When Students Have Power* (University of Chicago Press, 1996).

Shannon Siebert lives with her husband and two children in Henderson, Nebraska, where she substitute teaches in the area, sponsors a junior-high writing group, and does freelance writing. At the University of Nebraska—Lincoln, she is involved with a community/school integration seminar that links school curricula with community economic, cultural, and civic life. In the future, she hopes to help develop and participate in a rural writing project in this area.

Denise Stephenson recently finished her dissertation, "Blurred Distinctions: Emerging Forms of Academic Writing," in American Studies at the University of New Mexico. She currently directs the Writing Center at Grand Valley State University in Michigan, where she tries to subvert the imposter syndrome every chance she gets.

John Paul Tassoni has published essays on pedagogy and American literature in *Social Issues in the English Classroom* (NCTE), *Sagetrieb, Communication and Women's Friendships* (Bowling Green State University Popular Press), *ISLE,* and *Nineteenth Century Studies.* He teaches undergraduate composition and American literature courses at Miami University–Middletown.

Gail Tayko has published essays on pedagogy and postcolonial literature in *Social Issues in the English Classroom* (NCTE) and *College Literature,* and her poetry appears in such reviews as *Phase and Cycle* and *Painted Bride Quarterly.* At Miami University–Middletown, she teaches composition and literature as a visiting assistant professor.

Katharine M. Wilson is completing her degree in Professional Writing at Carnegie Mellon University. Her most recent scholarly work, "What Man Artow? The Narrator as Author and Pilgrim," in *Chaucer's Pilgrims: An Historical Guide to the Pilgrims in the Canterbury Tales* (Greenwood Press), appears this year.

Chris Zawodniak is a junior in English and French at The Ohio State University and plans to pursue a degree in secondary education. This is his first published piece.